11/96

 St. Louis Community College

Forest Park
Florissant Valley
Meramec

Instructional Resources
St. Louis, Missouri

GAYLORD

Beyond Traffic Safety

Traffic Safety Series

J. Peter Rothe, *Beyond Traffic Safety*. 1993.
ISBN: 1-56000-095-3.

J. Peter Rothe, *The Trucker's World*. 1991.
ISBN: 1-56000-551-3.

J. Peter Rothe, ed., *Challenging the Old Order:*
Towards New Directions in Traffic Safety Theory. 1990.
ISBN: 0-88738-828-0.

J. Peter Rothe, ed., *Rethinking Young Drivers*. 1989.
ISBN: 0-88738-785-3.

J. Peter Rothe, *The Safety of Elderly Drivers: Yesterday's Young in*
Today's Traffic. 1989. ISBN: 0-88738-728-4.

J. Peter Rothe and Peter J. Cooper, *Never Say Always:*
Perspectives on Seatbelt Use.
1989. ISBN: 0-88738-775-6.

J. Peter Rothe and Peter J. Cooper, eds., *Motorcyclists:*
Image and Reality. 1989.
ISBN: 0-88738-784-5.

wonder how we could have allowed the terrible carnage on our roads. Peter Rothe's brilliant book offers a new understanding of what is happening on our streets and highways. If we attend to what he says, perhaps we will find a better way of life.

DAVID MACGREGOR

Professor of Sociology
King's College
University of Western Ontario

solutions endanger the vital human rights that have taken Western society a millennium to achieve.

Peter Rothe shows that if we are to resolve one of the greatest and most tragic problems of the twentieth century, we will have to dramatically change our view of the world of traffic and of ourselves.

A few days ago I was enroute to a Ph.D. examination in sociology. An old John Denver hit was playing on the tape deck of my car. It was a beautiful sunny afternoon in mid September. Traffic on the four-lane divided highway was moderately heavy, and everyone was moving along effortlessly. I slowed instinctively as a huge mushroom of smoke erupted on the opposite side of the road. Truckers with extinguishers rushed into the flames. Within seconds the fire was contained. The busy highway turned into a combination parking lot and fair ground. People lined the road and stared at the fiery wreck of two automobiles, slewed into the ditch. I joined the onlookers and stepped into a field strewn with bodies. A boy twelve or thirteen lay on his side in the grass blowing bubbles of blood. His mother was on her back, a few feet away, knees up, her clothes covered with patches of blood. The lifeless driver of the overturned Honda Del Sol that shot across the median and collided head-on with the family of four in the Ford Tempo was hanging upside down in his seat belt harness. I left without seeing the bodies of the other victims, an eight-year-old girl and her father.

As Peter Rothe's study would lead you to predict, neither of the drivers in this accident had been drinking. Nor did they belong to other accepted categories of the "dangerous driver." All of the victims were wearing seat belts. The second-year university student was traveling at the posted rate of speed when the left wheels of his vehicle went off the pavement, hit the gravel, and the car leaped across the wide median. A strong wind might have caused his auto to swerve slightly when he passed the transport truck traveling on the outside lane. The driver of the Tempo probably did not have time to move the steering wheel or hit the brakes. The collision occurred at a combined speed of almost one hundred miles an hour.

This was a normal accident. Tragedies like this occur every-day in North America. Hundreds of thousands of people die annually, and many, many more sustain crippling injuries because of this modern plague. Sometime in the next century people will look back and

Foreword

Peter Rothe's *Beyond Traffic Safety* is an absorbing study of one of the most important areas of modern social life, the culture of the automobile. I believe Rothe will transform the way most of us see questions surrounding the individual, mobility, and social space. This book may change your life.

Rothe takes a problem from the realm of conventional, accepted reality and auto safety, and reconstructs it into a central means of investigating the human condition. Rothe challenges accepted accounts of traffic accidents that place the emphasis on individual behavior, whether that of the "drunk" driver, the aged driver, or the young driver. Instead, Rothe thrusts the analysis of traffic into a complex social scene that involves meanings and beliefs, institutional power, social engineering, and environmental factors. Our roads and highways comprise a constructed social scene, he insists: everyone is involved in creating a dense conflicted reality that is abbreviated and distorted by official statistics of road use, property damage, and death and injury.

Rothe's study is an example of the best tradition of renegade sociology. Like C. Wright Mills, Irving Horowitz, and Dorothy Smith, Rothe draws on the sociological imagination to reconstruct the social world. He uses a wide range of social theory, and an abundance of empirical studies, to demonstrate that everyday life is indeed problematic. No silver bullet exists for the urgent problems of traffic safety. Banishing the impaired driver, or the youthful driver, or the elderly driver from our roadways will not greatly reduce the toll in blood and human life we pay for our transportation habits. Nor will zealous enforcement of traffic law. Yet these conventional

Contents

Dedicated to Hilda and Siegfried Rothe
(Oma and Opa)

Library of Congress Catalog Number: 92-35666
ISBN: 1-56000-095-3
Printed in the United States of America

Library of Congress Cataloging-in-Publication Data

Rothe, John Peter, 1948-
    Beyond traffic safety/J. Peter Rothe.
    p.   cm. —(Traffic safety series)
    Includes bibliographical references and index.
    ISBN 1-56000-095-3 (cloth)
    1. Traffic safety—Social aspects. 2. Traffic safety. 3. Traffic regulations. I. Title. II. Series.
HE5614.R65   1993   92-35666
363.12'5—dc20   CIP

Beyond Traffic Safety

J. Peter Rothe

Transaction Publishers

New Brunswick (U.S.A.) and London (U.K.)

Preface

For the sake of continuity and because the position is widely recognized, I shall take as my stalking horse the premise that the study of traffic safety as presently practiced is intrinsically problematic. The position is a personal affirmation, a statement of one person's reaction to a field of endeavor in which he has invested twelve years of his life.

Traffic safety is compelling, exciting, and satisfying for intellectual and popular exploration. It is also serious and difficult with numerous definitional tangles. Because some matters are difficult in fact, they are difficult to portray. Traffic safety is a child of the medical, psychological, and engineering sciences, with elusive conceptual and symbolic boundaries. Its only consensus is a disposition toward positivism.

Traffic safety is a response to the puzzlement over the large number of vehicle crashes and fatalities. Usually empirical puzzles are solved through clever theorizing and collection of data. In traffic safety theorizing is limited, but volumes of new data are published yearly. Data are presented as facts and assumptions of methodological appropriateness on the part of the researchers are usually taken for granted. The assumptions reflect forms of thought that presuppose a specific or positivistic perspective on the subject. Yet who is to say a pregiven form of thought is the appropriate one? What epistemological tradition legitimates the assumptions made?

Consider the puzzle: Take six matches of equal length and form four triangles, all of which are equal in area. Immediately we assume that the triangles must be formed in just two dimensions on a flat surface. This assumption renders a solution impossible. Question the assumption: Why would they have to be formed in only two dimensions?   There is no mention of limiting ourselves to two dimensions in the statement of the puzzle.   The solution lies in building a pyramid in three dimensions where the four sides are all triangles equal in area (Wheatley, 1970).

The point about this puzzle is not to engage the reader in childlike play, but to demonstrate how taken-for-granted assumptions predefine an orientation and the resulting approach to puzzle-solving.   So it is with traffic safety.   By changing the dimensions a new design emerges, that of traffic safety within a societal/cultural context.

The idea of the book is to motivate the reader to think differently about traffic safety, to suspend for a moment all background epidimeological, engineering, and psychological beliefs.   Instead, the reader should think of it as a field of investigation that has much more than simply technical meaning.   It refers to symbols, values, and ideologies that have popular currency. It reflects an undercurrent of social process, collective behavior, and cultural meaning that are present in society. Once the leap in thought is made, an alternative mode of inquiry makes sense.   A different puzzle evolves that requires new investigative techniques and rational inquiries.

As long as relationships play an important part in people's lives, the study of traffic safety must focus on them as central issues. The concern is not to rehash stale debates about the merits of seat belt wearing, or epidimeological risk factors.   Rather it is to infuse traffic safety with vitality, and to construct a social context that provides it meaning and identity.

Acknowledgments

Acknowledgments are usually brief statements of credit. I forego this custom to illustrate that my acknowledgments reflect the help of people who went beyond all expectations to make this work possible.

For me, writing this book was especially difficult. Because I strayed from the beaten path, feelings of anxiety, vulnerability, and insecurity always reared their ugly heads. Finally, striving for originality where originality was needed, I became less and less bothered by comments to the effect, "That's not what Blumer said," "What does traffic have to do with sociology?" "You have strayed from traditional social theory," and "What would Marx say on the topic?"

I must acknowledge my gratitude to Ken Westhues, David MacGregor, Rick-Helms Hayes, and David Flynn, who helped me to steer my way through the sniping. They spent a great deal of time reviewing the manuscript and offering constructive criticisms.

My friends from across the the Atlantic, Guenther Kroj and Siegfried Werber made special efforts to assure that my work was accessible to the European traffic safety community. To them, special thanks for their support and genuine friendship. I also owe a great debt to Irving Horowitz for his ongoing intellectual support, critical astuteness, and genuine friendship. His faith in my vision and intellectual orientation never wavered.

Fortunately I am blessed with a sympathetic wife, Barbara, and two children, Blaise and Nicco. They must share the credit for this book because of their forbearance, understanding, and love. Whenever I felt like "shutting it down," they always unselfishly encouraged me on.

Finally I owe a considerable debt to Doug Tobin, Colin Goff, and Will van den Hoonard for motivating me to go onward. To all a heart-filled thanks.

1

Setting the Stage

*We are exceedingly stable about being
exceedingly imprecise.*

—Nettler

At first glance, driving a vehicle may be considered a nonevent, an action in which the majority of people in Western society engage in a casual, routine manner. It is considered by many as unreflecting action, and it is usually rejected as an unworthy topic of study (Bierenbaum and Sagarin, 1973). Yet while one need not be concerned with, or be anxious about, the familiar world of driving, a passionate drama about traffic has unfolded. For example impaired driving, speeding, non-seat belt wearing, youth and driving, motorcycling, and trucking have become highly visible issues. Public officials, traffic safety adherents, corporate representatives, and community activists have selected, labeled, and introduced particular groups of roadway users to the public as risk-takers, deviants, selfish, aggressive, and dangerous people behind the wheel of a vehicle (Parry, 1968). The indignation has become so prominent that it could be entered in any panic encyclopedia.

As the panic escalates, so do the contradictions. On television, a commercial reinforces viewer's perception that driving a Nissan sports car is like flying a fighter jet. A few hours later, news reporters announce that National Highway Traffic Safety Administration (NHTSA) research findings prove that motorists who speed are more likely to cause accidents and become fatalities than those who do not. A poster in the pharmacy reads "Speed Kills." Public service messages imply that risk-taking drivers are irresponsible people who live on the edge of ecstasy and dread, exuberance and threat of death.

Yet Reebok, a world-wide sporting goods manufacturer, in one of its television ads advises viewers to "play hard. Life's short." Pictured is a sky diver jumping out of an airplane with a surfboard tied to his feet. Others like the War Amps of Canada encourage people to "play safe." Breweries advertise that a preferred quality of life is synonymous with drinking a certain brand of ale. According to Postman et al. (1987) a Miller beer commercial implied that men like to play rough, take chances, and ignore (or find amusing) the costly and dangerous consequences of their behavior. Often, the messages imply the use of vehicles.

Yet activist groups like Mothers, Fathers, and Students Against Drunk Drivers claim that alcohol and driving is a potent mixture for catastrophe. People who engage in "vile acts" of impaired driving are society's enemies. Police departments warn motorists that they are certain to be caught at roadside checks if they decide to consume alcohol and insist on driving. Yet McEwen and McGuire (1981) reported that the perceived risk of apprehension for traffic offenses, including drinking and driving, is a remote possibility. On the average, a driver would have to engage in about two thousand impaired driving episodes before being caught by the police (Jones and Joscelyn, 1978).

There is ambivalence in society's attitude toward danger and risk-taking. A commonly held belief is that "real people" participate in sports like mountain climbing, hang gliding, and sports car racing, all of which involve elements of danger. The young are discouraged from being soft or timid. The impression left is that they should challenge fate and be bold (Macmillan, 1975). Yet the meaning of challenge is proscribed. Adventure in a high- powered vehicle on an open four-lane highway is considered to be a disregard for public safety, inappropriate and narcissistic actions, while taking risks in business, recreation, or gambling is glorified in the media as "good risks." Individuals are rewarded for seizing the moment to gain fame and fortune. But, when applied to driving, when a motorist "puts a tiger in her tank" enabling her to "get out of town fast," we define her as a risk-taker or wrongdoer who needs to be punished and/or reformed (Macmillan, 1975).

When it comes to public policy, the pigments of good risks are bleached out by the definitions of bad risk. The latter constitutes an absolute, and therefore needs to be controlled through an expanding legal shadow. Law enforcement agencies use modern technology such as the breathalyzer, aerial speed trap, laser monitor, or photo radar camera. The technology becomes the means through which legal personnel challenge and charge risk takers. The principle is simple and direct. Maximize the apprehension or even the perception of apprehension and you minimize the risk taking behaviors. By doing so the heartbeat of the roadway will be normalized and mobile society will become safer.

Such a representation of driving reality begs the question: Is the metaphor "safety" used in a sweeping fashion to promote the right of certain public and private agencies to exercise power? or Is it used in a narrow sense to promote the health and welfare of individual citizens (Fowler, 1985)? Is "traffic safety" a facilitating concept used to engender a need to educate motorists on the consequences of self choice and risk? If one assumes that language is constitutive of social practices, then the use of a term like safety may make it easier for citizens to accept practices, policies, and laws that they may otherwise question.

A survey of traffic safety literature and public announcements shows that a legion of experts or professionals have provided technical and moral opinion on the causes, consequences of, and the cures for risky driving. Spokespeople proclaimed that risk-taking in traffic leads to accidents, defined to be a major public problem that requires a determined public response.

Traffic Accidents as a Public Problem

The perspective taken to define traffic related problems plays a major role in the responses to them (Rothe, 1991b). Consider for a moment the often-announced problem that young drivers are overrepresented in automobile accidents. An age category ranging from sixteen to twenty four years is usually established to illustrate the number of accidents experienced by members (Harrington, 1973; Williams, 1984; Insurance Bureau of Canada public announcements, March 1992). To illustrate the seriousness of the safety issue, accidents and/or violations for this group, young drivers are subsequently compared to other age groups. The results show that young drivers, in comparison to other groups of drivers, are overrepresented in traffic accidents and driving violations.

Before embracing the findings as fact, some assumptions should be reviewed. Questions may be raised as to the credibility of age groupings representing standard characteristics and standard practices of everyday life. Are the young drivers' similarities contrived, much like pennies that happen to be in a bubble gum machine? More precisely, is a sixteen-year-old boy similar enough to a twenty-four-year old man to suggest they have similar characteristics? How do social factors such as community, family, employment, schooling, peer relationships, values, and self-image, influence or determine certain driving behaviors for sixteen and twenty-four year olds? Young people's perspectives on driving-related factors have not been properly clarified according to such features as roadway morality, commonsense behavior, transportation needs, social belonging, and symbolic value of the automobile to suggest that a broad young-driver category is valid and warranted.

An alternative assumption is that young drivers are a generation of people whose maturities, interests, values, and relevancies vary greatly by age and lived experience; people whose behaviors reflect concepts of sociability, independence, and social responsibility; and individuals whose rules of driving action reflect everyday concerns and circumstances. When this perspective is offered, the young-driver problem changes. Rather than intervene with punitive punishment or restrictions based on an age grouping, alternative strategies such as increasing driver safety educational opportunities or building community recreation facilities that allow teenagers to "hang out" within close proximity of their homes may be considered.

A recent speaking engagement at an Ontario university illustrates a prevailing attitude toward traffic safety. After urging students to reach beyond a simple "victim blaming" ideology toward young drivers, a senior student, representing a popular belief, responded that he cares little for social factors. According to him, a young driver who races down the street, cuts in and out of traffic and endangers other drivers, should be "nailed." He is accountable for his actions. No excuses—so the youth argued.

The following response was offered. Personal and social responsibility are undeniable factors in anyone's driving behavior.

However, it was suggested that the student, for a moment, think of having failed an important examination. After four years of successful scholarship he is in danger of not graduating. Should the professor take a firm stance and proclaim that it is entirely the student's responsibility to study and pass. No excuses! Or should the instructor review the outcome and consider factors such as unavoidable stressful events, testing apprehensions or other social factors that may have influenced the outcome? As the student speaker indicated, not only would he appreciate the professor's initiatives, he would lobby for it. The student was then asked to translate this hypothetical scenario to young drivers. He and others agreed that simple versions of responsibility may be spurious and misrepresented.

Before generalizing about traffic safety issues, it is prudent to first ask five simple questions:

1.   How was the issue defined?
2.   Who defined the issue?
3.   Who made the decisions for dealing with the issue?
4.   Who will benefit from the decisions?
5.   Who bears the cost of the decisions?

Answers to such questions provide the basis for painting a picture of traffic safety as a social process. They help unmask underlying values that shape the perspectives and decisions of those involved in traffic safety. The approach differs substantially from traditional practices that presuppose that people who deviate from a normative conception of a healthy and stable society are risk agents. They threaten the smooth functioning of the roadway system. It is assumed that speeding, impaired driving, or running a stop sign arise from drivers who made rational decisions to take risks against acceptable standards of society. People who engage in such actions are believed to be primary agents for causing the high rate of morbidity and mortality in the streets (Haight, 1980).

The view that self imposed risk causes traffic accidents is consistent with the public health philosophy (Jessor, 1987; Slovic, 1985; Waller, 1985). Health promotion literature introduces cigarette smokers, overweight couch potatoes, alcohol consumers, or reckless young drivers as health delinquents. Individual health is equated to

personal choice. Witness the following quotation by the Canadian
Public Health Association:

> Health promotion is the prevention of physical and mental health through the
> promotion of better personal health habits and the elimination of self-imposed
> risks. (1974: 140)

Working on the assumption that health is an individual choice,
researchers study driver actions and consequences by assessing the
degree to which drivers departed from rational norms; determining
what the consequences might have been had the drivers not departed
from the norms; and determining whether and in what measure
society was harmed by drivers who have departed from given norms.

The studies preclude any real understanding of driving as
perceived and experienced by drivers. Since driver behavior ranges
from the highly rational to the highly emotional, understanding driver
actions may require researchers to be not only rationally analytic but
also emotionally empathetic   (Weber, 1949).   One can better
understand drivers once it is known where they go, why they drive as
they do, and how they do it. The question is reduced to how do
drivers come up with a definition of driving that differs from the one
held by traffic safety agents and researchers.

Traditional initiatives in traffic safety fail to probe the stocks of
knowledge, standards, beliefs, and codes of conduct that drivers use
as cognitive blueprints.   Traffic safety researchers and agents
constitute, through a selection process, the very reality of traffic
behavior with which they are dealing.   What is noted is not
independent of the researcher.   There exists a relationship between
the researcher and the researched, and this reality-constituting
behavior is a matter to be investigated in traffic safety.

Traffic reality is a kind of Rorschach ink-blot test, tapping
sentiment of various kinds (Faberman and Goode, 1973). One form
of sentiment might be the "epidimeological" temper; another might be
a "psychological" bent; a third might be a "legal" sentiment; still a
fourth could be a "social" orientation. Because there are no immutable
stable reference points in traffic, it is represented by researchers and
agents according to one or another perspective. The key question
becomes, who has the power to have their construction of traffic
reality accepted as legitimate? Or, according to Becker (1963), who in

the "hierarchy of credibility" can suggest what is real and what is true in traffic?

A footnote must be introduced at this point. It is an illusion to consider the views expressed in this manuscript as neutral. Like those of previous writings, there are also premised upon certain interests, presuppositions, approaches, relevances, and choices. They reflect what traffic safety is and what it should become within the road users' everyday reality.

An Alternative Approach

The view taken in this book is that traffic arises from interaction between people at different levels. Traffic safety is a social process, created, formed, and changed in and through the activities of people (Blumer, 1969). It consists of multitudinous activities that individuals perform as they deal with successions of new situations. The individuals may be drivers acting singly, interest groups acting collectively, or researchers, policymakers, administrators and other stakeholders acting on behalf of, or representative of organizations and groups. Through interaction people negotiate traffic conditions, social norms, status positions, interests, role demands as drivers, social system requirements and cultural prescriptions in order to construct and guide their actions.

Drivers take account of various things. They note and forge a line of conduct on the basis of how they interpret them. According to Blumer (1969),

> the things taken into account cover such matters as his wishes and wants, his objectives, the available means for their achievement, the actions and anticipated actions of others, his image of himself, and the likely result of a given line of action. (1969: 15)

As drivers interrelate with others they partake of "joint action." Diverse people, such as law officials, policy makers, public administrators, and traffic safety agents, among others, interlink to articulate the meaning of traffic and traffic safety. Although the actions of a driver are repetitive, they are still meaningful to the individual. The recurrent practices are formed, sustained, weakened, strengthened, or transformed according to the needs of individuals within different traffic-related situations (Blumer, 1969).

An alternative approach to traffic resonates with different people's orientations to driving. It analyzes the constituted nature of traffic reality, its contextual meanings, values and sentiments, moral-political forces, meanings and actions of control, enforcement and punishment. The kind of approach offered here helps readers see that fundamental things such as trust, responsibility, risk, licensing, policing, speed, impaired driving, and traffic-related technology are arranged in different ways by different groups.

No attempt is made to shy away from controversial critiques or provocative positions. Instead, the goal is to stimulate reactions—disagreements and agreements that expand the reader's horizons and that provide insight into the question of why traffic safety issues have become so prominent in people's lives. New social boundaries are explored and old ones are crossed. The effort to search for greater elucidation of traffic reflects the following verse from Proverbs:

> The man who pleads his case first seems to be in the right, then his opponents come and put him to the test.

Having offered a general introduction to traffic safety, it is now imperative to present a brief review of the chapters that follow. The overview provides a feel for the coherence inherent in the presentation.

Chapter 2 explores how basic trust in traffic routines sustains an orderly traffic flow and how fiduciary trust leads to paternalistic intervention. Chapter 3 includes descriptions on responsibility and driving. Emphasis is on legal responsibility, driver intentions, and responsibilities drivers negotiate in everyday life. Chapter 4 speaks to social patterns of risk. Rather than concentrate on actuarial defined risk, the chapter describes how physical risks are negotiated to accommodate social expectations.

The task of outlining different ideas about social control in traffic is tackled in chapter 5. The purpose of the chapter is to show the role played by the driver license as a form of social control. Particular emphasis is given to the way in which different images of licensing convey different ideas about traffic safety. Chapter 6 describes the meaning of the driver license as defined by licensees -to-be and potential license losers. Chapter 7 focuses on the development of traffic laws—examining how laws affect the conduct of driving. Chapter 8 traces the roles discretion and tolerance play in police work, and how they influence traffic policing in general. In chapter 9 a dominant traffic safety feature, speeding, is selected for analysis. Similar treatment is offered for impaired driving in chapters 10 and 11.

Chapters 12, 13, and 14 address the presence of social control in traffic. More specifically, claim-making, technological support of the claims, and electronic surveillance as a counter to speeding are discussed. Chapter 15 offers a readable conclusion and introduces a series of questions that should guide future research, policy planning, and interventions.

Combined, the chapters support the thesis that when the whole of a motorist's behavior is studied, rather than a single aspect of it, and when interlinking social factors are distinguished, rather than isolated characteristics, traffic safety becomes a facet of social behavior worthy of in-depth study.

To reduce the task to manageable dimensions, the focus of the book is limited to drivers. Furthermore, speeding is emphasized throughout the book to avoid rehashing the literature on social pathology, impaired driving, and seat belt wearing. Although it has become a dominant topic in traffic safety discussions, speeding has not yet received the kind of thoughtful attention its deserves. For in the spirit of Thomas Jefferson, "we are not afraid to follow truth wherever it may lead, nor to tolerate any error as long as reason is left free to combat it."

2

Trust in Motoring

If we accept that we can see that
hill over there, we propose that from
that hill we can be seen.
—John Berger

Imagine someone traveling 70 MPH or 110 km/h along a divided highway like Interstate 5 in the United States or Highway 401 in Canada. While driving in the "fast lane" she does not expect oncoming traffic in her lane or to find a car parked there. Although there is always a remote chance that this may happen, the average driver does not act on the faint possibility. She orients herself to driving according to a socially approved set of rules and procedures for achieving typical ends (Schutz, 1973). Paraphrasing Giddens (1984), drivers have a "sense of trust" that traffic flow will continue as before, and other road users will continue to collaborate enough to produce continuity, reliability, and predictability in the ongoing nature of motoring.

It may be said that drivers have "ontological security," the unconscious need to believe that things are as they appear and that driving sequences are what they have been and will continue to be (Giddens, 1984; Turner, 1988). Anything less results in the pathology of normlessness, deregulation or anomie (Cohen, 1985). When the unexpected happens or when unanticipated events occur, drivers momentarily suspend trust. However, mistrust is short-lived as motorists reorient themselves to the activities of others.

Metaphorically, trust is like a social receptacle filled with expectancies of daily life. It lends commonplace scenes their familiar, life-as-usual character, giving the everyday world its order, stability, and regularity. Without it individuals would find it nearly impossible to sustain social engagements or encounters in a respectful and considerate manner. Every action, event, or move would have to be deliberated and confirmed.

Trust that the network of recurring patterns will continue and that the natural order of things will persist was clarified by Luhmann:

> Trust in the broadest sense of confidence in one's expectations is a basic fact of social life. In many situations, of course, man can choose in certain respects whether or not to bestow trust. But a complete absence of trust would prevent him even from getting up in the morning. He would be a prey to a vague sense of dread, to paralyzing fears. He would not even be capable of formulating distrust and making that a basis for precautionary measures, since this would presuppose trust in other directions. Anything and everything would be possible. Such abrupt confrontations with the complexity of the world at its extreme is beyond human endurance. (1980: 4)

Within the social repository of general trust in routines of daily activities is a tacit trust individuals have in other people's competencies and roles. For example, most people will tentatively trust a doctor they have selected from a phone book, should they be taken ill in a strange town, because the doctor's role projects an image of trustworthiness that transcends geographic boundaries (Wiseman, 1979: 255). Such trust reflects concern about personal health that requires faith in expert knowledge, technical facility, normative rights and responsibilities of a doctor. People trust that physicians prescribe solutions consistent with appropriate medical practice. If they discover that they were duped with a placebo rather than a drug, people may lose confidence in their physician but it is doubtful that they will not visit another doctor for future ailments (Bok, 1978). Furthermore, the trust between patients and doctors may be extremely intense. It is to doctors that many people tell their deepest secrets and trust that their confessions will remain confidential and private.

On the first day of classes, university students, as paying customers, trust that the person at the podium is a professor. There is no call for credentials or proof of contract. More commonly, citizens trust mail carriers, police officers, and teachers on the basis of typical roles they play, responsibilities they have, and the integrity and honesty bestowed upon the incumbents (Holzner, 1973). A trusting stance incorporates confident expectations that one acts without unnecessary fear of uncertain outcomes at the hands of another person.

Trust in Traffic

Driving includes standardized behavior that is at the root of community living.   It is lived experience par excellence that incorporates common reciprocal expectations people have of each other. Instead of calling forth unique actions at every step of the way, motorists use common schemes of reference to navigate the streets.

Cars, lanes, intersections, roadway markings, signal lights, and traffic signs are interpreted according to the significance they have for people's driving purposes. Although each road user is unique, for the purpose of public driving the uniqueness is superseded by collective meaning and action, often referred to as intersubjective understanding (Schutz, 1971). A large number of variations are possible—motorists are intoxicated or they experience individual urges or emotions. Unexpected driving events or critical situations happen that destroy the certitude of routines. These are matters of irritation or everyday crises in metropolitan society that may result in emotional and/or physical reactions. But they are usually taken in stride. To help manage the incidents, drivers assess them in some fashion, as for example, reckless, inconsiderate, or stupid. Whereas such interpretations guide future action, they do not shatter basic trust. Motorists continue to maintain trust that a more-or-less patterned set of traffic activities will take place. For example, they continue to believe that oncoming drivers will travel in right hand lanes and motorists will stop at red lights and proceed on green ones. Increased wariness on the roadway may occur, but it would not greatly influence a driver's usual response to the predictable features of operating a vehicle. If it were otherwise, the driver would succumb to the pressures of suspicion and mistrust and likely bring the traffic flow to a near standstill. This would create exceedingly worrisome situations.

Trust in traffic does not just happen. It is made to happen through habitual modes of behavior and thinking developed from previous experiences. To help manage a safe traffic flow, trust that drivers will comply with the norms of roadway engagements is essential. It minimizes idiosyncrasy, anxiety, and risk. For example, in North America and central Europe motorists drive on the right-hand side of the road unless they pass other cars. In the British Isles and Australia motorists travel on the left hand side. North Americans driving in these countries must suspend trust in traditional routines and reorient themselves to new patterns of driving. Difficulties in turning and parking speak of the habitual performances on which motorists have depended throughout their driving careers.

Trust in traffic behavior is similar to trust in a game in which basic rules or laws necessitate compliance (Garfinkel, 1967). Within the confines of basic regulations are preference rules. They can be demonstrated with a chess illustration, in which the basic rule states that any pawn or knight may be moved on White's first move. However, a player has the choice of moving any pawn or knight according to preference. So it is with traffic.

For example intersections are highly structured traffic situations in which road users respond to the actions of others, who perform expected actions in return. An intersection marked by four stop signs is structured by legal obligations. Motorists are expected to stop, scan the roadway, and proceed in a safe manner. The Ontario Ministry of Transportation defined an All-Way-Stop as, "an intersection where stop signs are located at all corners (3 or 4 way stops). The first vehicle to come to a complete stop should be given the right-of-way. If two vehicles arrive at the intersection and complete their stops at the same time, the vehicle on the right has the right-of-way and the vehicle on the left must yield to it" (Ontario Ministry of Transportation, 1992: 34).

In short, if three cars enter an intersection at approximately the same time, the law states that the car to the right of an approaching driver has the right of way. To ascribe such a generic characteristic to traffic is problematic. Drivers attach their own meanings to situations through the use of preference rules. Regardless of the legal right to proceed, it is not uncommon for motorists to guide each other's behavior by granting others rights and privileges in accordance with principles of fair play, safety, time, space, fear, congeniality, or privilege (Blau, 1964).

A driver, who can legally continue, may wave her rights and gesture another driver to proceed. There is implicit trust that the driver, although in a legal position to go first, yet granting the right to another motorist, will not change her mind. Temporary hesitation or doubt may occur because of a possible social fracture. In the final analysis, there is confidence that the "go ahead" gesture is a trustworthy concession made by a motorist. It is built on the tenet that granting and receiving rights is an honored tradition of driving. The practice is sufficiently observed that its contravention would be considered a breach of driving protocol.

Traffic exchanges not only reflect, but promote, trust. An integral part of most, if not all, driving behavior involves some assurance that each driver's role is respected and considered. For example, driver A trusts driver B to behave in a certain way and is willing to do what driver B trusts him to do; the same is true of driver B.

Residing in trust is commitment, of which there are varying degrees (Mermall, 1970). Commitment refers to the extent to which motorists are tied to conventional joint actions by virtue of social rewards that they obtain from acting in accordance with prevailing norms. It reflects questions such as: What should be done? and What is one's duty, responsibility and rights for one's self and other road users?

Mermall (1970) quoting the Spanish philosopher, Pedro Lain Entralgo, suggested that there are three levels of commitment which he termed minimal, circumscribed, and authentic, that can be used to characterize traffic. "Minimal commitment" occurs when drivers look inward, limiting their involvements in social exchange, and placing little interest on the moral order of the roadway. Motorists are absorbed in themselves, often lost in thoughts or daydreams. "Circumscribed commitment" is evident when drivers aggressively expect other motorists to accommodate their desires. The only expectations they have of other drivers is that they "get out of the way." Witnesses to behaviors arising from minimal or circumscribed commitment are likely to give discursive reasons or rationalize the conduct as out-of-the-ordinary. By doing so they uphold the efficacy of routine and entrusted roadway behavior.

"Authentic commitment" is evident when drivers negotiate exchanges while they are engaged in their driving projects. They are aware of the need to reciprocate advantages according to the pragmatics and expected values of the roadway. Because such drivers do not create undue anxiety upon other drivers, they reproduce trust through socially tactful driving. These commitments vary according to situations, drivers' intents, and trip purposes.

Fiduciary Trust

Trust in routine roadway behavior and in performance of roles entails fiduciary obligations and responsibilities (Barber, 1983). People trust others who they believe have a moral obligation to defend individual interests and community standards. They can be parents, government officials, professionals, or legal officials.

As an ideal, fiduciary trust denotes "universal otherhood," where everyone has fiduciary responsibility for the safety of everyone else (Titmuss, 1974). It corresponds to the Christian view of brotherhood and the Buddhist central premise of compassion. According to the Old Testament, people who fail to attend to the plight of their less fortunate neighbors are themselves ultimately doomed. Buddhist belief has it that one's ability to hear someone else's plight should be guided accordingly (Pepinsky, 1987). Alternatively, fiduciary trust can be realized as total state control, appropriately exemplified by Orwell's "Big Brother". The government operates somewhere between the two polarities. Officials are authorized to control certain people's behaviors, thought and relationships as part of the government's fiduciary responsibility.

The boundary between legitimate authority, supported by trust, and illegitimate abuse of power overstepping trust is a fading line in the sand. In an increasing bureaucratized society one which Horowitz (1989) classifies as public-sector dominated, technocratic and authoritarian, there is the temptation to pay homage to state power at the expense of people's interests. Officials act in a way that suggests the state becomes the "guardian of public interest over and against private interest" (Horowitz, 1989: 129). When this reality registers with people, their faith in state administrators to oversee their best interests may become eroded. Consequently, commitment to follow laws as the correct thing to do may give way to obligation for the purpose of avoiding punishment (Tussman, 1960).

Fiduciary trust reflects a utilitarian rationale that furnishes agents with rhetorical expressions and legitimizations that they can use to justify social practices and organizational behavior (Reichman, 1984). The basic principle is that community interests should be promoted because "doing so will redound to oneself as a member of that community" (Fagothey, 1976: 65).   Four basic pillars support the utilitarian platform:

1.   Utilitarianism seeks a satisfaction in which all will be satisfied rather than only the fortunate few.
2.   A person is social and thereby the safety of each person is tied up with the safety of all.
3.   Those charged with public welfare must seek the common good while at the same time protecting individual rights.
4.   Reliance is on education and intervention as a means of enabling more people to appreciate social reform.

From a critical perspective, Ewing (1962) reasoned that laws are not justifiable on utilitarian grounds.   They must be assessed according to situations and practicality.   For example, a traffic sign at a bridge reads "No Changing Lanes."   However, if lanes are clear, the traffic flow is 30 MPH or 50 km/hr, and a pair of cyclists riding two astride are traveling about 10 MPH or 16 km/hr, it is doubtful that motorists will abide by the letter of the law, refrain from passing, and follow the cyclists for three miles.   It is more likely that they will change lanes and pass, thereby breaking the law but reintroducing a normal traffic flow.

A second criticism presented to utilitarian-minded traffic officials is posed as a question.   How is the safety of the community or society determined?   Because it cannot be done by plebiscite, common safety is decided by individual road users according to their own tolerance and risk-taking levels (Lave and Lave, 1990).   Of course there are extremes.   But when it comes to acts of speeding, the range of exceeding the speed limit or the consensus of establishing a speed limit such as 50 km/h rather than 51,   52, or 55 km/h, is difficult.

A third criticism is that any enforcement of a traffic law today may affect future generations.   Assuming society is aging (Rothe, 1990a) how will, for example, traffic signs be obeyed in the future with an aging population that finds it difficult to read signs today?   Is the responsibility for disobeying a NO PASSING sign to be placed equally upon a young person with good eyesight, and on an elderly driver for whom the sign may be poorly placed or poorly marked?

Finally, when government regulators embrace fiduciary trust they emphasize the action component of individual choice. Conversely they deontologize the choice of lawmakers, engineers, sign erectors, planners and politicians. Drivers are expected to behave according to "the common good" as an intrinsic value and not as a state- enforced policy.

As anonymous "contemporaries," drivers likely do not have immediate experience of government regulators.   They only experience them by inference. Hence they impute typical attributes and have expectations that certain kinds of conduct are practiced (Schutz, 1971). For example, motorists expect government works departments to fill huge potholes or repair broken traffic lights. They expect the police to arrive at a traffic accident and to monitor driving behavior. But more important, drivers expect that the members of an agency have integrity and carry out their fiduciary responsibilities in competent and fair fashion. If this fails, people may suspect government regulatory agencies, possibly resulting in feelings of distrust (Barber, 1963). When this happens, drivers must rework their definition of fiduciary agencies, suspending formerly held trust. The pressure, therefore, is on the government agencies to justify themselves and to demonstrate their trustworthiness in defending community standards and people's self-interests within the confines of the community.

Fiduciary Trust as Paternalism

Over the last fifteen years, the boundaries of fiduciary trust in North America have widened. Witness the case of public health. Governments, seeing their task as protecting society from the damaging effects of risk-taking behavior, have embraced the idea that unhealthy and unsafe personal habits cause major accidents, thereby consuming a large share of health and welfare resources. Officials emphasize the need to change unhealthy and unsafe life styles in order to reduce the social burden of accidents and injuries and the potential damage to the individual transgressor. Laws and policies, based on a "new paternalism," were implemented in areas of smoking, alcohol consumption, and impaired driving among others (Bonnie, 1985).

As part of a paternalistic stance, government agents continue to implement legal interventions, education programs, and social policies designed to help prevent or discourage unsafe decisions or risk-taking behavior. However the extent to which controlling health risks may be generalized as a generic concern is debatable. The concepts of possible and certain harm lack too much precision. For example, an automobile that has no brakes because the manufacturer has chosen not to include them definitely affects a driver's safety. The same holds true for a drug that has been tampered with or a dangerous chemical for ingestion that has not been properly analyzed by government agencies. However, a motorist speeding down a highway is not certain to affect another driver's safety. The chance of him or her doing so is limited. This was featured during a 1992 discussion with three senior members of the German Safety Council. It was learned that unrestricted speeds on the autobahn are not considered a major safety problem. Instead, driving within the vicinity of roadway construction sites is the major autobahn-related safety problem. If possibility of harm was consistently upheld by government regulation, there should be no legal sale of cigarettes, alcohol, aerosol sprays, toxic insecticides, and participation in sky-diving, rock-face mountain climbing, or hunting should be prohibited.

From Trust to Distrust

When basic trust is eroded, forms and degrees of distrust can result. Garfinkel's (1967) "breaching experiments" illustrated what happens when people's trusted routines are disturbed. By manipulating trusted routine family affairs, Garfinkel and his colleagues illustrated the bewilderment, anger, and anxiety that result. As Garfinkel demonstrated, when individuals' trust in everyday routines is breached, people are burdened with the need to question ordinary affairs that had previously been accomplished with ease. Such questioning may lead to distrust, the extreme of which is labeled paranoia: a pervasive distrust of other people's motives.

Distrust may lead to increased wariness, which traffic safety experts suggest may be healthy. "Expect the unexpected," reads a prominent Canada Safety Council slogan. Defensive driving courses, based on the assumption that anticipation of problems must override basic trust in routine driving, are offered by the Canada Safety Council and the National Safety Council in the United States. Their effectiveness may be questioned because in part, people tend to construct their conduct through experiential scripts that are based on taken-for-granted trust. Drivers do not consciously consider every yard or meter of driving in order to maintain problem-free driving. People somehow learn to drive without thinking about it or being consciously aware of it. They simply drive to get to their destinations, much as one walks to the corner store to get a quart of milk. To illustrate, drivers are supposed to engage in a three second count when following vehicles, so that they can make sudden and unexpected stops without crashing into vehicles in front of them. People do not tend to follow these rules because they are accustomed to styles of driving in which it is believed that "everything-will-be-alright" (Jacobs and Dopkeen, 1990; Werner and Rothe, 1984). Counting for safety is not a natural part of routine driving and a distrustful orientation to motoring does not easily fit with drivers' customary behavior.

Conclusion

Basic trust is a resource in traffic safety that has not yet been properly explored. Drivers are expected to, and expect other drivers to, maintain the sanctioned features of the roadway—its routineness, reliability and predictability. If it were otherwise, millions of drivers could not proceed to their destinations safely and reasonably quickly.

Furthermore, motorists believe that officials charged with fiduciary trust over traffic will take care of traffic safety issues. Although organizations may be far removed in time and distance from the driver, they are major partners in defining traffic behavior. They represent the "anonymous other" that people believe constructs safe roads, develops appropriate traffic laws, enforces laws fairly, and in the process upholds the integrity of the driver.

Unfortunately, the version of reality displayed by contemporary and anonymous organizations is likely to differ from that of drivers on the roadway. Consider the following example. A trucker waves to a motorist behind him that it is safe to pass. He pulls over slightly, but not enough for the passing driver to clear the truck without straddling the center lane. The motorist trusts that the trucker follows basic rules of tact, and thereby passes. If it happens that it is unsafe to do so and a crash results, the passing driver will likely be charged in violation of safe passing. The breach of trust in the trucker's practices may not be considered when a formal investigation of the facts is made. The law becomes the standard measurement of evidence.

3

Responsibility and Driver Conduct

No system promises a shift from ordinary human fragmentation to twenty-four-hour-a-day clarity.

—Will Ferguson

There is no question that traffic is patterned behavior. A collection of rules, albeit often unstated, serve as socially approved boundaries within which drivers operate their vehicles. If it were otherwise, chaos would reign on the roadway. One such boundary is responsiblity. The questions that need to be addressed are: How is responsibility invoked in drivers' lives? How is responsibility interpreted and maintained as a significant feature in traffic safety?

Responsibility in traffic can be thought of in three connected yet conceptually distinct ways—personal, social, and legal. The extent to which one view dominates over, or interrelates with, others depends upon the analyst's perspective on what is considered to be appropriate and permissible behavior.

Personal responsibility denotes drivers as objects of their own actions. It focuses on individual motorists as it pertains to personal feelings, motives, wants, goals, conceptions of self and visible conduct. Driving is regarded as a behavior resulting from individual decision-making. The singular driver becomes the medium for the fulfillment of responsible behavior.

Personal responsibility is routinely invoked by traffic agents when they speak of driver error, negligence, or driver fault. The rationale is as follows. Once drivers choose to drive in some way or other, they must accept the consequences of those decisions. Because drivers are considered to be the authors of their own behavior, they are often labeled speeders, drinking drivers, or risk-takers. For many traffic safety agents, the rationale is beyond compromise. Witness Haight's (1980) example of a traffic safety official who told him that even if there is a ten- foot pit in the middle of a freeway, falling into it would be "driver error." It is the driver's duty to stay out of it.

Social responsibility refers to obligations people meet in everyday life while playing different roles in different situations. In a general sense people fit their lines of conduct with those of others. For example, parents attend to crying children in cars, friends defend each other's images as drivers, and bus drivers stop at undesignated parts of the street for the convenience of ailing senior citizens.

People master social relationships and maintain accepted patterns of group life without fanfare. They live up to expectations of a normative or behavioral order found in all peopled places, whether it be public, semipublic, or private, organized or merely routinized (Goffman, 1967)

At the microlevel, social responsibility comprises the extent to which people exercise competent and acceptable interaction. The lines interactants maintain, the concerns they share for each other's image, and the extent to which they sustain an expressive order of events connote taken-for-granted social responsibility (Goffman, 1967; Lyman and Scott, 1970). Failure to live up to one's social responsibility may produce ostracism, reprimands, broken relationships, or loss of image.

In traffic, social responsibility is recognized in situations where, for example, drivers merge from two lanes to one. To deal with the problems of a lane closure due to construction, motorists cooperate according to the common task of mobility and social tact. Universal symbols such as raised hoods are interpreted as car trouble, against which passing motorists take precautionary action, or stop to offer assistance. Such social actions shape driving, whereby drivers adjust their behaviors according to the responsibility they share to maintain patterns of joint action. Although they are recurrent, they may be illegal. One example is parents, who, on a thousand-mile vacation trip, unbuckle their seat belt to attend to bored children sitting in the back seat, or who unbuckle children so that they may lay down and rest.

Legal responsibility may be viewed as an ideal, constructed on the belief that laws are social contracts between drivers and the state. They provide the institutional context for drivers, obliging them to behave in a way that provides benefits for all drivers.   Bentham wrote:

> The art of legislation (which may be considered as one branch of the science of jurisprudence) teaches how a multitude of men, composing a community, may be disposed to pursue the course which upon the whole is most conducive to the happiness of the whole community by means of motives to be applied by the legislator. (1970: 293)

Because drivers operate in the public domain, they are expected to live up to their social obligations, one of which is to abide by traffic laws.   Legal responsibility connotes the government's judicial and legislative powers under which legislators set generic standards intended to help assure safety, order, and efficiency.   It is based on the traditional belief that following the law will avoid accidents and thereby drastically reduce social costs.   If statutes are broken, the persons held responsible are blamed and punished.   From a judicial perspective it is incumbent on drivers to adhere to the laws as a form of involvement in the collective conscience of all road users.

Traditional View of Responsibility in Traffic Safety

Traffic safety agents share the assumption that drivers are responsible for themselves; the safety of other drivers; and adherence to traffic laws, statutes, and policies at all times under all conditions. Responsibility is measured through accountability, whereby motorists must answer for breaches of roadway behavior that is in conflict with the law.

The doctrine of responsibility as fault and negligence for which drivers are held accountable provides a moral argument that rests on the character of drivers: they failed to meet a standard of right conduct (Gusfield, 1981).   They did what they should not have done. Hence they must answer for the consequences.

A rational version of driver accountability and responsibility leaves untouched the construction of a judicial system that demands efficient processing of responsibility.   At most traffic courts there is an extended list of cases to be dealt with. Judges, naturally, wish to proceed with business as efficiently as possible. The constraint of time may have an important bearing on the decision of responsibility and the extent to which details of cases are offered as evidence (Hood, 1972). To save time, benches generally agree on appropriate measures to deal with ordinary cases. The assignment or dismissal of responsibility may become routine, rather than a studied legal decision. Macmillan (1975) and Hood (1972) aired kindred thoughts when they announced that courts, which hear traffic offences, are geared to unanimity of guilty pleas and stock fines.

A long-standing legal source of discouragement for drivers failing to live up to their responsibility is the threat of tort law (Friedland, Trebilock, and Roach, 1988). In tort action the identified irresponsible driver, in theory, stands liable for losses sustained by a victim in the form of foregone future income, medical costs, and pain and suffering.

The threat of civil liability operates on the same principle as the threat of fines. Both are intended to punish prospective wrongdoers. It is expected, that a driver choosing to engage in driving conduct considered to be irresponsible, will weigh the expected costs of an accident against the costs to her adopting some alternative conduct. In theory this calculus should lead to legally defined responsible driver behavior on the roadways.

By using the threat of legal sanctions as a negative stimulus, society hopes to force drivers to drive according to the canons of traffic laws. The consequences for their decisions to drive otherwise carry sanctions such as fines, demerit points, and the eventual suspension of driving privileges. There is a shared belief that punishment can deter and that lack of punishment will generate law violations (Gusfield, 1981). Driver responsibility, as defined from the perspective of legislators and supporting traffic safety agents, becomes regulated and enforced. The assumption is that motorists who drive within the limits of the law are error-free drivers, safe drivers who do not have accidents—at least they are not responsible for any (U.S. Department of Transportation, 1970).

The explicated link between driver responsibility and accident involvement, so dominant in traffic safety, seems at first glance "normal" and "natural." It meets the prevailing concepts of fault, traditional in American and Canadian law. However it is not above criticism. Although it is difficult to deny that drivers take responsibility for their actions and consequences, the issue at hand is the extent to which driver responsibility is a universal condition. To clarify, the Department of Transportation (1970) reported that the majority of drivers are guilty of formally defined driver error, a situation considered to be normal by the government department even though such behaviors depart from, "standard, correct and ideal behavior" (U.S. Department of Transportation, 1970: 189). Also, emotional stress may influence drivers' actions and create violations of the law or accident proneness (Norman, 1962).

An earlier study by Norman (1962) set the stage for the Department of Transportation announcement that each driver makes about two hundred observations per mile, twenty decisions per mile, and one error every two miles. As a result, near collisions are experienced about once every five hundred miles and a collision once every sixty one thousand miles. To generalize, fallibility is an inherent of the human condition that overshadows strict responsibility (Friedland, Trebilock and Roach, 1988). Fault, for which the driver is considered to be responsible, may not be considered as self-evidently wrong. It may be little more than a momentary act of inattention or distraction, devoid of any illegal intent. In short, fault may be considered to be part of normal driving.

The character of perception and conceptualization inherent in causal responsibility assigned to drivers deemphasizes responsibilities for the safety of the community assigned to other groups, organizations, or institutions. For example, do car manufacturers have responsibility to construct vehicles that are maximally safe? Do engineers have responsibility to construct safe highways? Do governments have responsibility to provide a social ethos that encourages safe driving and reduces the need for risk-taking? As Haddon (1973) has wisely demonstrated, even if the post office drops a tea cup, it makes better sense to wrap the tea cup than to train the employees of the post office how to handle tea cups. Correspondingly, Haddon (quoted in Gusfield, 1981: 47), suggested that the problem in traffic safety may not lie in the foolishness or drunkenness of the driver but in the failure of the auto industry to construct an automobile designed on the assumption that drivers would be foolish or drunk, a point of view shared by consumer advocate Ralph Nader at the 1985 Community Leaders Conference held in Vancouver, Canada.

Responsibility and Intention

Intentionality suggests that any acts in which drivers engage, objects they see, or events around them are not objectively out there. They are perceived and interpreted according to what they mean to motorists while they are driving. The perceptions and interpretations may change over time; nevertheless drivers act upon or behave according to them.

As a springboard for reflection, four levels of intention are presented which accord meaning to driving acts and responsibility. The first is "actual intention" in which drivers consciously choose to behave a certain way by invoking reasons for the decisions. Motorists pay attention not merely to what they are doing but also to why they are doing it. For example, someone may decide to party and get drunk for the purpose of having a good time, being fully aware he will be driving home inebriated.

Virtual intention is one that was once made continues to influence the driving act. But it is not present in the motorists' consciousness at the moment of performing driving acts (Fagothey, 1976). For example, a motorist plans a trip to a specific destination. Although there is a plan for the overall trip when starting out, after driving awhile circumstances present themselves that although linked to the original plan of the trip become features in and of themselves. Making a right-hand turn at a busy intersection while the mind wanders or turning on the radio and tuning into the music for enjoyment illustrate such situations. Within the overall plan for making a trip, there are a whole series of acts that bring the original intent to flourishen but while engaging in these, the driver need not be thinking at all times of the intended trip.

A habitual intention implies habit. A driver has always driven a certain route while commuting, or consistently engages in unreflective behaviors such as smoking cigarettes or failing to use signal lights for turns. It all seems like second nature. The intent is to abide by the habit for convenience and comfort rather than find the energy and will to escape it. This point was well illustrated by a New Brunswick police officer. Near Oromocto, workers removed a ten-year-old stop sign and placed it at another corner. Although the need to stop was eliminated, many drivers still stop there as they have done for years.

An interpretive intention is one that has not been originally made but presumably would have been made if the motorist was aware of the circumstances. If the literal application of a traffic law causes more harm than good in relation to the driving project, a driver may relax the law. For example, a highway maintenance crew stops traffic for a period of time, causing the driver to arrive late at her destination. Had the driver been aware of this situation she might have left earlier or have taken a different route. But being caught in the traffic congestion and needing to be at a certain destination on time may encourage the driver to speed.

Although intention does not negate legal responsibility, it modifies it. It clarifies circumstances of intent that underlay driver actions. They are traditionally defined as personal responsibility.

Modification of Legal Responsibility

A working assumption is that a driver's responsibility is a reflection of the degree to which the driver acted voluntarily. The question becomes: What renders legal responsibility imperfect, reducing the specifically human character of the driving act and making the driver less responsible? To address this question, five potential modifiers referred to as ignorance, passion, fear, health, and habit will be discussed.

Ignorance

Lack of knowledge about some law or policy can be and is frequently invoked in varying degrees by drivers. The rationale is as follows. A driver, capable of knowing the laws, but lacking knowledge of them, has an obligation to know. For example, professional truckers are expected to operate their rigs with full knowledge of the capabilities of the equipment, just as sea captains are expected to know navigation. The possession of a driver's license is considered to be standard proof that   drivers have benchmark knowledge about the law and features of driving on which they can be held accountable. A motorist's ignorance of the law therefore, is not a reasonable justification for negating driver responsibility.

A follow-up issue is the extent to which drivers have proven knowledge about laws, but do not use that knowledge. For example, the owner of a driver's license knows for all practical purposes the meaning of traffic signs.   However, because of unforeseen circumstances such as a parked truck, a sign is, or cannot be seen. Is this person to be held responsible for a violation, or more extremely, the cause of an accident?

One argument is that the driver lessens responsibility because he cannot act according to something that was or could not be seen. Alternatively, the driver increases the burden of responsibility because, as a license holder he is expected to thoroughly scan the roadway for signs and act accordingly. A third argument is, can it be proven that the driver did or did not see the sign? Law officers usually assume that not seeing a sign is little more than an excuse to be relieved of responsibility (Rothe, 1992).   The driver will, in all likelihood, be held responsible for disobeying the sign as a result of the legal assumption that there is no invincible ignorance.

Passion

Passion is defined as the experience of an all-powerful emotion that reduces self-control.   A driver's senses are heightened as reactions to sudden feelings of joy, anger, hatred, grief, shame, pity, disgust, and the like. These feelings may occur without the drivers' will or against their will.

In criminal court, passion can be used as a defense by pleading temporary insanity. It can take the form of antecedent passion or engagement passion.   However, in traffic court the presence of passion before an undeliberate or violent driving act is not generally accepted as a legitimate excuse for escaping responsibility. A person who is experiencing a heightened state of emotion because of life events such as divorce, loss of job, or the death of a close friend or family member should refrain from driving. Paradoxically, the state of passion itself negates the rational deliberation required to abstain from driving.

In some cases the automobile is used as a resource to feature passion. A broken romance may create the need to dramatize the extent to which someone's feelings are hurt. A tactic may be to jump in a vehicle, burning rubber as the wounded lover demonstrates the emotion over perceived mistreatment at the hands of another (Rothe and Cooper, 1989). One may conclude that the manipulation of passion through engagement is voluntary and purposeful, increasing a person's responsibility (Fagothey, 1976). Passion that arises spontaneously during driving may only lessen but not negate legal responsibility.

Fear

Fear can be a separate modifier for legal responsibility. It can be an emotion, the appearance of a sudden fright-producing reflex, or an impulsive act of avoidance. In this sense fear is a sensation similar to passion.

There is another kind of fear that may not include heightened emotion. A trucker may decide to cut off a motorist on a freeway to "make time," because the driver is fearful of losing a future load due to tardiness. A male driver may decide to refrain from speeding because his mate has threatened to break up with him, or a young driver may decide not to drink and drive because she fears that if caught her parents will take away her car.

It is true that the emotional type of fear can throw drivers into a panic, that they lose self-control, or freeze entirely.   But the intellectual type of fear does not produce such an effect. Drivers calmly look about for an escape from a threatened evil. Based on their interpretation of events, they yield to the fear instead of resisting it. From a legalistic perspective they may be considered to be responsible for the actions they take, regardless of whether they are more or less safe.

Driving under duress and intimidation has fear as a motive. This may vary from peer pressure and a potential loss of face to a threat that if someone does not drive as demanded, the drivers physical health is at risk. From a philosophical point of view driving under duress and intimidation may be considered responsible acts.   A person could refuse and take the consequences.   Threat of bodily harm can be nullified by the law.   However, the extent to which this form of reasoning reflects people's behaviors in fear-producing situations is debatable.

Health

A person's state of health is anther focus for arguing against legal responsibility.   Certain chronic health conditions have been identified as being potentially dangerous while driving.   Some of these include insulin- dependent diabetes (Frier et al. 1980), epilepsy (Harvey and Hopkins, 1983), head injury or neurosurgery (Jennett, 1983), stroke (Quigley and DeLisa, 1983), and any condition that reduces the extent of the visual fields (North, 1985).

If the condition was diagnosed and treated prior to driving it is considered to be the individual's responsibility to take precautions suitable for the ailment.   This may include taking appropriate medicines, or following doctors' orders for healthy and risk free activities in which the patient can engage.

If the doctor fails to advise the patient of possible dangers, and the patient is unable to decide on risk and impairment, the responsibility lies with the medical professional.   Also, if a condition such as a heart attack or a stroke happen during driving, motorists are discharged from all legal responsibility, unless they failed to take proper medication earlier.

Habit

A habit is defined as a constant way of acting resulting from repetition of the same act.   People who have acquired habits will engage in actions spontaneously and nearly automatically.   Deliberate guidance is unnecessary.   A habit becomes a pattern that can be reproduced with an economy of effort.

Some motorists may have a habit of tailgating, in which they follow cars in front without sufficient space for a safety cushion. Excuses of habit for such driving behavior do not suffice to free drivers from legal responsibility. The counter is that it is up to the driver to make the effort to eliminate a habit.

In traffic safety habit carries a dual meaning. From a positive perspective the habit of seat-belt wearing is a responsible behavior. However, if it is a negatively assessed habit like speeding, motorists are warned to change their behavior. Habit, therefore denotes both responsibility and irresponsibility.

Responsibility as Everyday Life

By moving into the everyday world of drivers another perspective on responsibility is noted. Traffic safety agents have points of view on responsibility that may differ from that of drivers. The highway as a portion of the everyday world is shared by everyone. There is a fundamental agreement that people have to live with each other before they enter a vehicle, while driving, and after they step out of the car. The necessity of getting along with people is a common fact, a pragmatic motive. Within this world, responsibility becomes a lay formulation and not an objective or professional formulation such as a law, statute or policy. It is a folk feature upon which people place great emphasis, so that their experiences are representative of the experiences of others. Everyone in society relies upon, attends to, and uses responsibility as a basis for action (Zimmerman and Pollner, 1970).

Within the reality of everyday life, responsibility may be in rhythm with, antagonistic to, or transcend legal responsibility. It depends on the settings. In North America, motorists live up to their responsibility of driving on the right-hand side of the road, unless the lane is closed in which case they forego the law and drive momentarily on the other side of the road. They turn their blinkers for turns, unless they are in the habit of not doing so. As such, responsibility relates to the habit or routines of driving as it has always been done under the purview of the law.

Social responsibility may be antithical to the law when, for example, concern for family, friends, or associates overrules adherence to a statute. Although there are hundreds of examples to choose from, two obvious ones come to mind. Packing in more passengers in a car than legally allowed or than there are available seat belts may carry a social responsibility of pleasing friends, but it negates legal responsibility of abiding by the seat-belt law. Stopping on the side of a highway marked "No Stopping" to allow a child to urinate can be interpreted as a socially responsible act from the perspective of family obligation, but it contradicts the absoluteness of a no-stopping rule. The possible stigmatization or injury to one's identity as a reasonable, tactful individual overrides the endorsement of legal responsibilities. Such measures are interpretive or strategic actions that enable drivers to cope in the world, but that also place them in conflict with the law (Blumer, 1966).

A reading of the daily newspaper will likely produce instances where drivers act according to their interpretations of social responsibilities rather than legal ones. For example, on January 21, 1992 a medical doctor appealed a speeding ticket to the Quebec Superior Court after losing in a municipal court earlier. He received a $132 speeding ticket while rushing to the aid of a sick baby (Kitchener-Waterloo Record, 1993). After having been denied the appeal the doctor told the newspaper: "If this judgment holds true, many children will die. When the Superior Court makes the speed limit, at 7 A.M. on an empty street, more important than the life of a baby, something is wrong" (Kitchener-Waterloo Record, 1993: A 2).

Equally important is the point that, according to one's sense of social responsibility, drivers may outperform the letter of the law. For example, the law may state that the speed limit on a street is 30 MPH or 50 km/h. However, when there are children playing on the side of the road and there are parked cars that obstruct vision, a motorist is expected to drive slower, regardless of the law. Drivers are expected to assess the risk according to their social responsibility for the safety of children.

Conclusion

Many folk responsibilities in traffic are difficult to reconcile with the rationale and dictates of legal responsibility. As was outlined in chapter 2, to have the relatively smooth flow of traffic that occurs on unhampered highways requires a faith or trust that drivers are responsible enough to follow basic rules and patterns of driving. It could not be any other way. If some motorists engage in unlawful driving, it is in all likelihood not on an ad hoc basis. It may not necessarily mean a defect in responsibility, but negotiation of legal responsibility for the sake of social responsibility as interpreted by the driver. Ultimately, the driver is judged on the basis of the law. Still, upon closer analysis, the rules of social responsibility as departures from legal responsibility warrant closer investigation in traffic safety.

4

Street Risks

*Common sense is that collection of prejudices
accumulated by the age eighteen*

—Einstein

"It is probable that . . .," "chances are . . .," it's likely that . . ." are three expressions people commonly use whenever they are uncertain about the future, but have to decide on future events before they occur (Thygerson, 1977). They represent general modes of conduct that crosscut a great number of social situations. For example, motorists are faced with everyday life decisions such as deciding which route to take during rush hour traffic so that they can arrive punctually at their destination, or playing the odds that they have enough gas in the tank to reach the next filling station. Such guesswork need not be admonished. It is indicative of everyday risk taking and risk avoidance, an intrinsic part of people's driving lives.

Although risk taking is objectively ascertained by experts according to psychological characteristics of sensation seeking and thrill seeking, and actuarial projections of probabilities and cost, risk taking as social behavior has not yet received rigorous attention.

Despite Douglas and Wildavsky's (1982) treatise that acceptable risk taking has strong cultural and social bonds, limited effort has been spent in traffic safety to investigate their thesis, because culture and social realities have been thought of and treated as self-evident (Douglas and Wildavsky, 1982).

This chapter originally appeared in *New Ways For Improved Road Safety and Quality of Life*, Tel Aviv, Israel, 1991.

To illustrate, Jacobs and Dopkeen (1990) reported that their computer search of risk literature did not reveal a single entry under risk and self assessment, qualitative studies, or everyday life. Risk analysts have stayed with an individualistic orientation conceptualized in terms of economics, human life, and health cost benefits. People's perceptions of risks continue to be measured according to psychological processes that determine the extent to which risks are acceptable (Short, 1984).

For the sake of simplicity, risk analysts measure risk according to one of three dominant schools of thought. One group studies versions of gambling, aiming to clarify which aspects of gambles make them seem risky. A second group concentrates on dimensions of risk judgments about events that are not likely to happen within people's personal experiences, as for example, the risk of a nuclear power plant accident (Sande, 1987). The third group of analysts attends to judgments of risk events in which people have personal experiences (Brehmer, 1987). This is the school of thought most applicable to traffic safety.

Traffic safety has become the home for an array of risk experts. Insurance company actuaries, epidemiologists, cognitive psychologists, decision analysts, and economists apply mathematical models of probabilities to assess factors of risk and consequences for regularly occuring driving events. Psychologists like Fuller (1984), Wilde (1982), and Naatanen and Summala (1976), and economists such as Peltzman (1975), outlined models of risk analysis in traffic that assume a direct link between motorists' perception of risk and their driving behavior. However, according to Adams (1985), each risk-taking theory is little more than common sense, glamorized as intellectual endeavor. To Adams, the various psychological and actuarial models are little more than formalized speculation about mental states and processes that escape empirical verification.

Implicit in risk analysis models is the assumption that drivers have an optimal level of risk compared to acceptable risks in society. Behavior, judged to fall below a threshold, needs to be managed. For example, by 1981 many countries passed seat belt laws on the basis of studies showing that seat-belt wearing reduces the severity of injuries from 30 to 60 percent. Underlying the establishment of seat belt wearing legislation is the assumption that drivers need to be protected from themselves because they are hesitant to voluntarily engage in safe behavior. By not wearing seat belts they are risks to themselves. It is further believed that by enforcing seat belt wearing laws, lives will be saved and in the process the net aggregate good of society will be maximized. Risk analysts support the idea that a system of deterrence, comprised of seat belt wearing statutes and communication plans for announcing risk indexes about not wearing seat belts to drivers, will decrease the levels of risk. Measurable decreases in the number and severity of fatalities and a concomitant reduction in social health costs will follow (Cohen, 1983).

Statistical calculations of risk, like those used to rationalize mandatory seat belt wearing legislation, imply that mortality and morbidity are preventable. Although diagnostic models have contributed to a better understanding of risk, they have precluded the social context of driving. From an everyday perspective, growing up and surviving in North America means competition, of which risk is a main ingredient (Nash and Spradley, 1976). Driving is part of surviving. Anchored in drivers' practical consciousness are thoughts of rewards for successful risk taking, such as saving time, gaining status, satisfying egos, meeting challenges, gaining skills, winning favors, or maintaining social ties. The degree of risk may vary with situations; some are personal, others involve people. As Barber (1983:8) correctly wrote, the fundamental considerations for risk analysis are " the expectations that social actors have of one another in social relationships and social systems." These expectations constitute trust.

It is doubtful that risk indexes change motorists' behavior in light of the millions of risks they experience daily (Adams, 1985). This conclusion sounds very similar to one provided by Avis, Smith and Mackinley (1989). Trying to establish a correlation between individual preception or risk and objectively determined risk, the researchers concluded that once people know "objective" information about risk, they are no more likely to change their behavior. Something else is clearly going on. As was discussed in chapters 2 and 3, drivers are more likely to make decisions based on preferential rules of conduct than they are on objective information. Such shared meanings arise from a cultural concern of how people wish to live with others and how they wish others to live with them (Wildavsky, 1987).

Giving shape to social reality includes people sharing taken-for-granted rules of "proper" social conduct. Through the use of preference rules, individuals sustain a standard of self respect and considerateness with others that in certain circumstances may overshadow consideration of laws. Although drivers' preference rules may increase the chance of accidents, they are essential for maintaining social relationships, or according to Goffman (1967), they are a form of savoir faire or social skill.

Standing inside their own culture, motorists can only look at their driving behavior through culturally fabricated lenses.   There are moral and social issues underlying driving decisions that bear on the analysis of risk. For example, driving on public streets is an orderly affair structured subjectively by participant's trust, socially established norms of responsibility and morality, social pressures and community cultural standards of appropriate behavior. According to Zimmerman (1970: 233), people's behaviors are based on how they "satisfy themselves and others concerning what is or is not reasonable compliance in particular situations." In the following pages I describe on how drivers negotiate social and physical risk and in the process construct a picture of orderly conduct regardless of laws and formal definitions of risks.

Managing Risks on the Roadway

The data for this chapter came from three major British Columbia studies, one each on young drivers, seat belt wearers, and elderly drivers.   Information came from open-ended interviews with 150 young drivers (Rothe, 1991c), and 130 elderly drivers who were victims of injury producing accidents (Rothe, 1990a).   Also, 200 drivers who considered themselves to be regular seat belt-wearers were interviewed at length (Rothe and Cooper, 1989).

Behavior cannot be fully understood as mindless and must therefore be phenomenologically grounded. In other words, behavior must be seen as intentional and as based on meaning (Gutenschwager, 1989). If drivers engage in risky driving behavior, one must analyze the meaning and intention behind that behavior to better understand it.

If motorists appear to be acting dangerously, one must understand how this behavior could appear, to them at least, to be legitimate and acceptable, if not rational and logical in a positivistic or scientific sense.

To describe motorists' meanings and rules of behavior, a series of interviews were conducted to address drivers' versions of crash involvements, self-images, routine and preferred driving behaviors, life-styles and risk taking. For consistency in description, Douglas's (1976) recommendation of social validation was acknowledged. Relevant others, such as family members, friends, driver trainers and examiners, and groups of random people were also interviewed. Combined, the research produced descriptions of preference rules used by motorists to account for street risks as "good risks" (Thygerson, 1975).

Common Preference Rules

On a daily basis people construct and employ social rules in connection with circumstances and situations in which they find themselves. They act upon or are guided by the rules. By standing back for a moment, one can discern patterns, trends, and adaptations that comprise group life. They are shared to the extent that people in a given society have similar backgrounds, learning experiences, understandings of the everyday world, expectations, and language. The same holds true in traffic. Four basic general rules or principles were extracted from the interview data to account for drivers' versions of risks as normal street risks. Respective examples are "regard for others overrules personal safety," "image of self competence outweighs self doubt," "good driving warrants risk taking," and "risks for good reasons are normal." Any scheme of risk taking as rule-governed behavior is influenced by an evaluation of the odds—is there enough potential gain to assume risk (Thygerson, 1975)? Such rules are helpful is understanding how drivers engage in risk taking to fulfill social obligations and satisfy self-concepts.

Regard for Others Overrules Personal Safety.

A careful reading of the interview data shows that drivers are attentive to sociability, responsibility, congeniality, and smooth social encounters. Maintaining smooth social lines, or social tact often overrules canons of safe driving and the law.

Consider seat-belt wearing as a well-accepted safety procedure. After years of public relations, media presentations, educational intervention in schools, and the passage of mandatory seat belt legislation, researchers independently established that provincial seat belt wearing rates rose from about 50 percent in 1985 to 85 percent in 1992.

Studies based on surveys by federal and provincial government agencies and university researchers generalized that 75 to 85 percent seat belt use represented an accurate account of regular seat belt wearing.

Follow-up interviews with drivers who defined themselves as "regular seat belt wearers" illustrated that regular seat belt wearing is not a constant. Its meaning depends on emerging situations in which people make decisions through negotiation. Consider the following example. The British royal family officially opened a park in New Westminster, British Columbia. Teachers organized parent-run car pools for children to witness the momentous affair. The school principal notified parents that all those wishing to join the transportation pool must abide by the seat belt law, namely, one child per seat belt.

On the day of the royal visit the restraint rule fell apart. Decisions were compromised. Witness several examples given by teachers:

> There were five safety belts all right but only four of them worked. One of them in the back seat was hopelessly stuck between the seats. So I buckled the two smallest children together and we were on our way.

> When you count the driver, there were only three belts available, not four like we thought. One kid kind of scrunched down on the floor in the back.

> It ended up that there were three kids in the car. Two buckled in the passenger seat and one behind the seats. (Rothe, 1991b)

To get all of the children to the affair, parents and teachers routinely transported more children than there were available seat belts. Instead of confronting parents, teachers remained conciliatory. They wanted to avoid creating disharmony with parents and preserve normal relations with community volunteers. Consider the following account presented by the head organizer of the car pool:

> One of the mothers who signed up to drive pulled up in a Corvette. I told her that there weren't enough belts, but she said she always rides with her son or daughter in the back. I didn't want to do it, but I thought she'd make a fuss if I pushed her. She does a lot of volunteer work around the school. The kids she was going to drive were best friends of her daughter. It ended up there were three kids in there. Two buckled in the passenger seat and one behind the seats near the window. That's the way she wanted it and that's the way she got it.

Within the parent-school context, interpretation and enforcement of the seat-belt statute was very flexible. It was negotiated to help avoid conflict between the school and community.

It was not unusual for self-proclaimed seat-belt wearing motorists to describe situations in which they permitted more passengers than there were seat belts. One mother reported her experiences in a car pool in which where she always transported one more child than there were belts. With seven children in the pool, four always sat in the back seat. According to the woman, to engage the car pool with one less family would have increased each parent's driving time and it would have left one family "out in the cold."

A reoccurring theme in the young driver testimonies was that regardless of the number of seat belts in a vehicle, everyone present gets a ride. To do otherwise would be a major breach of social expectations,   resulting   in   ruptured   friendships   and   strained relationships. Nearly all of the young people interviewed experienced situations in which there were more passengers than seat belts. They knew that having more passengers than seat belts in a vehicle was illegal. But they considered the practice to be routine, a natural occurrence in teenagers' lives. They did not consider the behavior dangerous, nor did they attach any meaning of risk to it. It was impossible for them to avoid the practice, given the adolescent need for peer acceptance and group involvement. Said one teenager,"If you're leaving a party you pretty well have to take everyone who wants to leave or people will think there's something wrong with you."

For young drivers, automobiles are like living rooms on wheels, social environments where norms of social interaction must be obeyed (Marsh and Corbett, 1986). Whenever young people drive with friends they can theoretically withdraw themselves from conversation (Goffman, 1967). Few do so. The preference rule of maintaining a smooth state of affairs with peers is too embracing. Young drivers reported that they normally engaged in animated interaction with passengers because of the social expectation that in-car social gatherings demand it. To do otherwise carries the threat of being labeled a social boor, moron, or nerd. Invariably drivers who interact with passengers become less attentive to driving. Momentary inattention caused by talking with passengers can lead to reduced road wariness and increase the risk of a serious mishap (Rothe, 1990b).

The need to maintain proper social relations and thereby incur safety risks was also a prevalent theme with senior drivers. Senior motorists, sixty five years and older, recognized that they experienced driving limitations such as slower reaction times and health problems that naturally creep up with age. Experience has taught them to compensate for poor eyesight and hearing. Senior drivers left the impression that they forego high risk-driving conditions like fog, rain, snow, dusk, night and rush hour traffic.

Upon further questioning, it was learned that compensating for high-risk driving was open to negotiation. For example, to help friends and/or family members, seniors willingly disregarded dangerous driving conditions. They were prepared to drive in terrible road conditions because they promised to, "take a brother-in-law to therapy," "pick up a parcel for a friend," or "give a neighbor a ride to church or the community center." For some, keeping a promise is sanctified—breaking one is disrespectful. A promise made means meeting obligations, regardless of personal risks. Senior drivers explained that they would rather inconvenience themselves or put themselves at risk than they would inconvenience others. They were prepared to face almost any driving conditions before they would abandon their social responsibility.

Images of Self Competence Outweigh Self Doubt.

Drivers in the presence of others manage information about themselves, their feelings, their relationships, their character, and social status, that conveys particular impressions they wish to make (Stoddart, 1988). They offer impressions of themselves that create an outward image of driver competence and confidence regardless of the doubt they may feel inwardly.

On numerous occasions young drivers revealed that they feared certain roads and felt anxious driving through bad weather conditions. However, there was widespread concern that their fears and anxieties, although real, were inappropriate.   Teenagers described how they would encounter contempt and antipathy or become objects of ridicule or scorn if their friends discovered their feelings. For example, a sixteen year old boy was about to receive his driver license. He already knew that his friends expected him to drive them to Long Beach for picnics. He was "really scared" at the thought of driving on the "treacherous" road because his grandfather "ran off it last year." The boy's fright was never shared with others because, he thought, once his friends knew of his fears they would think less of him.

Another student, aged seventeen, was afraid of driving in downtown Vancouver traffic because of "all the one-way streets and the parking hassles." But, he "wouldn't want this to get around because people would think he is a fool."

Young drivers' initial anxieties about driving in certain circumstances is compounded by the pressure to actually experience them, to appear to be in control and look "cool."   Consider the following example: A boy received his license in the winter. Within weeks it was his turn to drive his friends to Whistler for a day of skiing. As was reported in Rothe and Cooper (1989), "I was a wreck when we got there," he said. "I've never driven on the highway before and I've never driven in snow, and all the while I had to be cool."

Operating a vehicle includes the need for a smooth social performance. This is further proven in seat belt wearing. Passengers may decide not to wear seat belts to support the self image of drivers who believe themselves to be competent and reliable. One motorist, a self-proclaimed regular seat belt wearer, will not wear a belt as a passenger because, "I trust people I drive with; they're good drivers. The people I drive with can handle themselves in any situation" (Rothe and Cooper, 1989).

Some drivers felt that a person's image as a competent driver may become tarnished if a passenger wears a seat belt. A group of motorists portrayed their driving character as virtuous and honorable, attributes they expect passengers to honor. As one boy said, "I never wear seat belts when I'm with my dad. He doesn't believe in them. If I put them on he accuses me of not trusting his driving and he acts hurt. Sometimes my mom puts them on just to get at him" (Rothe and Cooper, 1989).

In some cases the driver's image as a good driver rests on passengers reinforcing the self-concept by not wearing seat belts. Smooth performance of the faith-in-the-driver principle is a preference rule that is usually unspoken and taken for granted. As one interviewee stated "it is one of those things you know you just feel. It's there."

Whereas young drivers typically discussed driver competence in terms of their physical skills and abilities to handle a car, seniors presented competence as courteousness, considerateness, and patience. Most of the senior drivers who were interviewed defined themselves as competent, because they possessed social and not physical qualities.

Senior drivers idealized themselves as competent drivers who have learned to be attentive to the feelings of other motorists, to patiently wait to see before they enter a roadway, and to be wise enough to allow other drivers to do as they wish. By defining competent driving in terms of social tact, senior drivers deemphasized age-related problems such as declining health and technical driving skills.

Good Driving Warrants Risk Taking

For many interviewees able driving was considered to be synonymous with technical skills, and personal histories of accident-free driving. Nearly all of the young drivers' parents that were interviewed considered themselves to be patient, alert, cautious, and/or technically able. Some parents constructed their definitions of themselves as good drivers on the basis of never having received a traffic violation. Good driving was depicted as being "street smart," anticipating where speed traps are, or where police officers may be looming.

During interviews with youths a contradictory message was given about parents. Fathers were featured as individuals who had total disregard for the law and safety (Stoddart, 1988). Fathers' driving was repeatedly characterized as speeding, beating red lights, running stop signs, ignoring pedestrian rights, not wearing seat belts, and driving while impaired. Some youths defined their fathers as driving maniacs who rationalized their actions by saying "I've never had an accident so I know what I'm doing."

Several examples extracted from the interview data illustrate the gravity of the finding. On the way to a football game one boy's father was, "going over seventy in a fifty kilometer zone." The father told him, "Cops never stop an old man in a T-Bird [make of a car]. Never got a ticket. Besides we don't want to be late for the game do we?" (Rothe, 1991b).

Another boy described how his dad evened the score with a tailgater. He swung around between parked cars, slowed down to let the other driver pass, then proceeded to tailgate himself. At the red light the other driver jumped out of his car, whereupon the boy's father, "took off like a bat out of hell" (Stoddart, 1988). The father reasoned that because "he really knew how to handle a car he could teach the other driver a lesson" with little risk to himself.

These same fathers teach their sons how to drive. They instruct them how to become confident-enough drivers, to take the occasional risk without creating dangerous situations. The fathers shared the view that signs of "real driving" are not found in driver manuals or motor vehicle acts. They are found in experience; this is similar to some parents' life philosophy that youngsters are expected to take chances to get ahead in life.

The majority of young drivers interviewed also regarded themselves as cautious drivers. They seldom judged themselves as the guilty party in the accidents in which they were recently involved. The young drivers were "just going forward," "waiting for the light to change," "starting to proceed after looking to see if everything was clear," or "making a proper turn" (Rothe, 1991c). Buried in the statements was the claim that the other drivers was the guilty party. They violated rules of cautious driving by having made unusual, unexpected, and sudden moves, tailgating, slamming the brakes, passing illegally, turning suddenly, or running a stop sign/a red light. According to the accounts offered by young drivers:

> This guy came through a red light. He just came out of nowhere.
>
> He just pulled out to make a left turn.
>
> He suddenly pulled out and turned.
>
> He was going faster than fifty.
>
> His car weaved into my lane and hit me. (Rothe, 1991c: 61)

For senior drivers, most of the crashes in which they were victims were described as anomalies or one-time affairs; an unfair basis for judging a person's driving competence. They did not claim responsibility for their accidents. A common rule senior drivers invoked was that their "real self" or "true self" as good drivers is defined by history. Most had not received traffic citations, nor had they experienced accidents in the last five years. Their accidents, usually described as their first, were the result of the other drivers' actions and perhaps momentary lapses of attention "that can happen to anyone." They considered their crashes as fate that operated randomly and not in a programmatic way. As one senior expressed it, "Nobody's perfect." Eventually, "everyone's number comes up" (Rothe, 1990a).

Risks for Good Reasons Are Normal

In normal driving situations, motorists continuously make decisions that reflect their interests at hand. Their rationality reflects Cohen's (1960: 38) thesis that "our actions are often guided not by what we feel is more likely but what we feel is less likely to happen." Cohen's rule became evident during interviews with young drivers. Most attend weekend parties and consume alcohol. Some have verbal agreements with their parents that says, "If you have been drinking, call us and we'll pick you up, no questions asked" (Stoddart, 1988). The informal contract implies that parents will not punish or discipline teenagers who telephone for a ride after they had been drinking and partying.

Despite parental assurance, most parents who answered student calls did engage in judgment or discipline. Rather than focus on the young driver's decision not to drink and drive, parents moralized about the company the youths kept, the parties they attended, or the time of night in which they caroused. As one girl put it, "My mother would die if she could see what used to go on at those parties" (Stoddart, 1990). A dominant perspective was that students would "get into trouble" if their parents thought that they were associating with a "drinking crowd."

To call parents for rides was considered by most to be unthinkable. Because their parents are somewhat suspicious of their friends and association patterns anyway—a phone call to them would confirm their suspicions and result in "even more restrictions." The fact that the students who called, avoided drinking and driving, is replaced in importance by parent displeasure about students' social circles. For some young drivers, the outcomes of revealing information to their parents, would meet with severe consequences such as "grounding for eternity," refusal to allow teenagers to "hang around with those people ever again," and "never being allowed to use the car again."

For others, parental disappointment would take the form of degradation ceremonies. Equally serious, but less explicit were the parents' visible and sometimes exaggerated emotive reactions. They would show disappointment, displeasure, failure, hurt, shame, or repugnancy, followed by silent treatment, lecturing, and constant questioning because of what parents considered to be a broken trust. Because of these likely parental reactions, some youths believed that driving while impaired was a risk worth taking.

Parents' negative reactions was a certainty in young people's minds. Becoming involved in a car crash, or being caught by the police for impaired driving, was at best a remote possibility. Consequently, the youths preferred to risk a possibility than confront a certainty. Some would wait out the drunkenness for a short time, while others would drive home on back lanes, side streets, or gravel roads where there was less likely chance of being spotted by the police. They have good reason, for as one father said, "I don't know if he could call me and be honest because he might be too afraid I would never let him have the car again" (Stoddart, 1988; 193).

Some youngsters decided to risk impaired driving because their parents would suspect them of ulterior motives. For example, if a daughter failed to get home on time, parents would become suspicious that she is engaged in sexual activity. Witness: "I had to drive home with him because if I stayed out all night or until he sobered up, my parents would think I was sleeping with him "(Rothe, 1991c).

Youths concentrated on the here and now, consisting of normative or probable parental reactions to their behaviors. They were prepared to take risks to avoid sanctions at home.

Taking risks for everyday reasons was also dominant with seat belt wearers. For example, child rearing is considered by many to be a more important social responsibility than seat belt wearing is a legal one. Mothers and fathers who described themselves as regular seat belt wearers would not hesitate to unbuckle to help a crying baby or tend to an energetic toddler while the car was moving. Indeed, mothers stated that they were prepared to remove colicky children from their baby seats and try to stop the crying. This was especially true if the driver complained about the noise. Furthermore, a front-seat passenger is seldom reluctant to unbuckle in order to retrieve a bottle, map, book, umbrella, or cassette from the back seat.

Although the reasons differed, the taking-risks-for-good-reason rationale was noticeable among senior drivers. Some motorists reported that they risk making left-hand turns at busy intersection because they expect other drivers to recognize them as elderly and take appropriate actions. Some seniors drive according to the expectation that motorists are more cautious around the elderly.

Status was a dominant factor for some seniors. They expected special consideration or respect from younger drivers because they fought in World War II, helping to preserve democratic ideals that young drivers now enjoy. These expectations encourage some senior male motorists to take risks to which they believe other drivers are not entitled.

Conclusion

Motorists are not isolated individuals. Their social life should be included in the analysis of how they think and behave. By following preference rules, they demonstrate how risks are managed for social reasons. Suffice it to say that an awareness of people's behavior that departs radically from formalized explanations of risk helps us better understand the power of social conventions. As social beings, people are aware of social rules that must be followed to retain social tact, propriety, and responsibility in customary ways. When these rules trample formal laws or basic rules of safety, an area of distinct interest emerges. It is a sense of society that motorists themselves make, a symbolic exposition that street risks, as qualities of social organization, pre empt rigid categories of tightly controlled models in risk-taking analyses.

5

Licensing Strategies, Common Sense, and Public Interest

Can we know the risks we face,
now or in the future? No, we cannot;
but yes, we must act as if we do.

—Mary Douglas and Aaron Wildavsky

The driver license is intended to regulate drivers-to-be. All citizens must have knowledge of laws and regulations, minimal driving competence, physical health, and be of minimal age. They must meet these criteria before they can drive motor vehicles on public streets. Their knowledge retention is evaluated on the basis of standardized written tests composed of questions taken from a driver's manual. Driving ability resides in a road test in which driver candidates have to demonstrate that they posses minimum skill handling a motor vehicle over a designed course on public streets. Physical condition includes vision, hearing, and other problems that a medical report suggests may be dangerous for driving. The last area of control is minimum age. Whereas most provinces in Canada and states in the United States have proclaimed sixteen as the minimum age for obtaining a standard driver license, some jurisdictions have raised the age to eighteen (Friedland, Trebilock, and Roach, 1988).

Absence of Benchmarks

Although the driver license has been heralded as proof of minimal driving competence, a careful reading of the literature illustrates that license examinations have little validity in predicting who will and will not be safe drivers (McKnight, 1985). For example, Wallace and Crancer (1969), concluded that driving knowledge is not a valuable predictor of driving behavior when measured by violations. Conley (1976) agreed that there is no systematic correlation between driving records and test scores. More recently, Atkins (1984) established that scores on written examinations cannot accurately reflect driving behavior. Thorpey (1988) followed with a similar conclusion. After having analyzed available research literature, no correlations were found between test scores and drivers' follow-up records.

Of all the knowledge required to understand driving, only a small amount is presented to candidates for study. Faced with a situation of so much to know, license candidates are expected to develop a short-term perspective—learning what is likely to appear on the examinations.

Unlike apprenticeship programs, education courses, internships, or technical skills training schedules, license candidates in North America are not required to engage in formal preparation for a license. Although driving schools provide training, they are not compulsory. Therefore, the problem of so much to know in driving is compounded by the absence of learning objectives, and teaching techniques such as problem solving, decision making, and skills development. There is only a short-term examination for proof of knowledge comprehension and driving ability.

The complexity of the subject matter that is not addressed provides a "training for uncertainty." These uncertainties stem from incomplete mastery of the vast and growing knowledge in traffic safety, information about up-to-date road markings, laws, technological changes, and human behavior. License candidates study a handbook to prepare for the examination. By memorizing select facts and demonstrating predefined skills on a given day, driver examinees take on a "cloak of competence." They believe that passing examinations gives them control over traffic situations and lessens the possibility of making mistakes. There are no possibilities for students to learn "cool driving," namely the ability to react confidently and skillfully to novel traffic scenarios. Yet traffic safety agents expect them to master uncertainty and anxiety engendered by various traffic features.

To overcome the burden of operating up to standards that have not been properly defined, taught, or accurately measured, traffic jurisdictions have introduced designer licenses. They are intended to help convince new drivers that the licensing experience is serious.

Because of poor predictive validity, McKnight and Edwards (1982) questioned the value of knowledge tests for screening out bad drivers. They recommended that the test should become an incentive to learn traffic regulations and other critical information pertaining to safe driving practices. Tests can then act as inducements for new drivers to acquire knowledge of driving laws and safe driving procedures (McKnight, 1985).

The suggestion that the driver's license does little to limit dangerous driving activities has been well accepted in traffic safety circles (Jacobs, 1989). The present-day licensing system is not designed to screen out unreliable and unskilled drivers. Instead, according to Reese (1971), it serves as little more than a means to raise revenues and register the driving population. With application costs and five-year renewal costs appropriated from drivers, the government is assured of a consistent net income and a well-placed monitoring process.

Licensing has also become a stage for sorting potential drivers into categories based on generalized risk factors, health, driver characteristics, and driving skills. For example, young and novice drivers, motorcyclists, and senior drivers are considered to be different enough to incur special treatment. Members of these groups had standard licensing practises revised in order to stabilize their behaviors that officials considered to be risky and dangerous. The differences are clearly expressed in designer licenses that recognize a cognitive distance between normal, experienced driving and abnormal, inexperienced driving.

Designer Licenses

Designer licensing schemes were introduced to modify novice young driver risk taking, to restrict their range of operation. One example of a designer license is the probationary license.

Probationary drivers receive documents that clearly mark their driving status. They can quickly be identified and punished. If they accumulate more demerit points than experienced drivers over a defined period of time, punitive actions can be taken against them. The emphasis is less on guidance and supervision and more on surveillance and threat of punishment—seeing to it that probationary drivers behave as required under conditions in which where their infractions stand out as being more serious than the infractions of other drivers. As Mayhew and Simpson (1990) correctly point out, probationary drivers are subject to tighter suspension rules than nonprobationary drivers. They receive warning letters after the first loss of points rather than after six points; no interviews at all as opposed to interviews at nine points; and mandatory suspension at six points rather than at fifteen.

Waller already noted the ethical pitfalls of probationary licensing in 1974. The characterization of inexperienced drivers is synonymous with social maladjustment, meaning lack of proper safety attitude, questionable psychological characteristics, and lack of standard abilities. Coppin (1977) questioned the intents underlying the granting of probationary licenses by suggesting that it is designed,

> to develop in the driver the correct approach toward driving. If the person can be induced to drive safely in the first year of driving, he (she) is more likely to continue the practice in later years. Further it is considered that the threat of immediate cancellation does have a beneficial psychological effect in accidents, particularly the high accident rate with young drivers. (Pg. 44)

Consequently, probationary drivers are more likely to receive harsh penalties for an offense (Waller, 1974). It is consistent with the behavioral modification scheme of imposing negative reinforcement. Combs's (1979) response to behavioral modification in education may prove enlightening. He compared the process with a fencing-in technique for controlling behavior, like that used in stockyards to move cattle from one place to another. Moving cattle is a simple matter of exerting pressure from the rear to make them move forward through the lane prepared. Although the method works fine for cattle, people have "an annoying habit of climbing over fences or discovering gates that we forgot to close" (Combs, 1979: 56).

A second designer license of note is the provisional license, a form of probationary license that is typically applied to young newly licensed drivers. Whereas the probationary license threatens punishment for driving errors committed by novice drivers, provisional licenses impose restrictions on driving privileges (Mayhew and Simpson, 1990). Tighter license suspension rules than those imposed on experienced drivers, restrictive driving times, and mandatory completion of a one-year violation-free driving period are measures invoked by the authorities.

As of late, attention is focused on "graduated licensing schemes," which are designed to provide new drivers the opportunity to gain experience under conditions that minimize the exposure to risk (Mayhew and Simpson, 1990). The presiding assumption is that experience increases driving proficiency. As experience and competence are gained, the opportunity for exposure to risky situations is gradually phased in (Mayhew and Simpson, 1990). Boughton, Carrick and Noonan, (1987) included the following stages:

Stage 1	Supervised day driving only, no passengers, zero or low BAC (Blood Alcohol Concentration)
Stage 2	Supervised, may carry passengers during the day, and may drive at night, zero or low BAC
Stage 3	Unsupervised during the day, passengers day or night if supervised, zero or low BAC
Stage 4	Unsupervised day or night if solo, supervised if carrying passengers at night, zero or low BAC

Australia has now practicalized the conceptual stages of a three-year graduated license scheme. Learners begin with a learner's permit for twelve months at minimum age sixteen, after which time they receive a "probationary" Red license. It restricts them from driving with no more than one passenger per car, any blood alcohol concentration count, and eight-cylinder, turbo-charged or modified cars and soon-to-come nighttime driving. If they have a year of violation-free driving and pass a computer-based test they are upgraded to a Gold license.

Several issues come to mind. Although the stated intent is to ease "novice" drivers into driving, the case made for a graduated license is "age-related." According to Boughton, Carrick and Noonan, "the model developed for discussion purposes addresses the main problems of alcohol abuse, night driving and passenger carriage, which are the major common factors in crashes involving young drivers" (1987: 354).

It appears that the graduated licensing scheme, although rhetorically intended for new drivers, is in reality a de facto design to identify and control the young. Despite Mayhew and Simpsons' (1991), argument to the contrary, one of its latent purposes is to penalize problem drivers, namely those under the age of twenty.

Before the graduated licensing scheme is embraced, it may be fruitful to question the assumption that supervision of new drivers assures that they will become safer drivers. Once students' descriptions of their parents' driving patterns is considered and research that suggests the majority of drivers speed and break laws is reviewed, a shadow is cast over the claim that driver supervisors, whoever they may be, are positive role models in the search for risk-free driving. If the bulk of research has credence, then a follow-up question may be asked: Should guidelines be placed on potential new driver supervisors?

With reference to Goffman (1963b) young novice drivers become like discredited persons. Although they passed all of the prerequisites for driving, they are assigned characteristics that distinguish them from other drivers. All new drivers, the majority of whom are teenagers, have been grouped on the basis of experience and statistical tabulations that show new drivers are a threat to themselves and the well-being of society. Based on statistical reports governments consider them to be less trustworthy than older and more experienced drivers. New drivers get caught in a preventive philosophy under which they experience interventions for behaviors in which they personally may never have engaged.

The strategy can be compared to a classroom. The teacher, after having left the classroom for a few minutes returns to find a disturbance was created. To her chagrin the culprits refuse to identify themselves and the class prefers to stay silent. Consequently the teacher punishes everyone. The motive of wanting to preserve order and discipline in the classroom is sound, but to punish both the guilty and the innocent can be considered unjust (LeMaire, 1982). Two questions come to mind. Do the innocent suffer with the guilty? Where is the fine line that allows traffic administrators to negotiate community safety standards while preserving individual freedom?

The call for marking novice drivers is a call for special treatment. To help pave the way for designer licenses, a stigma theory on novice drivers was developed. It explained their inferior skills and limited driving experiences, which, when added up are believed to produce dangerous driving, resulting in huge economic, medical, social, and psychological consequences. As it turned out, young novice drivers have been characterized as being cognitively and/or perceptually deficient. They are suspected of having questionable motives for driving, less experience, and lesser talents than more experienced drivers (Simpson and Mayhew, 1991). But most important they are perceived to be more dangerous. Witness Mayhew and Simpson's introductory statement on probationary licensing:

> We began this report by demonstrating that young drivers continue to be overrepresented in both minor and serious road crashes in Canada. . . . In this context, we examined previous work in this field and determined that two principal causal sources have been cited: one of these was the cluster of attributes and characteristics that are unique to youth; the other involved the cluster of variables related to driving experience (or lack of it). . . . Results of our analyses showed that both age-related and experience-related factors are linked to collision rates. (1991: 117)

All three licensing programs reflect a control ideology. McKnight (1985), an influential traffic safety policy researcher, illustrated the extent to which the ideology is prevalent. He announced that provisional licensing schemes must include restrictions that are distasteful to drivers in order to be effective. It was thought that the negative stimuli would motivate new young drivers to change their "typical" way of driving.

The intervention strategies contradict Moynihan (1986), Bronfenbrenner (1979), and Baumrind (1978), all of whom agreed that the powerlessness of young people should be redressed. Their rights and privileges should be increased and negative sanctions should be decreased. These recommendations presupposed that the youth are a disenfranchised minority; victims of society. The views were shared by Coleman (1975), who referred to the youth as a "subordinate nation." Unless an ethic of private fulfillment and radical autonomy is balanced by an ethic of civic commitment and interpersonal caring, a sense of alienation occurs (Bellah et al., 1985). The estrangement from society cannot be solved by imposing further restrictions without risking further confusion and alienation (Baumrind, 1987).

Regardless of evaluation findings and literature on youth rights, social interventions have been introduced by way of restrictive licensing practises. For example, in Maryland, Pennsylvania, New York, and Louisiana curfew laws were implemented that prohibit young novice drivers from operating a motor vehicle during nighttime hours. They were considered on the basis of research by Williams (1985), Karpf and Williams (1983) and Williams and Karpf (1984), who concluded that young people's nighttime rates of fatal crashes are higher than those of older drivers.

Lower speed limits have been introduced in Australia. Provisional drivers are not allowed to exceed maximum speeds of 80 km/h. The logic used to support the innovation was that reduced speed is a safer speed. The risk of getting into accidents is reduced and the severity of injury to drivers involved in crashes is lessened (Drummond and Torpey, 1985).

Passenger restrictions, or lowering the number of passengers that the holder of a junior license can transport has also been implemented in Australia and at the time of writing this book, is being considered in parts of the United States such as Pennsylvania and New York. The reason given for the restriction is that internal distractions, particularly those with passengers, precipitate crashes among young drivers (Robertson, 1981).

It should be noted that restrictions such as night curfews, reduced travel speeds, and passenger limits were introduced without new drivers having been given opportunities to become educated about such risks. While it has been generalized that new drivers engage in risk-taking behaviors, the accused have not received formal access to education or training for high risk traffic situations. There is no opportunity to master the complexities of driving and achieve standards of learning required to cope with the many traffic exigencies. The criticism gains significance in light of Payne and Barnack's (1963) research findings that early detection and avoidance of emergency situations can reduce the accident involvement of normal drivers. Yet opportunities where teenagers can learn cognitive and physical skills needed to maneuver in dangerous or high-risk driving situations are conspicuously absent. Few financially feasible opportunities exist for new drivers-to-be to study decision making, values orientations, attitude development, driving risks, or drivers' legal and social responsibilities.

Designer license restrictions are passed *to* young drivers, not *for* them. They become after-the-fact compensation measures for an inherent weakness in the driver preparatory phase. Through provisional licensing schemes young drivers are restricted from participating in activities for which they have not been properly educated, trained or assessed. The restrictions are external impositions, conducted without the co-operation or involvement of the people whom they are supposed to serve and with little thought given to individual needs and expectations. The issue becomes not what to do to whom, but how to extend participation in decision making. It concerns the extension of power in decision making rather than the preordination of that power (Wilkins, 1984).

The noninvolvement of "marked" people follows a pattern in which "faulted" or "discredited" persons are acted upon and not acted with (Goffman, 1963b). Their driving identities are externally produced and compensatory actions are developed accordingly. Instead of a dull laundry list of restrictions, agencies can develop a bold plan that addresses the empirical findings on young driver problems, social concerns for safety and young driver perspectives.

It may prove useful to attend to the important aspect of social development, that of dealing with the novice driver's ability to adopt the perspective of the other road user. The ability to assume the position of other drivers is a prerequisite for a proper understanding of road safety practices.

How Well Are Designer Licenses Doing?

Traffic agents or officials claim that licensing restrictions contribute to a common goal—a reduction in the number of automobile crashes. In light of this spoken aim, it is worthwhile to see how the claim holds up. McKnight, Hyle, and Albrecht (1983) assessed the Maryland provisional licensing program that stressed a late-night curfew between 1:00 a.m. to 6:00 a.m.. They found no significant effect on nighttime accidents among the sixteen and seventeen year olds in the program. The change they did demonstrate was reasoned as an overall part of a downward trend in nighttime accidents among sixteen year olds relative to older drivers. However when Preusser, Zador and Blomberg (1984) analyzed the same data, they found substantial effect of curfews. As Mayhew and Simpson (1991) pointed out, unfortunately the researchers failed to consider the overall trend in nighttime accidents that was originally calculated by the McKnight team. Nevertheless, concerned organizations such as STAYSAFE (1988) drew their own conclusions, suggesting to the Australian government that road safety benefits from curfews are uncertain. They only contribute to personal costs of reduced mobility and freedom without proven benefit of improved safety. Disregarding the STAYSAFE argument, the government introduced provisional licensing legislation.

Not content with the finding that restricted nighttime travel by young people had little effect on reducing nighttime crashes, Williams, Lund, and Preusser (1985) recommended more stringent measures. They called for curfews to begin at 9:00 p.m. rather than twelve midnight. The authors rationalized that by introducing even more severe restrictions, youths would be dissuaded from getting their licenses, thereby providing a chance for critical improvement in age-related accidents. Their response reflects the American fascination with behaviorism. Failure to show reductions in the rates of condemned behavior can be taken as proof of the need for further escalations; or the greater the threat, the more likely a change in driving behavior (Jacobs, 1989). This partisan stance illustrates that although uncertainty in outcome continues, decision makers or those advising decision makers prefer increased control. The judicious combination of rationalization, elements of scientific determinism, and ideological preference for state control places the experts in a powerful position to make serious recommendations for increased state authority.

A similar pattern exists for lowering novice driver speed limits. Mayhew and Simpson (1990) reported that measured safety benefits resulting from lowered speed limits for new drivers have not been established. Their confession is accentuated in light of the treatise that speed variance and not pure speed is a significant variable for crash risks (see chapter 9). If speed variance claims made by researchers like Solomon (1964), McCarthy (1988), and Garber and

Gadiraju (1988), among others are valid, then the rights of novice drivers have been curtailed for risks that have not been convincingly defined.

Doubts may also be raised about the issue of the number of passengers in cars.   Johnson (cited in Waller, 1986) presented evidence that the crash risk among young drivers is lowered when they have less than two passengers.   After a thorough review of the literature Mayhew and Simpson (1990) concluded that at most, restricting young drivers from carrying passengers "could" or "may" result in safety gains.   There is little profoundness in the conclusion. Common sense suggests that if any drivers transport less passengers a decrease in the number of roadway fatalities is assured.   More important, the conclusion neglects to mention the social design of motor vehicles, which encourages people to socialize.   The minivan, for example, is advertised as a suitable unit for driving family members and friends in comfort.

Although restriction of passengers is being studied by a number of jurisdictions in the United States and Australia, several important factors require critical reflection.   First, many young drivers transport family members while they are learning to drive and after they receive their license.   Second, a passenger restriction could have the unintended consequence of encouraging young passengers to license early and to drive their own vehicles resulting in an even greater affront to safety than the number of passengers carried by young drivers (O'Connor, 1986).

The special license format for young and novice drivers reflects the paradox that society must segregate in order to integrate. Despite limited evaluative evidence of success, new drivers are aggregated, isolated, recorded, and analyzed according to predefined criteria. Through segregation policymakers expect novice drivers to become socially approved, problem-free drivers, resulting in the reduction of crashes.

The principle of segregating novice drivers has striking similarities with the framework called "Techniques of Neutralization," developed by Sykes and Matza (1957).   By renaming it "Techniques of Accusation" the rationale for categorization and special treatment would look something like the following:

1. *Accusation of Responsibility.* Policy setters declare that because of statistical analysis and categorization, young drivers are responsible for the accidents they have caused and therefore they must be controlled to change their driving behavior.

2. *Accusation of Injury.* Traffic agencies suggest that young drivers will hurt other roadway users simply by their presence and behavior on the road. The analysis of aggregate data prove this.

3. *Accusation of Victim.* Because young drivers are categorized as having the greatest number of accidents, as a group they deserve to incur driving restrictions regardless of driver training, individual maturity, values, competencies, history and social/economic needs.

4. *Condemning the Condemners.* It matters little that researchers have produced evaluation findings that fail to prove the effectiveness of control measures, young drivers must be controlled through licensing.

5. *Appeal to Higher Loyalties.* Traffic agencies rationalize that they are engaging in increased control of young drivers as part of their fiduciary responsibility. By increasing the safety of young drivers, the overall safety of society is enhanced.

The argument traffic safety agents use to explain safety and accident-free driving has validity, but if reviewed carefully, it lacks depth in thought. The basic rationale given is that safe driving prevents accidents, and people who do not have accidents are safe drivers. So far the reasoning makes sense. The critical point about the rationale is that safe driving is defined entirely in terms of outcomes. It says little about the act of driving, or behaviors that can be changed to prevent collisions. It negates the issue of drivers whose behaviors may not place them at personal risk, but whose actions may increase the overall risk on the roadway. Of note are motorists who drive 50 km/h on a 80 km/h two-lane highway. Such drivers may be termed safe on the basis of speed, because they are not likely to get involved in accidents. However, obstructing the traffic flow may motivate other drivers to take risks in order to pass.

Conceptual schemes based entirely on outcomes reflect a narrow definition of safety—one that can suffice for concrete policy change. A comment made by a provincial government official and echoed by others was, "Something has to be done, and done quickly to lower the carnage on our roads. We'll try whatever we think works and won't cut too deeply in the government purse strings."

The Licensing Context

The process of licensing cannot be discussed in a social vacuum. It belongs to a social context, one in which the automobile has become the mainstay for mobility in North America. As president Warren Harding said in his 1921 message to the United States Congress, "the motor car has become the indispensable   instrument in our political, social and industrial life" (Flink, 1975: 140).

Harding spoke of what may be called "automobility". It is symbolized by a transformation of national culture, changing thought, and language. As the Lynds (1929) demonstrated, the motor vehicle has come to symbolize quality of life, good times, and employment. Car ownership has become commonplace. It is seen by citizens as symbols of self-respect, material prosperity, and individual mobility.

With the extensive use of the automobile, urban life shifted from the inner-city community to the suburbs. It eliminated the necessity of locating the place of residence and work in close proximity. Shopping   centers,   factories,   and   other   business   establishments decentralized (Gold, 1982). To retain their jobs, workers had to drive. A major change in social relations resulted. One's neighbors now worked in locations at the other end of the city and one's co-workers no longer lived in the neighborhood.

Suburban development, distant work sites, destruction of mass transportation such as electric cars and trains and a dramatic increase in highway construction motivated or even forced people to become car drivers, giving way to the automobile culture. Graham (1989) provided some figures that outline the extent to which motor vehicle use in the United States has increased. In 1945, 31 million cars were registered and the annual miles traveled were 250 billion. In 1965 there were 89 million vehicles registered and the distance traveled was 888 billion miles, compared to 1985 when 163 million automobiles were registered and annual distance traveled was 1.7 trillion miles. In the province of Ontario the estimated number of kilometers driven in 1931 was 5,602,000 and in 1980 it rose to

72,419,000 kilometers (Ontario Ministry of Transportation and Communications, 1980).

The steady increase in distance traveled per year demonstrates that people have come to depend on the automobile as the primary means of accomplishing their travel projects. Citizens shop, commute to work, visit, search out medical assistance and enjoy recreation opportunities through driving (Rothe, 1990a). With the increasing emphasis on automobility, people have come to regard driving more as a right and necessity to fulfill functional needs than as an earned privilege or luxury for the select (Shinar, 1978).

There is a societal expectation that nearly everyone has the capacity to and will operate a motor vehicle. Consequently the driver license has become a symbol of livelihood and life-style. In the United States the Supreme Court ruled in *Dixon vs Love*, 431 USA 105 [1977] and *Mackey vs Montrym*, 443 USA 1 [1979] that there is a substantial property interest in a driver's license, an interest that cannot be easily infringed on (Jacobs, 1989).

The license represents access to employment, recreation, medical help, everyday sustenance, and familial gatherings. For most people in North America, driving a motor vehicle is the only reasonable answer to distance, suburbanization, regional sprawl, and limited mass transit. Without it, lives would be restricted and some people such as rural dwellers, would be trapped within a transportationless environment.

The Social Meaning of the Driver's License

Although the driver license represents formal authority for a citizen to operate a motor vehicle, it has come to mean much more to individuals. The license symbolizes a "coming of age," or becoming "a person of consequence." It designates a major shift in status. Persons who were passive passengers are now active drivers. They enjoy independence and the freedom to partake of personal mobility. In the words of Berger and Berger (1975), the individual has gained a new identity that was obtained through the deliberate effort of acquiring a driver's license.

The driver's license or miniature certificate of identity has come to be an extension of a person's self (Eisenhandler, 1990). It gives shape to a person's behavior outside of motoring. For example, as a form of identification it is used and expected to be used when people cash cheques, or when they wish to enjoy a few drinks at the local tavern. The driver's license is considered to be evidence of age by most liquor establishments.

Financial institutions often match signatures on checks with those on driver's licenses. For those licenses that have the holder's picture on the top-left hand corner and vital information on the bottom, the license verifies who the holders are in comparison to who they represent themselves to be. Crossing the border from Canada to the United States does not require a passport;   sufficient proof of Canadian citizenship is a driver's license. Without one, Canadian travelers may be denied entry into the United States.

It follows that for individuals living in North America and other developed countries, the possession of a driver license is an important socialization document. It brings the world to them. People are recognized through it.

Furthermore the driver license is a symbol of trust and integrity. The government grants owners the right to drive without being continuously observed. To do otherwise would be overly expensive and impossible. The driver's license affirms a jurisdiction's trust that the holder of one has internalized the demands of proper driving and that this internalization will control the person's conduct on the roadway. The licensee is expected to understand driving through the silent voice of the driver's license, which says, "Do this" and "Don't do this."

Conclusion

By constructing a critical perspective on the driver's license one can confront a number of general concerns. The first centers on the question, What is a license worth? The answer to this question may well determine the nature and course of future licensing strategies. As an attributional approach to this query suggests, earning a license in North America does not mean competence, tactfulness, breadth of social and technical learning, or safety consciousness. It simply signifies coping at the lowest level of vehicle operation.

The limited worth of a driver's license comes as no surprise to motor vehicle department personnel. They are fully aware of the limitations. In keeping with their interest in affording maximal participation in automobility, government administrators prefer to select empirically demonstrated high-risk groups such as young novice drivers and develop control strategies for them. They believe that by doing so, safety will be enhanced. For officials, the strategy provides least political opposition and conveys a willingness to deal with the problem of accidents.

To support a strategy of control for certain drivers-to-be, governments introduced designer licenses such as probationary, provisional and graduated licenses. By doing so they invoke a form of stigmatization. Young novice drivers as a collective group are evaluated as not having the attitudes expected of "normal drivers." They have a spoiled identity based on a series of statistical analyses. Little is done to provide opportunities for young novice drivers to learn problem-solving, and decision-making techniques that will help them overcome supposedly negative assessments.

Investigating the legal right to drive in a social context of automobility is particularly complex. So much in daily life depends on driving. In many cases, especially for those living in rural areas, the need to drive cannot be taken lightly. It may well mean economic survival for some people. To change the rules could have social ramifications beyond the constructive good of imposed designer licenses. To date the latter have not proven to be effective in evaluation studies.

Equally important is the view that a driver license means more than simply an assessment of skills and knowledge. It is an extension of self, proof of identification in certain business arrangements and a symbol of social competence. These factors should be considered when driver's license policies are considered.

6

Becoming a Driver and Ex-Driver

I slept and dreamt that life was Beauty;
I woke, and found that life was Duty.

—Emerson

As was described in the previous chapter, the driver's license is a public artifact whose meaning extends beyond legality. That is, its meaning reflects the ways in which individuals see the license, the ways in which they are prepared to act toward it, and the ways they are prepared to talk about it (Blumer, 1969). Accordingly, the value placed on a license can be illustrated through descriptions on what it means to get one.

To flesh out the significance of a driver's license, 200 young licensed and unlicensed students, fifteen to nineteen years old, were interviewed in group sessions as part of a major young drivers study (Rothe, 1991c). Although many themes were explored in the original study, the social meaning of the driver license was not one of them. For the purpose of this book the essential theme is expectations students have of earning a driver's license and the meanings they attribute to possessing one.

At the opposite end of the spectrum, losing a license is another life situation that is significant and meaningful. To establish the extent to which losing a license effects senior citizens, data from a survey of 904 senior drivers, focus group interviews of 230 elderly people, and 130 open-ended interviews with senior motorists who recently experienced injury-producing accidents were re-analyzed from an original study by Rothe (1990a).

Becoming a Licensee

In discussions about becoming licensees, teenagers embraced self-accepted views that served as key dimensions of meaning. They were neither rare nor esoteric. They were rules of thought that supported their involvement in driving. The most emphatic of those offered was, "I can't wait."

Can't Wait to Get One

Throughout the analysis of the data, one was repeatedly struck by the passionate expressions of anticipation. Status was put on the line. Students could not wait to get a driver license, because they assumed it would have a positive effect on their social life, association pattern, employment opportunities, opportunity for romance, and independence. The legal right to drive was represented as a milestone, one that signaled a new era of adulthood.

With few exceptions, teenagers in grades ten and eleven planned to pass the driving test on their sixteenth birthday or as soon as possible thereafter. For those licensed, anticipation was described in retrospect. It was only a matter of days after their sixteenth birthday that they received their license. One teenager was disappointed that his birthday fell on a Saturday when the Motor Vehicle Department was closed. Another boy claimed that he started a countdown-to-driving 100 days before his sixteenth birthday.

The majority of boys characterized themselves as being unable to wait, claiming that they had been thinking about driving ever since "getting over" riding the BMX bicycles and walking the streets (Stoddart, 1988). Some claimed that the last couple of years had been boring, as they had given up some of their "younger" pursuits like BMX riding. They expected that driving would fill the gap and open new possibilities.

Students shared the view that "getting-a-license-by-sixteen" was normal. In contrast, not getting a license at or near the magic age of sixteen was translated as abnormal. One teenager, exemplifing the characterization of normality uniformly agreed to by others, insisted that those teenagers who do not get a license shortly after their sixteenth birthday would be embarrassed and possibly try to hide the fact. He said that, "only geeks don't want to drive." Another boy referred to those not getting a license at the accepted symbolic age and date as "wimps."

One student described the social repercussions he experienced for not having received his license on his sixteenth birthday. As "punishment" for coming home drunk at the age of fifteen, his parents decided to restrict him from getting a driver license on his birthday. For three months he had to wait in "agony". In his own words he "felt like a fool." All of his peers knew his birthday had arrived and that he was not able to drive.

Although the majority of boys expressed an unbridled enthusiasm for licensure, a collective view shared by most of the girls was that they did not feel the urge. They did not feel bound by the social expectation to be licensed by age sixteen. Licensure was a low priority, something that could wait. Rather than methodically preparing to get a licence, girls were content to depend on their friends, boyfriends, and parents for transportation. Indeed, whenever girls spoke of getting their license it was with a more considerate and low key approach, one that suggests moderation and life facilitation rather than life changing (Stoddart, 1990). However the common expectation shared by both boys and girls was that a license means symbolic participation in adulthood. It was assumed to enhance their quality of life.

Social Life

The typical scenario described by nonlicensed students, approaching the legal age of licensing, involved their inability to participate in extracurricular activities such as sports, clubs, and bands. To become involved meant asking parents or friends for rides. This scenario had special significance for rural students who live miles from the school and who are cut off from public transportation.

From their point of view, getting a license is "the ticket" for considerably more freedom and a "much richer social life." They can break free of parents who do not want to drive them to events, wait around and transport them back home, or whose work schedules make it difficult to drive their sons or daughters back and forth for extracurricular activities.   Because of these difficulties,   students described themselves as being "stuck" once the school bus dropped them off at home. They cannot keep up with their extracurricular calendars.

Some students portrayed their hardships with precision. One girl was heavily involved in competitive figure skating and ARCT piano lessons. She needed to make extensive transportation demands on her parents.   Supportive as they are, she said, "they can only take so much" (Stoddart, 1988).   She anticipated that her parents would finance her driver's license and might even buy her a small car. Several students claimed that it was natural for their parents to drive them around when they were younger, but no longer.   They felt parents were getting "fed up."   Mothers and fathers occasionally complained about being their sons and daughters' taxi service. For some, the concessions they had to make were too great. For example, one father liked to have a few drinks before dinner "but cannot on those evenings when his daughter has softball practise" (Stoddart, 1988).

Students are at the age at which they want to move beyond "sitting at home and watching television," which in the case of some living in rural areas meant staying glued to one or two channels watching programs like "The Tommy Hunter Show" or "Jeopardy."

Changing Association Patterns

Sixteen is a featured age, a "coming out" celebration, a theme consistently offered by interviewees.   Sixteen meant social and physical changes, one of which is friendship selection. At this age students search out and select friends of interest and not of physical proximity.   Whereas they used to typically "hang around with whoever lived nearby,"   now their friends lived in different communities or municipalities, ones that could not be easily reached by foot or bicycle.

Because secondary schools are more centralized than elementary schools, students who befriend each other here may live significant distances apart. This factor is especially relevant for rural teenagers. After-hour events or get-togethers among schoolmates are considerably more difficult, if not impossible, without a car.

The changing association patterns are also significant because, during the teenage years, socializing is more important to students' self-esteem and growth than at any other time in their lives. Hanging out with others takes on major significance. For most students, inability to do this produces anxiety and personal unrest.

Interviews with teenagers revealed a shared concern about having "little to do" within walking distance from their homes. To make matters worse, shopping malls have security guards who students believe are told by storekeepers to "shoo" them away. Finally, the community centers offer few programs that teenagers enjoy. Most of the planned activities for teenagers are managed by adults whose versions of a good time are not synonymous with young people's needs and wants. The generational difference is usually solved in favor of the adult interpretation. According to the young people, the ability of adults to assume the position of teenager is far from adequate.

Criticism was directed at the municipal administrations for not providing enough youth-oriented facilities. They ignored the high value young people place on being together, listening to music, associating, or hanging out. The youth prefer facilities such as teenage nightclubs or Happy Days-style hangouts within close proximity, where they can be "cool" to "what's happening" with their generation. Still, some students would need access to transportation.

Dating

A prerequisite for teenage social development is dating. To say that students, especially boys, are eager to drive to make dating easier is a dramatic understatement. Driving makes the physical act of transporting a date easier; it also promotes close physical encounters between daters, and it sustains an image of maturity as boys drive their dates home.

With the advent of driving, students are no longer dependent on parental or public transportation. As one young man put it, "Have you ever tried to fool around with a girl on the bus?" Another made the same connection concerning the lack of opportunity to fool around in parents' chauffeured vehicles. Some students refused to date when parents drove because the embarrassment would be too great. The image of mother or father chaperoning in the car is too difficult to "live down" in front of peers. "After a while you start to feel like a fool," said one boy, a view supported by others (Stoddart, 1988).

Girls tended to rely on boys, girlfriends, or boyfriends for transportation. Like boys, they would also like to have use of cars for privacy and retaining an acceptable image before other girls. However, the car need not be theirs and they need not be the driver. A boyfriend or girlfriend's car was considered perfect. They did not oppose parental transportation as vehemently as boys, but it was, nevertheless, considered as something to think about before they agreed to date a boy whose parents might be driving.

A further footnote to the discussion should be added. Gender differences in views on dating were detected. Girls appear to possess a more comprehensive repertoire of social skills than boys. They were less inclined to date. For many, a "good time" was a likely to be a group of girls driving to a party or dance than it was going with a boy. They elaborated on the theme of developing independence as a way of not being "hung up on one guy" or being controlled by parents.   Nevertheless, access to an automobile was a desirable feature for managing their life-styles.

Freedom from Parents

For boys, receiving a license meant that they could drive around out of their parents' watchful eyes, or escape from being under the parental thumb. They could drive around with friends without the need of parental approval. Also they can get to see the friends they wish to see without prior parental evaluation of the character of those friends. Although many boys like to spend time with their friends on weekends, they prefer that it not be at home. To accomplish this socially vital goal, they need a driver's license.

Licensed and recently licensed girls commonly spoke of parental influence in ways that suggested they were not as preoccupied with the goal as were boys. They were not as ready to dismiss the chance of girls getting together in one another's home. But, they felt, there had to be opportunities when friends could get together to talk about private matters outside of the parents' visual reach.

Some licensed students explained that once they received their license, parents placed greater restrictions on them. Their whereabouts, driving behavior, and curfew time were more closely monitored after licensing than they were before. Unlicensed drivers dismissed this "gloomy picture" and "still couldn't wait to drive." They felt that the opportunity to drive outweighs any life-style cramping imposed by parents. They would "just feel better."

Employment Patterns

Teenagers routinely invoked economic interests, or more commonly, the need for part-time employment at off-hour fast food locations or gas stations. Without a license would-be workers have little flexibility to drive home late at night. They would not, or could not depend on parents for their transportation needs during late hours. For teenagers, the answer was self-evident. A driver's license and access to an automobile would offer them the advantage of employment opportunities and allow them to be totally independent in the process.

Waitressing at pizza shops, cafes, or roadside diners, scooping ice cream at drive-throughs, flipping hamburgers at fast food outlets, or pumping gas at service stations were defined as made-for-teenagers work opportunities. Unfortunately the businesses are usually located in adjacent communities, municipalities, or in parts of the city a "fair ways from home." To get there teens needed to drive.

By focusing on how young people construct their expectations of obtaining a driver's license, readers are in a better position to appreciate the value that is placed on it. A license is not just a toy with which children play in the park; one that agents can manipulate as they wish. It is a necessary and vital feature of teenagers' everyday reality that has a profound impact on their definition of self, sociability, and economic potential, a fact that becomes evenmore pronounced when a person is faced with the eventuality of losing a license.

On Becoming An Ex-Driver

Embedded within the inventory of an individual's life-span is a cluster of experiences referred to as stressful life events (Gentry and Shulman, 1988). Ones typically referenced are marriage, the birth of a child, retirement, and widowhood, the latter two of which are usually documented as stressful. Retirement results in a loss of self-respect and social status, lowered morale, and problematic identity. Widowhood results in the living spouse having to re-orient his or her life toward single living. While retirement and widowhood are usually specified as significant life events that have major ramifications on the senior citizen's social involvement, coping abilities, and well-being, a third one that may be featured is the loss of driving privileges (Rothe, 1993). It is an all-pervasive mentality that makes the loss of a driver's license a major stressful life event.

The Efficacy of Driving Termination

A theme detected in the research was self-efficacy and driving termination as it related to personal control and system responsiveness (Gurin and Brim, 1984). Based on the research, a generalization can be distilled. Although senior citizens are aware that the possibility of losing the right to drive exists and that they have little choice in the matter, they do not believe that the probability of losing a license is likely to happen, and if it does, they will be so old that it matters little. Consequently, they are reluctant to prepare for the eventuality, believing that if it should happen there is little they can do about it.

Senior citizens consider the laws relating to driver termination to be beyond their control. Political institutions, medical organizations, and vehicle control agencies are believed to have the power to make unilateral and binding decisions. A typical response produced by interviewees was, "I have little control over the matter." According to Mirowsky and Ross (1986) and Wheaton (1983), loss of control of one's own life can diminish or decrease coping effort, or "enabling potentials" (Shotter and Gergen, 1989). Prospects or visions of what might be are transformed from the possible and probable to the permitted.

Fatalistic comments such as, "I guess I'd stay at home, that's it" or I would just pack it in" were often given. Most translated the loss of the right to drive as "devastating," "frustrating," "heartbreaking," or "a frightening experience like losing a right arm, or dying."

Generally elderly drivers try to ignore the impending finitude of driving and hope for the best. One elderly male recognized that as you age you "lose your abilities in the method of your driving." Being seventy-one years old at present, he does not believe any decline in driving ability will occur until he is between the age of eighty and eighty-five. By then "we'll have the life span up to ninety and ninety-five and I may not start worrying about it at eighty."

The elderly drivers recognize the impending physical and mental problems associated with aging and driving but they try to rationalize the moment away into the future. Much like Flaherty's (1987) concept of duration dragging, elderly drivers aged sixty-five plus chronicle temporal driving realities as lasting well into the future, despite recognition of present driving limitations. For some the future date is marked by calendar time—seventy, eighty years of age; for some it is translated into onset of special medical ailments—stroke, high blood pressure; while for others the moment is measured by self-analysis of incapability to drive:

> I can't imagine life without driving. I know someday it will come. When you get older you can't drive, but my mom is 87 and she is still driving. So I have lots of time yet.

> The basic thing is to make sure you're not subject to a stroke which can kill not only yourself but a number of other people. I think the medical side is the only reason to give up your driver's license. Luckily I'm healthy.

A point for consideration is offered. Elderly drivers recognize that they may have to stop driving because of certain physical impairments that hinder their driving. Nevertheless they believe that their ability to compensate for certain impairments allows them to continue on. For example, for some elderly drivers, the inability to turn their heads is considered to be a signal for driving termination. Others with such a problem disagreed, because according to them, experience, not physical impairment is the key factor:

The ability to turn your head is a very good point for quitting. There again experience is a factor. You have two rear view mirrors, I use them fully— you have blind spots, but not if you recognize the factor when you are going. It's a matter of learning to be patient. Always park in a parking lot to move ahead. Never get caught backing up.

It is the understanding of self at an older age, rather than objective age itself that is important.

The reason they put a mandatory sixty-five on things, it's a name, a number when you retire. But a lot of people are great at sixty-five. At sixty-seven they're not as good as they used to be. They think so. Who's gonna tell then they're not. Who's gonna tell me I'm not when I'm eighty.

The sense of future and the loss of driver's license indicates a strong attachment to self, whereby elderly drivers define themselves as having the capacity to compensate for perceived physical or mental difficulties (Kalish and Knudston, 1976). Elderly drivers often try to prolong the "inevitable" by choosing to drive in a certain way, but they recognize that the acute event of driving termination hovers over them regardless of their present-day activities.

Because of the low self-efficacy on planning for their loss of driving status, the seniors regularly invoked the Canadian Charter of Rights as a benchmark rationale for defense of their beliefs. They repeatedly provided accounts that claimed they had the inalienable right to drive until a serious health problem arose, which was considered to be a remote possibility. The seniors argued that withholding the right to drive is a clear illustration of prejudicial action against a defined group.

Senior drivers felt that they were being denied control in the decision to quit driving because government agencies are predisposed to objective data such as written and/or road tests. Presently, most provincial and state motor vehicle department make termination decisions solely on the basis of a medical evaluation and/or a road test, both of which exclude involvement by the senior drivers. The elderly drivers agree that deteriorating health is a consideration for removing driving privileges, but, they were quick to point out, seniors have learned to compensate for it by avoiding risky driving scenarios.

Respondents answered that they avoid troublesome driving circumstances such as fog, rain, snow/sleet, nighttime glare and long distance travel.   Over the years they have matured, driving more defensively and cautiously.   Overall, senior drivers believed that they have become more conscientious and serious about driving. These qualities were considered to be adequate compensations for the onset of health problems that come with age.

Some of the senior drivers had the impression that as the number of seniors on the road increases in the future, the likelihood of government agencies increasing their power over them also becomes greater.   To counter the suspected trend and to retain a say in future decisions on driving termination, the seniors would like to see the establishment of a safety net such as an appeal board.   It would resemble a Workers Compensation Appeal Board, comprised of experts and senior lay people empowered to review driving termination decisions.   This process would help assure that senior motorists' self-perceived competencies and personal efficacy is considered.

Whereas the majority of senior drivers try, as one male driver said, "to shove the thought about never driving again to the back of their minds," they realize that cessation of driving because of health reasons could happen. When they were asked about life after driving, it again became apparent that they did not plan for a reorganization of life-style after loss of license.   Rather, they considered possible or plausible vignettes of life after driving, often in desperation.

On the Buses

The obvious alternative to driving a vehicle is to ride the bus. The option, however, is one many would choose reluctantly. In the focus group interviews and discussions held with accident victims, it was established that the quality of passengers ("vandals" and "rough, loud people"), or the number of passengers on buses (overcrowding and standing) makes riding on transit buses an experience often described as "hated" and "dreaded."   Witness the following representative quote:

> I went a couple of times to Vancouver and you get these bunch of kids in the back and then they start screaming, it's enough. Like once you get older you don't want to be with this, someone screaming at you all the time. You kind of want to be like semiretired, you want to be left alone you don't want this.

Although taking a bus may solve conventional transportation problems, it contributes little to the elderly person's yearnings for sociality. They could not go "golfing," on "picnics," or "hunting":

> Well it would put a real crimp in my retirement wouldn't it? I'd be stuck. I couldn't get out for golf or anything. Carry clubs on the bus? No way!

They would find it difficult, if not impossible to visit friends or family because the latter live "far away" or they reside a long distance from a bus line. Evening visits would definitely be out of the question.

Researchers such as Adams (1971) and Butler and Lewis (1977) wrote that there is a link between morale, life satisfaction, and enjoyment in the later years of life, and the interaction and maintenance of relationships with friends and intimates. Friendship is an integral factor in the adjustment processes of older adults. They are better equipped to cope with the role of becoming "old" when interaction with friends and intimates is possible, or when friendship relations maintain role continuity (Blau, 1973).

Reliance on busing to retain a friendship circle was considered by some senior motorists as, "ridiculous," "totally stupid," or "crazy." In short, it cannot be done because of considerations such as bus scheduling and routes that do not provide easy access to most communities or suburbs. As a result, 57.1 percent of the elderly surveyed answered that rather than take the bus to retain their friendship circle they would stay close to home or become less social (48%). There was little that could compensate for the loss of driving and visiting friends or family.

The longing to retain some form of mobility after the loss of a driver's license was also described in terms of walking, the most elementary, yet vital form of transport.

Walking

For two thirds of the surveyed population, walking is an obvious alternative to driving, but a confined one. It becomes a practical choice only if the distance to a destination, weather, health, and geography are considered, factors that are uncontrollable by the individual.

One elderly man aged seventy has no access to a bus and would find walking an unproductive choice if his license was taken away. He said,

> We don't have a bus. I'd have to walk down to St. Johns or up to the Comox light. If you go downhill you have to come back up. Going uphill is not easy at my age. I have a very difficult time getting up this hill.

Some elderly drivers have health problems such as poor blood circulation in their legs or a heart conditions that keeps them from walking great distances. One elderly lady suggested that because of her inability to walk she would have to "sit at home and write letters or something like that." Others are scared of walking in the winter because they might slip on the ice. To go shopping on foot would require many trips because the elderly cannot physically carry a week's supply of goods and walk home.

To adapt, some elderly people suggested that they might move to a city condominium within walking distance of shopping facilities or near a bus line. They considered the possibility of such a move as stressful from life-style and cost of living points of view. Because of changes in their driving careers, the elderly are, according to a respondent, "pushed into doing something that's really not needed. It's trauma, really."

For most people, a move is a short term crisis that over the years becomes normalized. For the elderly, the eventual reorganization is long-lasting. This is especially true for those living in the rural districts or city suburbs. If they were forced to move it would be a cultural challenge (Rothe, 1990a). The need to make new friends, to discover community services, recreation opportunities, and shopping facilities without benefit of an automobile becomes a lasting time of disconnectedness, even social alienation. Their hopes are on hold and their life in the future takes on new twists and turns, events most elderly drivers prefer to avoid.

Some elderly drivers defined walking as a continuum of driving. They take the car to the woods or the park to take leisurely walks. This scenario produced an image of a healthy self-concept, characterized by "getting away" and "exercising." It reflects a vibrant life-style experience.

Once the vehicle is removed from the event, walking loses the health or recreational meaning. The elderly lose the need to "get out and get away." Instead of voluntarily walking in the park or forest for relaxation, the seniors are expected to walk city streets to buy groceries or other necessities.

Taking a Taxi

As a usual means of conveyance, taxi use does not rate high on the seniors' list of transportation preferences. Taking a taxi is an expensive option very few senior drivers were willing to consider. Some recognized that "taking a taxi" is a choice, but one they would be reluctant to make. If all else fails, taxis may be used, as for example in an emergency health care situation. As an everyday alternative, riding a taxi does not fit with the elderly person's on-going plans.

Conclusion

The license to drive a vehicle is synonymous with self-respect, social membership, independence and quality of life. As one senior explained, "It means enjoyment of culture, the arts, everything, church, friends. It's the avenue of life."

Drivers maintain a continuing claim to identity and membership in the larger community through the laminated driver's license. It bestows formal recognition of social competency and maturity, documenting personal identity and worth (Eisenhandler, 1990). To withdraw the right creates a crisis, a stressful life event for the senior driver. It points to the proposition that the quality of an older person's life is largely dependent upon the means of personal transportation (Scheidt, 1984).

The driver license shores up a personal and social identity that belies chronological age. For the young, the driver license represents a range of benefits—independence, convenience, access to myriad social roles, and necessary transportation. Holding a license verifies that one has managed to meet a series of formal expectations.

The symbolic tie between having a driver license and being part of the larger active world is instrumental in keeping identity intact and robust at the same time that it may present danger to the individual and others (Eisenhandler, 1990).   Therein lies the crux of the problem. To what extent should the novice or new driver, searching for independence and social status, be subject to arbitrary rules that governments impose on driving practices?   The right to drive is eagerly awaited among the young and not surrendered willingly among the old (Eisenhandler, 1990).

7

Constructing Traffic Laws

*Societies somehow 'need' their quotas
of deviants and function in such a way
as to keep them intact.*

—Kai Erickson

Nearly three hundred years ago a group of Dutch settlers brought a game to North America called "ninepins." It proved to be a hit. Nearly everyone played it in bars, taverns, and wherever people gathered. It spread like wildfire across the continent.

To extinguish the fire, because of the gambling it produced, Connecticut and New York passed laws against it. Players were subsequently charged and if convicted they were fined or sent to prison. As a result, would-be players felt constrained to enjoy the game because the police, for a time, spent considerable energy on enforcing the law. Taxes were raised to subsidize the catching of ninepin players.

In hindsight the enactment and enforcement of the ninepin law proved to be wasted attention. People were so determined to play this game that they introduced an extra pin and made the game legal again. They started playing it once more and they have continued playing it ever since, calling it ten pin bowling. The game survived. The law died. In retrospect, making the game a violation of the law seems questionable. Will future generations say the same about some traffic laws?

The superintendent of the Ontario Provincial Police (cited in Willett, 1974) noted in a provincial workshop on traffic safety that the exigencies of modern driving conditions often force people to break the law. He cited the rush-hour conditions on Highway 401, which often force motorists to speed and follow too closely. He concluded that

> where the law is in such cases so out of touch with the realities of the driving experience, people are merely bewildered by it as it is often applied. (Cited in Willett, 1974: 19)

Consider the trend. In Canada, over the last ten years or so, over 1 million drivers per year were convicted under the Highway Traffic Act (Friedland, Trebilock, and Roach, 1988). This was five times higher than the number of persons charged under the Criminal Code, and it only represented those "dumb enough to get caught" (Macmillan, 1975: 42). Feest (1968) found that only 20 percent of drivers stopped at stop signs when there was no danger.

Chambliss and Seidman (1971) noted that as societies change and become more industrialized and complex, laws that regulate the encounters of individuals become necessary. To assure order, and to bring some predictability and coherence in human behavior, government officials introduced control measures that may be bent, but not broken.

The need for increased social control in the sense of "where things are going" is personified in traffic laws. Consideration of which driving behaviors are high risk and should be controlled, necessitates a discussion of how and why state authorities can and do proscribe some roadway behaviors while allowing others. To help assure that the life of traffic continues to be a smooth, ongoing process, officials have enacted a legal strategy composed of a series of decrees that rationalize driver behavior, differentiate and classify drivers into separate types and categories, increase segregation of drivers into penitentiaries (e.g., drinking drivers) and other rehabilitation institutions (e.g., driver retraining courses), and invoke a philosophy of deterrence. The strategy featured a shift from the principle of compliance—which attempts to prevent violations of the laws from happening to the principle of deterrence—which allows violations of the laws to occur so that the violators can be punished (Reiss, 1984).

Lave and Lave (1990) introduced an interesting observation that traffic laws not only achieve order but they may also enhance mobility. If legal controls were removed, drivers would have to engage in elaborate procedures to signal their respective intentions, which could slow traffic to a standstill. As a result, the disappearance of regulations in an urban setting may be more safe than unsafe. Without the facilitation of traffic laws, traffic flow might become so slow and burdened that damage from accidents would be limited or it would virtually disappear (Lave and Lave, 1990). Unfortunately, in a modern urbanized society built on speed and efficiency, the idea of a lawless roadway would be at best a utopian ideal, completely removed from the lived reality.

Traffic laws exist to identify and encourage driving behavior in accord with a smooth functioning roadway, and to deal with nonconformist drivers who aggravate the hazards of traffic movement. From another perspective, traffic laws, like all laws, may be perceived as a form of social engineering in civilized society (Quinney, 1970). Witness the following announcement made by the Ontario Registrar of Motor Vehicles:

> Primarily it may be said that the traffic laws are intended to provide an environment for orderly movement of traffic as to minimize congestion and frustration and to ensure the fastest point-to-point movement of motor vehicles. Coupled with this, an atmosphere of predictability is engendered, largely eliminating the need for intuitive or diagnostic thought by the driver as he faces traffic situations. As a result of these effects, there is a reduction in potential vehicular conflicts which may develop into collisions resulting in loss of life, injury and property damage. (Centre of Criminology, University of Toronto, 1972: 46)

Through the Ontario government's bifocals, traffic laws are seen as reducing personal or intuitive thinking, thereby increasing the chance of coordination, conformity, predictability, and orderliness. In contradistinction to the individualistic perspective, which is commonly assumed to be chaotic, uncoordinated and accident-prone, governments are committed to conscious planning and coordination in which the welfare of every road user is assured. These goals are expressed in daily life through social institutions, organizations and public agencies. Schutz (1971), noted that people often experience the world as prescribed by such social institutions as law makers,"I find myself in my everyday life within a world not of my own making. I experience these transcendencies as being imposed on me" (245-46).

Legal statutes transform the individual self into an idealization of the collective. To clarify the shift from driver as individualist to driver as collective participant, several features were catalogued. Although they appear as dualities, they are usually not featured as such in drivers' lives. Motorists may find themselves leaning one way or the other in their beliefs about traffic and the law.

Driver as Individual	Driver as Collectivist
Self as driver follows libertarian ideals	Self as driver follows collectivist ideals
Self as driver desires impulsive driving	Self as driver desires constraints through external controls
Self as driver is loyal to self	Self as driver is loyal to the collective
Self as driver adheres to standards of personal will	Self as driver adheres to social standards of driver conduct
Self as driver is discovered and explored	Self as driver is achieved and attained
Self as driver is concerned about the present	Self as driver is concerned about the present and future
Self as driver participates in driving as expressive movement	Self as driver participates in driving as self-control entrenched in institutional structures
Self as driver uses personal standards for judging safe driving behavior	Self as drier uses collective standards for judging safe driving behavior

Central to the viability of a collectivist ideal is that individual drivers surrender some of the differentiated privileges and attributes, so that they may lie peacefully in the maternal bed of society (Cooley, 1966). Today's traffic laws emphasize control of driver individualism for the safety of all drivers and efficient mobility. Impaired driving, speeding, and non-seat belt wearing laws continue to be the most popular regulations (Friedland, Trebilock, and Roach, 1988). They fall within a penal style of control. That is, penal control prohibits each of the above behaviors, and it enforces its prohibitions with punishment (Black, 1976).

The processing of alleged offenders is not only the result of faulted driving behavior. It also arises because the behaviors in question violated a collectivist law that forbids those behaviors (Durkheim, 1953). For example, speeding, identically performed in different locales with the same material consequences, is sanctioned according to whether or not a rule forbids it, and the extent to which law officers interpret the behavior as a violation of the law. Their tolerance levels determine how speeding is considered routine or cause for sanction (for a lengthy analysis of police tolerance, see chapter 8). Speeding, condemned in normal driving, is permitted in time of emergency. Exceeding the speed limit by 20 KM/H or 12 MPH may be considered routine on the freeway but not on suburban streets (Rothe, 1992). These examples illustrate the impossibility of a neat scheme. Situations that are problematic and for which existing laws are interpreted and negotiated, constantly arise within the scope of traffic

To help specify how traffic laws are intended to establish forms of joint action, three groups of prescribed conduct can be discussed. Group one includes laws of "position." A set of laws allocates the use of parts of the roadway according to normative driving behavior such as distance between moving cars, lane changes, direction and speed. Group two determines the order of presence at intersections (Ross, 1960). Examples are statutes pertaining to stop signs, rights-of-way, traffic signals, and similar devices. The third set of laws includes driver and vehicle appropriateness. The conditions of drivers and vehicles is emphasized. For the driver this includes intoxication, driver disabilities, wearing seat belts, having insurance coverage, and possessing a driver's license. Laws pertaining to the automobile regulate standards of safe brakes, lights, tires, installation of seat belts and other mechanical devices.

Traffic Laws and Accidents

Although the three sets of traffic laws are usually invoked to establish common safety, they become problematic when related to traffic accidents. They cannot be considered a homogeneous class of events with common circumstances and common causal factors (Macmillan, 1975). To begin, most violations do not result in accidents. Imagine that it is twelve o'clock midnight. There are no nearby vehicles in the vicinity. A driver runs a red light. A violation occurred without an accident. This is not an idle point easily dismissed as being obvious. There are many situational factors at play to question the legitimacy of claims that violations cause accidents. For example, relevant intervening factors such as traffic flow, time, location, purpose of the trip, and the state of the driver must be recognized to establish how and when drivers disobey laws without causing accidents (Gusfield, 1981). Because motorists drive according to how they define the traffic situations in which they are called to act, violations without accidents occur frequently.

While on the streets drivers have reciprocal expectations of each other. They take evasive action to avoid collisions with other drivers regardless of who is violating a traffic law. Besides, violating drivers are not mechanized automotons. They also take evasive actions, such as sudden application of brakes, last-second steering maneuvers, or quick acceleration to avoid crashes. Although it may be said that violations increase the possibility of accidents, it is questionable to assert that violations increase the certainty of accidents, or conversely, that accidents are normal outcomes of violations.

Not all violations discovered in connection with accidents contributed to those accidents. An appropriate example is possession of a driver's license. Suppose a driver who is involved in an accident has forgotten her driver license at home. Driving without a license is a breached traffic law. However, it is doubtful that an accident would have been avoided if the driver had had the operator's license in her possession. Another example is an intoxicated driver waiting at a red light who is rear-ended by another driver. Although the victim driver is guilty of impaired driving, the accident was such that it would have occurred even if he had been sober. It would be highly unlikely that driving under the influence of alcohol at the time of the accident was a contributing factor of the accident.

Violations also occur without recognition by drivers. For example, motorists may be unaware that they passed a highway sign with a reduced speed limit, or that they failed to see a stop sign. This occurrence should not be shrugged off as yet another excuse for errant driving. If Hughes and Cole (1986), Milosevic and Kajic (1986) and Shinar and Drory's (1983) research findings are taken seriously, up to 50 percent of people's visual attention is directed toward non-driving-related objects, and only 50 percent of all road signs are perceived by drivers. Drivers may look at a road sign but they may not register what it says. Rather than a willful attempt to violate the law, there is a reasonable chance that the action resulted from normal lack of alertness to the driving task (Hughes and Cole, 1986).

Yet in a court of law, the crown in Canada or the district attorney in the United States would likely suggest that there is a general speed for the entire province or state on rural highways and interstates, in cities, towns, or villages with which drivers should be familiar. The need to give evidence of situational variations of speed is not required. Regardless of the physical location of speed limit signs, it is assumed that drivers' familiarity with speed limits should be sufficient for them to drive within the speed limit (Hutchison and Marko, 1989). In the Provincial Offences Act, section 81, the statute reads that ignorance of the law by a person who commits an offence is not an excuse for committing the offence (Kastner, 1987). The principles are:

1.   allowing a defense of ignorance of the law would involve the courts in insuperable evidential problems;
2.   it would encourage ignorance of the law where knowledge of the law is socially desirable;
3.   every person would be a law unto himself, infringing the principle of legality and contradicting the moral principles underlying the law; and
4.   ignorance of the law is blameworthy in itself. (Stuart, 1982: 261-68)

According to Hutchison and Marko (1989), the suggestion that all drivers know the laws and bring their behavior within its confines is nothing more than legal fiction or wishful thinking.

At the risk of sounding redundant, nearly everyone disobeys traffic laws occasionally. Some motorists may interpret a speed law as an infringement on individual freedom. They may not consider the potential or actual harmfulness of breaking laws. In the words of Lyman and Scott (1970), they excuse their actions as acceptable because of the irregularity and infrequency of accidents they experienced when they have engaged in previous law breaking. A buried statistic worth unearthing was originally presented by the American Bar Association. For the year 1955, in 889 American cities, there were 21 million traffic cases filed, of which 8.5 million were "moving" violations (Ross, 1960: 235). A series of typical motives can be assigned. Some drivers were habitual traffic law violators and got caught in the process. Others were out to seek thrills and excitement. Some were unaware of the law within certain situations (Ross, 1960).

Other reasons can also be entertained. For example, drivers may have violated laws because they deemed social responsibility to have been more important than legal policies. Traffic signs may have been missed because of perception difficulties. Drivers may have been unaware of their speed after having driven extensive number of hours on highways, and so forth.

Some law violations may result from lack of minor skills. Motorists may have misjudged the slickness of a roadway surface or have not properly steered a vehicle through a tricky part of the roadway (Ross, 1973). Furthermore, momentary inattention, or poor depth-of-field perception may have caused some drivers to misjudge the speed and/or distance of oncoming vehicles.

The examples are not presented to be dramatic or to illustrate the extraordinary. They reflect a usual state of affairs in driving (Wilkins, 1964). Although these examples illustrate everyday drivers experiences, they conflict with the strict letter of the law. The judiciary reconstructs the reasons for violations as, for example, failure to abide by the law, knowledgeable negligence in driving behavior, purposeful disregard of the law and safety, and/or premeditated misuse with mal-intent of the automobile. Furthermore, if a driver, as a result of one or more of these reasons is unfortunate enough to become involved in an accident, the violation becomes the cause. Intent or awareness become irrelevant and insignificant.

If one assumes that all drivers violate traffic laws, it should come as no surprise that Jimmy Carter, the former president of the United States, was clocked at an average speed of 72 MPH for a twenty-two-mile trip from Metro Airport to the Detroit Plaza Hotel. Apparently, arriving at a campaign appearance on time took priority over following the 55 MPH doctrine (Bedard, 1983). Yet, the former president, while in Oklahoma, stated at a town meeting, "I think the law (55 MPH) should be enforced I think it saves a considerable amount of energy and I also think it saves a considerable number of lives" (Bedard, 1983: 70).

On Trial

Motorists have a mental picture of proper trial procedures. They expect that the charge against them will be judged on legal merits, that the case will be compared with the evidence, and that they be presumed innocent until proven guilty. But, when a motorist's driving behavior brings her in conflict with the law, the intent to violate a law or drive negligently does not have to be proven by the prosecuter. The burden of proof is on her to show "due diligence" or reasonable effort, under a regulatory scheme (Hutchison and Marko, 1989).

The rationale underlying the legal process is more concerned with efficiency than with legality. Officials consider gathering proof for intent or " mens rea" as impractical because of cost, time, and lack of standard (Hood, 1972). Court officials perform a needed service. To do so effectively they neutralize barriers that are considered to be hindrances. According to Morton and Hutchison (1987), the burden of proof on the motorist is questionable. It negates the fundamental assumption that a person is innocent until proven guilty.

Traffic Laws as Deterrence

A point regularly made by law officials is that deterrence works (Friedland, Trebilock, and Roach, 1988). In brief, the cost of undesirable driving behavior is deemed to be a function of the expected probability of apprehension, conviction, and severity of punishment (Friedland, Trebilock, and Roach, 1988: 198). If any of the variables are increased, the targeted behavior will diminish (Tittle, 1980).

Discussions on simple deterrence and traffic bring to mind concerns expressed by Bittner and Platt (1966). The two sociologists advised that punishment based on deterrence is inherently unjust. If examples are made of some persons to deter others from deviant actions, then the former suffer, not for what they have done, but on account of other people's tendencies to do likewise.

Still, legal officials invoke simple deterrence through the development of legal strategies that are believed to help reduce the number of crashes and fatalities on the road. To promote the common good and harmony of society, the courts must penalize and be seen to penalize conduct to deter others from engaging in it.

In a way, individual drivers are responsible not only for their own behavior, but also for the behavior of all drivers. The notion has a strong resemblance to the essence of the great Dostoyevski's ethic that each person is responsible to all, for all.

In the search for greater control, simple deterrence of a charged driver has been linked to general deterrence. Drivers are warned that regardless of who they are, if they commit a violation they will be punished (Ross, 1982). The extent to which the warning is workable, practical, or honest is open to debate. Friedland, Trebilock, and Roach (1988) responded with a passage taken from the Canadian Sentencing Commission:

> Deterrence has to rest, at least partly, on mystifications . . . The criminal justice system is led to bark louder than it can bite in order to sustain the public's belief in the certainty of the legal sanctions. (Cited in Friedland, Trebilock and Roach, 1988: 41)

In order to insure that a justice system's "loud bark" is heard, the spotlight is directed on the media. Through news reports, public service announcements, editorials, public debates, and feature presentations, justice is shown to work and the long reach of the law is shown to be ever-present. Community police blitzes on seat belts and impaired driving reflect the theme that a driver who fails to follow the law is certain to be caught, because the police are out in full force for the defined purpose of stopping the lawbreaker. The rationale usually includes a footnote, carrying out traffic laws is not an end in itself for the police, but an effort to further the safety of the community.

Some sober reflection is required. Imagine, for a moment a situation where there was no law enforcement. Would the accident rate increase? Carr and Schnelle (1986) assessed such a claim by analyzing data from a 1976 Kansas study. Their conclusion from the retrospective study was that wide variations in the overall level of enforcement have no measurable impact on the frequency or severity of accidents. Their study supported Gardiner's (1964) research in four Massachusetts cities. He concluded that there was insufficient evidence to support the theory that large number of tickets produce low accident rates, or that high accident rates cause the police to adopt stricter ticketing policies. Similar findings were reported by the National Academy of Sciences (NAS) when a team of researchers analyzed data from fifty American states for the years 1974 to 1983. Based on an independent analysis, the Federal Highway Administration (1976) concluded that the level of police enforcement had little or no apparent effect on the mean speed or on the accident experience in their study sample. Campbell and Ross (1968) reported that an unprecedented crackdown on speeding in an eastern state had no discernable impact on automobile fatality rates. Later, in 1973, Ross concluded that there is no effect on subsequent driver history for those appearing in traffic court and those having received warnings. On the basis of these studies it might be prudent to reserve judgment on the idea that the use of law enforcement as a strategy to prevent accidents is effective. Deterrence, at best, may give favorable short-term results but these soon regress to numbers established prior to increased enforcement (Friedland, Trebilock, and Roach, 1988).

Another critical issue concerning the law and deterrence is long-term versus short-term gains. Enforcement deals primarily with negative motivation, causing people to avoid certain types of driving behaviors. Strict enforcment may be an effective means of breaking drivers' bad habits, but is less effective in creating good habits. The latter is not a goal of deterrence philosophy.

Attitudes toward Traffic Laws:
A Guide to Behavior

If you start with the assumption that attitude helps explain behavior, there is merit in uncovering the attitudes a problematic group like teenagers have toward traffic laws. In the words of Blumer,

> The attitude is conceived to be a tendency, a state of preparation, or a state of readiness, which lies behind action, directs action, and moulds action. Thus, the attitude or tendency to act is used to explain and account for the given type of action. (1969: 93)

The intent is not to establish a direct relation between attitudes toward traffic laws and subsequent driver behavior. Rather, the attitude provides an orientation upon which drivers judge, define, and organize driving actions. A description of attitudes toward traffic laws is, therefore, a useful strategy for developing a social construction of traffic laws. As a basis for description, 200 hundred young people's responses to open-ended questions about the law and normal violations were analyzed. Although they were originally collected for a book on young drivers (Rothe, 1991c), they were re-analyzed for the purpose of this manuscript.

Views of the Law before Licensure

Based on the group interviews, it appears that an attitude towards traffic laws already exists when young people, not yet licensed, formulate for themselves the kinds of drivers they will become. Their constructions of future selves as drivers suggest principles, actions, and rationalizations emulated from acquaintances and parents.

Unlicensed teenagers consistently defined how they expect to drive as their friends do. They described how their experiences as passengers had influenced them to the point that they are likely to speed and disobey traffic signals whenever the need warrants it. For them it was a matter of situational ethics. Numerous illustrations were offered that outlined the premise that ignoring traffic laws or traffic controls was a reasonable and normal thing to do if someone was in a hurry and needed to arrive somewhere on time.

The boys conceded that once they were licensed they were likely to violate speed limits. They revealed that a disregard for speeding laws was normal, defined by them as "minor," "no sweat," a form of driving that "everyone does." They did not consider themselves to be an exception to the rule.

The unlicensed girls' collective attitude on speed laws differed from the boys. They were less willing to accept the boys' assumptions that speeding is normal behavior. Some expressed fear of driving fast, while others adopted the collectivist ideal that lawbreaking is immoral behavior. As one girl expressed it, "if a law is to be broken the driver better have a damn good reason for it." Worthy reasons were presented. For example, an emergency such as injury to someone in the car, or the need to arrive in time for work or for a test could justify breaking the law. Another scenario girls offered was being caught in a situation where "a guy suddenly cuts you off." There are no alternatives and precautions that could not have been reasonably taken. Whereas the girls tended to emphasize legal responsibility, the boys argued that legal responsibilities should be negotiated according to situations and circumstances.

The difference in attitude may reflect the different meaning driving has for boys and girls. Based on the interview data, boys are more likely to use the car as recreational vehicles and the streets are more likely to be recreational sites. Risk taking is a vital ingredient in recreation. Girls are more likely to engage in purposive journeys such as running errands or reaching specific destinations for specific reasons. They are less inclined to take lawbreaking risks and more likely to concentrate on orderly, goal-directed driving.

Licensed Young Drivers and the Law

The overall impression gathered from licensed boys is that regulations and laws constrain their movement or "cramp their style." There was little evidence to suggest that they internalized a need to obey laws. They claimed to comply with laws "when necessary," meaning when there was a reasonable chance of being observed by the police. The boys expressed that they speed regularly—though usually not dramatically—when the chance of being spotted by the police is minimal.

Low commitment to compliance of traffic laws also reflected in their assessment of driving situations. In good driving conditions, such as proper visibility, nice weather, and low traffic density, speeding was considered to be a safe thing to do. Seldom did students relate the importance of obeying laws to safety. For them the featured attribute of traffic safety is to drive like an expert, meaning that drivers know how to get out of tight spots through quick reaction moves.

Some licensed teenagers reversed the logic of safety. They thought that by compliance with the laws drivers may be unsafe. There were discussions of how drivers who followed "the letter of the law" cause accidents. An illustration that re-appeared in the interview data concerned drivers who keep within the speed limit, but who fail to keep up with the flow of traffic. Teenagers reasoned that these drivers force others to slow down against their will, creating an urge to pass, which if not done properly is unsafe.

During the interviews young drivers were not hesitant to invoke their parents as displays. They assessed their parents' driving as being "less than perfect" and often in violation of statutes. Most observed that their parents consistently break traffic laws. One teenager stated, "My dad's always watching out for cops. The way he drives he has to." Another said that his father told him—in the course of teaching him to drive—that it was not important to follow the laws at all times. His father's interpretation of compliance with the law was reflected in his remark, "that's the way old women drive." Several students suggested that it was their mothers who helped maintain orderly driving. As one teenager claimed, his mother is "always after" his father to slow down when they are on the highway. To further illustrate the point, the parents of some students drive cars equipped with radar detectors. Fearing they would become illegal, one father went out and purchased a spare, "just in case."

"Do as I say and not what I do," was the advice parents gave to young drivers. Some young people "drive as they were told by their fathers." They were taught that it is not just a matter of respecting the law, but being practical about it. This may mean going through a stop sign if no one else is around, or breaking the speed limit when the need arises. The onus is on drivers to minimize the chance of being observed by the police. A licensed grade ten student, claimed that his father, while teaching him to drive, encouraged him to speed up in order to "get the feel of the car."

A violation commonly committed by young boys is the "taxi-stop." They think it is foolish to make a full stop at a stop sign when there is no need to. With few exceptions, taxi-stops were identified as routine driving practice. Equally consistent was "loading up a car with people," many more than there were available seat belts. Like their unlicensed counterparts, licensed students claimed that this was necessary and not optional. Not to crowd in all the friends who want a ride was considered to be a breach of moral obligation. "You can't say no," said one.

Girls displayed a greater readiness to stop whenever the law required them to do so, slow down where needed, and accomodate laws such as seat belt wearing. A greater number of them would at least think first before allowing more passengers in a car than there were available seat belts. However, in the final analysis, girls like boys, leaned toward the social rule of "giving everyone a ride." Girls who found themselves in vehicles packed with boys and girls had to be on the alert for "roving hands," something the girls disdained. As a result many of them refuse to enter cars overloaded with teenagers of mixed gender.

Audience Segregation and the Law

For teenage boys, driving is a performance before an audience. They put on different displays for friends, dates and parents. The one for friends is more dramatic and frequently in violation of traffic regulations. The one for dates is "coolness," while for parents they put on a two-hands-on-the-wheel show, a "smooth stop and start" version. Before friends it is not unusual for them to round corners a little quickly, and to speed on residential streets to dramatize expert driving status. With girls they are more likely to speed, but with confidence and savoir faire. In front of parents expert driving is restaged as traveling within the parameters of the law: slow and safe.

While boys claimed to perform out of role before parents and in role before friends, girls tended to be more consistent in their driving performances. They preferred to "take it easy" regardless of who is accompanying or observing them. They like to think of themselves as responsible and law-abiding. Some noted that complying with their legal obligations instills within them a sense of pride and social duty.

Views of Impaired Driving

Impaired driving has special significance in traffic safety. Traffic safety researchers and agents consider it to be a leading cause of automobile accidents and fatalities. It is singled out for media treatment, police enforcement, punishment, deterrence, and educational programs. It is *the* social problem for some community activist groups. In short, impaired driving has become the spectacular issue in traffic safety.

In their discussions on the topic, teenagers tended to separate the objective from the subjective. From an objective perspective, boys and girls considered impaired driving to be a potentially dangerous practice. However it would be a grievous error to assume that young people's attitudes toward impaired driving is a law abiding one. Some supported penalties such as like roadside suspensions and loss of license.

From a lived experience point of view, most licensed and unlicensed drivers knew of someone who had been charged with impaired driving: uncle, brother, friend, father. Conspicuous by their absence were aunts, sisters and mothers. Although several tales about females engaging in impaired driving were presented, they were in the definite minority. The matter was quite gender specific. Males were usually characterized as having been involved in impaired driving and confrontation with the law.

Accounts of personal experiences with impaired driving often included versions of social criticism. One grade twelve boy related that a family he knew "was thrown into welfare," when the father, a truck driver, lost his licence because of impaired driving. For him, the price paid by the family—disintegration and upheaval—had exceeded the crime committed. Others had their fathers charged with impaired driving, resulting in mandatory license suspension and loss of jobs. One father lapsed into an alcoholic depression and "hasn't been the same since." Equally severe was another story about a father suspended for impaired driving. The grade eleven boy felt that this was unfair because his father only had a few drinks, which did not make him drunk. "He's a good driver and he's driven a lot worse than that," he said. Because of a driving suspension, his father, a logging truck operator, "had to go back into the bush" resulting in "a heart attack" which put the family "almost on welfare." The young man inferred a direct causal relationship between the punishment for impaired driving, his father's health, and the family's trying economic status.

Punishment was usually documented as impact on the family. The questions posed were: Why should families be "ruined" by "one little mistake" made by a father? Why should the law damage a family beyond repair? A ruined family was designated as one that became financially troubled, socially stigmatized, stressed, disintegrated, or one that became dependent on the charity of others for its transportation needs.

From students' points of view, the law on impaired driving should be applied with reason, tempered with a degree of humanity and consideration for the family of an arrested party. Some suggested that the law should be more of a teacher, educating drivers about their negligent behavior, but not punishing them into "oblivion." What the law *will* do to the victims of a family is no better than what an impaired driver *may* cause on the roadway. Others thought that the law should be less legalistic and more socially based. Judges should determine whether a serious social problem exists with the accused—whether, for example, a driver or family requires help in order to meet their needs. To do so judges should take all the circumstances into account when they impose severe penalties.

Some teenagers proposed that the courts should emphasize driver competence rather than depend entirely on the results of a Breathalyzer test. They assumed that people can drive "alright" when they are impaired, or according to one student, "My father says that you can sometimes drive better when you're a little bit drunk." There was general agreement that impaired charges should be laid only when or if the driver is "really" impaired in an ability-to-drive sense. Unfortunately, the students could not specify how such an assessment should or could take place.

One teenager proposed that his brother drives better after taking a few drinks than he does when he stays sober. Better driving results from fear, or as he said, "He's so afraid of getting caught that he drivers real slow and follows all the rules." Another teenager supported the claim, suggesting that his friends are more cautious drivers after they have been drinking. "They're so afraid of getting stopped they drive more normal than they usually do." These student claims should not be written off as legitimizations. They were supported by traffic officers, one of whom suggested that today's impaired driver is more likely to drive slowly to avoid detection (Rothe, 1992).

Students supported the impaired driving laws and sanctions in principle, but once the laws were personalized, agreement evaporated. Most agreements with the law were expressed by girls. A few felt that the penalties were not severe enough. They wanted higher fines and longer license suspension terms. But, more importantly, they disagreed with the it's-ok-to-drive-with-only-a-few-drinks rule espoused by the majority of boys. They called for zero tolerance and no breaks for those caught. Drinking even the smallest amount of liquor was considered to be dangerous. Rather than apply an experiential base for their assessment, the girl's "proof" was collected from sources like the media and/or school programs on impaired driving.

Impaired Driving as Normal Violation

The majority of licensed and unlicensed students, regardless of gender, have been exposed to impaired driving as passengers with lovers, friends, and/or parents. The difference arose with actual involvement in impaired driving. The general rule for the boys was that they are likely to drive after a few beers, but not if they were drunk. Girls are more inclined to follow a safe pattern by not participating in impaired driving.

For boys, driving impaired is not like driving drunk. On numerous occasions they presented a picture of confusion between drunk and impaired. They would never drive drunk, yet they are willing and actively do drive after having "a few beers in the pub."

Conclusion

Laws do not emerge from nowhere. Other events lead up to, prepare, and set the stage for them. Accordingly, a social canvas of traffic safety should include the development and unfolding of traffic laws, the contingencies of their development, and the delineation of groups involved in the activities. A description of the context of traffic laws provides for a deeper understanding of drivers' personal reactions to traffic laws and how these reactions are interpreted by traffic safety officials.

8

Policing Traffic Laws

You can't carry water in a sieve.

—G. Nettler

Along with their responsibility to prevent violations of traditional criminal laws and to enforce and gather evidence of those violations, the police are charged with achieving community conformity with rules designed to make collective life minimally workable. One function of this charge is to regulate traffic, so that modern commercial life can prosper and a semblance of order can be maintained.

Some police officers have traditionally defined their performance in traffic safety as a service function—a nonprofessional role. It requires meeting constant comments of resentment from people who committed traffic offenses, but who do not believe or agree that they deserve to be penalized. Drivers frequently offer opposition to a traffic citation because of the innocuousness of the offense (Skolnik, 1966; Rubinstein, 1973; Ross, 1960).

Skolnik (1966) wrote that assigning the police to traffic detail may be considered a strategic move to improve or maintain a jurisdiction's economy. Municipal administrations and courts have been known to utilize police authority to meet budgetary requirements rather than enforce public order. This strategy is not lost on citizens, who suspect that speed traps are used to engender high fines rather than maintain public order or enhance traffic safety. It has become a

This chapter originally appeared as a paper presented at the Qualitative Analysis Conference, Carlton University, Ottawa, Ontario, 22-25 May 1992.

lucrative "cash cow" for jurisdictions, without the bad publicity that comes with tax increases (Skolnik, 1975).

More recently Eagan (1990), a retired police officer-turned-author detailed how speeding tickets are vital to the economy. They help pay for an army of civil servants, including police officers, court clerks, accountants, judges, secretaries, stenographers, bailiffs, computer operators, programmers, attorneys, and more. Munici-spalities draw on revenue from traffic tickets to purchase radar units, police cruisers, pens, pencils, and file folders. In the private sector, lawyers and insurance companies receive massive revenues directly and indirectly from speeding tickets. In fact, according to Eagan (1990), if everyone stopped speeding tomorrow, taxes would skyrocket and massive unemployment would begin. In a backhanded way, if elected officials were honest they would tell people that they owe it to their country to speed.

Smith and Tomerlin (1990) further supported the premise that tickets are economically valuable:

> Enormous increases in revenues since the passage of the national maximum limits, in conjunction with federally supplied radar guns, have made traffic enforcement an important funding source for state and local governments. Many jurisdictions now budget a year in advance for money from traffic fines, relying on such revenues for a major part of their operating expenses. (P. 4)

Still, at the street level, police officers believe that enforcement is a necessary and worthwhile strategy to maintain public order and increase safety. To do it successfully, officers must employ both discretion and tolerance.

A Commonsense Focus

A large part of policing traffic is to interact with motorists. Officers communicate, interpret, and adjust their acts according to the motorists they meet. Action unfolds as officers and drivers take each other into account. As Skolnick (1966) and Rubinstein (1973) discussed, traffic encounters are the single most frequent reason for contacts between the police and citizens. Because the majority of road users are motorists and truckers, they are the main subjects for officers' attention.

To highlight the essential elements of police-driver interactions Lyman and Scott's (1968) concept of coolness is used. As related to police work, *coolness* is defined as "poise under pressure in situations of considerable emotion or risk, or both." Paraphrasing Goffman, Lyman and Scott described *coolness* accordingly:

> The capacity to execute physical acts, including conversation, in a concerted smooth, self controlled fashion in risky situations, or to maintain affective detachment during the course of encounters involving considerable emotion. (1968: 93)

Smooth performances differ with respect to truckers and general motorists. They carry different meanings, rules of conduct, and intents. For example, when truckers are stopped, the meetings resemble a cultural ceremony, a form of plea bargaining, a staged interaction. Police officers and truckers are likely to negotiate common ground through mutual respect of roles; conversation in a concerted, smooth, self-controlled fashion; and willingness to negotiate each other's rights, responsibilities, and privileges. Constables are more inclined to treat truckers as professional street partners who, like the police, make a living in a tough environment.

Motorist encounters with the police are more regulated, and officers maintain an affective detachment during the course of encounters so that charges can be laid with minimum difficulty. Constables are more likely to impose their views on events or on drivers through tightly controlled interaction strategies. Traffic officers stage encounters by managing an appearance that they are preserving the sanctity of the law. To help them succeed they attempt to refrain from empathizing with particular cases. They take precautions to avoid being played for a fool and thereby risk losing their image as objective law enforcers.

The exhibition of coolness with truckers occurs for three basic reasons. One, officers view them as blue-collar colleagues who should be treated with respect. Two, police officers recognize the truckers' strategic value in policing the highways. For example, because truckers are radio-equipped and they ply the roads in great numbers, they can assist the police spot wanted vehicles, help in accidents, or warn officers of dangerous stretches of highway. Three, most police officers are insufficiently trained to properly check truck maintenance such as brake alignments, and they do not know the many intricacies of trucker log books. For some officers, trucks are intimidating and best left alone. They are not worth the risk of losing one's image.

Whenever truckers are stopped, police officers tend to establish a negotiated interaction during which they often make decisions as to what charges should be laid. Hence it is incumbent on truckers to make strategic interaction moves that they believe may lessen the chance of being charged.

As one long-distance hauler from Portland coolly remarked, "When the man stops you, you have to know how to play the game, how to play it right so you don't get burnt too bad."

As the trucker metaphorically stated, officers stopping truckers for violations of the law represent a game. For the purpose of this chapter, the game is a roadside encounter, marked by a series of moves (Goffman, 1967; Lyman and Scott, 1970). Hence this chapter describes the methods truckers, motorists, and police officers use to stage coolness, and in the process sustain a vision of order and appropriateness (Goffman, 1961). Although charging truckers and motorists are compensatory acts for those who violate laws, they take on observable patterns of social construction. From an analytic perspective, the encounters consist of "searching out a partner," "avoiding roadside encounters," "engaging interaction," "negotiating a way out," and "terminating the encounter."

Searching out a Partner

Before police officers engage drivers in roadside encounters, they have already done some thinking about who, and who not to catch. The filter they use for selection is discretion. Some traffic laws are written so vaguely and in such abstract terms (e.g., careless driving, unsafe conditions, inattentive driving) that by their very nature they must be dutifully interpreted to be enforced. For example, it is absurd to think that a speed limit is specific enough to include the many situations drivers experience. It is up to the officers to exercise discretion on reasonable exemption (Davis, 1975).

Discretion is the canopy of decision making. It is the basis for answering policing questions such as: Who is defined as a violator?

Who gets apprehended and who does not? Under what circumstances should the violator be apprehended? Once the decision is made to apprehend, and all of the variables are considered, will the driver be charged, warned, or let off?

Discretion underlies officers' personal tolerance levels, or standards of law violation with which "officers can live." Although parameters of lawbreaking are prescribed by the police departments, personal tolerance may override them. It is, as one officer stated, his "gift to the driving public," albeit a hardly visible or concealed one. If it were publicized, officers would be called on to present the moral, legal, and cognitive grounds for their tolerance, a possibility they want to avoid lest they lose their credibility as objective or neutral law enforcers.

Speeding is the most often used reason that the police pull over drivers—and speeding is synonymous with an officer's personal tolerance. As a rule, police officers are not likely to stop a vehicle for exceeding the speed limit by 10 MPH or less, although according to some officers they have the legal right to do so. Tolerance, ranging from 10 to 15 MPH over the speed limit is the significant factor. As a rule, officers are not likely to stop motorists who exceed the speed limit but who drive within an officer's tolerance level, unless other factors such as "blowing a red light" are involved.

Tolerance represents a personal judgment, one that is not formally prescribed by the police department. In the case of speeding, the tolerance level resembles a yardstick for apprehending traffic violators. Once the officer sets it, it becomes the standard, the line that one police officer suggested "motorists dare not cross." He continued:

> I can see going 10 over the limit. That's just the feel of the foot on the accelerator and stuff like that. But if you're 15 or 20 over on a street like this you gotta know you're speeding. No ands, ifs, or buts. If you don't you shouldn't be driving. You're responsible.

A common assumption shared by members of the traffic squad is that all speeders break the law and they could, objectively, be pulled over and charged. Like a "little white lie" motorists bend the rules. However only those motorists that exceed the officer's tolerance level are marked. This becomes a standardized rule. For example, the police radar is not set at the speed limit. Rather it is marked according to the individual officer's tolerance level. Anyone traveling above the speed limit but below the tolerance level does not merit official attention. Anyone driving over the tolerance level becomes a target with little opportunity for negotiation. Those drivers caught are almost certain to receive traffic citations. As one law officer stated, "Everybody gets a break up to 20 (km/h). Then its over. That's it. No way out."

One member of a traffic division constructed his own creative version of tolerance. He took action against motorists driving 15 km/h over the speed limit. Although he applied a lower tolerance limit than his colleagues, he did not charge drivers with true speed readings. If a motorist drove 80 km/h in a 60 km/h zone, the officer would likely register 74 km/h to prevent the driver from paying a higher fine and from accumulating three demerit points on the driving record.

Once travelers are spotted violating the traffic officers' personal tolerance levels, they are stopped. Charges are likely to be laid. As one officer said,

> I don't really care whether the guy beats or not. If I feel its the right charge, then I'm gonna lay it. If he beats it, he beats the system. He didn't really beat me.

Tolerance is a major factor for officers who assign violations on the basis of what they see. For example, a motorist may be spotted rolling through a stop sign. Each individual officer must decide whether the motorist will be apprehended. As one constable advised, "Its your tolerance whether you'll accept a 1, 2 or 5 km/h roll through a stop sign." Interestingly, the focus of his statement was not whether the driver did or did not stop, rather it was based on the speed at which the motorist rolled through the stop sign. Obeying stop signs has evolved to the point at which most officers do not expect drivers to make a complete stop, engage in a three-second count, and leave safely. According to one officer, when someone approaches a stop sign, "You kind of have to cheat on the corner a bit. Nobody does the 1001, 1002, 1003 count, like nobody. You'll be counting forever."

Whereas tolerance suggests the acceptable variation of breaking laws according to officers' personal standards, discretion refers to the officer's flexibility or freedom to select tolerance levels.   All the members of traffic details involved in the study agreed that they have a great deal of discretion within the loose structure of organizational norms. One officer was succinct.   He equated enforcing traffic to selling brushes.   Just as sales agents must sell so many brushes per month, constables must charge so many motorists.   In light of the traffic scene, where "six out of seven" drivers speed, filling a quota is easy.   According to the officers, there are plenty of opportunities to select the drivers they need, or as one said, "There are plenty of fish in the sea."

Safety is another roadway feature that warrants police discretion. Officers judge traffic conditions according to how safe they are for apprehending violators.   For example, while directing a track radar at oncoming traffic, a readout may show a driver speeding above the officer's tolerance level.   Rather than give immediate chase, the constable quickly assesses the volume of traffic, and the ease with which a U-turn can be made. Witness the following police account:

> I don't bother in town where there's a lot of traffic. You gotta be aware of the guy behind you when you make a U-turn. You gotta be watching for guys ahead, cars turning. Its fine at eleven at night when there's only 3 or 4 cars. See I got a guy in my blind spot right now. [Laughs] He'll just sit there right up to the next light.

Certainty of making a charge stick may also be a consideration before a charge is laid.   As a rule, catching a motorist for running a yellow light is considered to be a" waste of time."   Based on troopers' experience there is little certainty of getting convictions in court. So most police officers do not bother with motorists who drive through yellow lights. Although a constable may document a driver's actions, the speed of travel, whether the motorist was accelerating or decelerating, the location of the front wheels in relation to the intersection, and whether there was a crosswalk, he may still " lose it on a technicality."

Discretion as to who is stopped and charged is also reflected in how an officer assesses the fairness of a traffic law. Officers are not apolitical automatons. Rather, they consider the principle of fair play during law enforcement. One example is location.   Several officers did not run radars on certain streets because of what they perceived to be "unreal" speed limits. One location observed was a four-lane roadway with a 50 km/h limit. It was downhill from an expressway, with clear visibility, no housing development, and "bush on both sides." One patrolman reasoned:

> To my way of thinking, and I probably don't do this right, I say, ok the speed limit is 50. But it should be 60 to my way of thinking or 70. I have trouble going to that location with radar.

Although police officers pledge to uphold the law, they acknowledge that some traffic laws are not designed for safety or smooth traffic flow. They are political in the sense that "somebody knows somebody on council and gets the speed limit dropped." Hence drivers on such streets are less likely to be stopped than motorists driving on roadways that have speed limits more agreeable to the police officer's sense of appropriateness.

Conversely, other streets located near school zones, public parks, or senior housing complexes are considered to be dangerous. Here motorists may find two or three police cruisers at a time intent on apprehending and charging speeders. Officers would frequent these locations whenever they were bored and sought some action, or when they needed to fill their quota quickly. Some members of the traffic division referred to these sites as "fishing holes."

Discretion may be seen as the officer's individual "middle ground," upon which she decides to act. It substantiates the constable's sense of morality. An excellent example was provided by an officer:

> I have a lot of discretion. Oh yeah, unless you're heartless. I guess its kinda hard. You get a guy at two thirty in the morning, wife and kids in the back and he's been out picking worms all night, driving a '72 Chevy thats falling apart at the knees, blows an intersection. Are you gonna charge this guy or a guy making $150 thousand a year driving a Lincoln?

A motto one officer invoked to rationalize his actions was, "You got to live with yourself, too."

Seeking impaired drivers at night varied among officers. Each member used a personal standard of morality and drew on experience to assess the extent to which impaired drivers were high priorities for enforcement. For some, any driver who exceeded the tolerance level for speeding or drove in an exaggerated manner was assumed to be an impaired driver. Others believed that impaired driving had changed over the years. Nowadays impaired drivers were considered to be less inclined to speed or drive dangerously, because motorists knew that this kind of behavior increased their chance of apprehension. This group of officers did not assume that speeders at night were impaired drivers. However they did share the same perspective as their colleagues—drinking drivers must be removed from the road.

Although there was a concern for impaired driving, it did not reflect a zealous position that all impaired driving must be stopped. Some officers felt that it is not their job to "rid the world of all the social ills." They are just doing their job with the least amount of conflict and trouble as possible.

Once motorists trespassed an officer's tolerance level and became targeted, they were stopped and asked to meet with the officer at the roadside. There was little chance for avoiding the meeting. Drivers could either stop or run. "Ninety nine point nine percent of the time they stop," said a member of a regional traffic division.

Different rules of operation were invoked with truckers. They were not considered to be part of "working traffic" in the sense that truckers were herded into the officers' version of common violators. A different sense of discretion and tolerance was observed. It begins with the officer's opening move of selecting a trucker. In the United States the police cannot pull over truckers without "due cause." In Canada they are more flexible. For example, whereas in the United States the police cannot stop truckers for seat belt violations, they can do so in Canada. Unless it is a planned roadside or weigh scale inspection, state troopers must, by virtue of the law, be selective about which truckers they can stop. Although they may suspect that a trucker has falsified his log books, an obvious law must be broken before a trucker can be stopped and questioned about log books. The American police are, therefore, on the lookout for ways to stop truckers whose vehicles or drivers look suspicious, but whose driving behaviors appear for-all-practical-purposes legal. In Canada this process is de-emphasized.

Truck investigation officers have a stock of knowledge upon which they draw to fulfill the "due cause" principle. One cause officers used was the presence of misaligned or worn-out trailer mud flaps. By law, mud flaps must cover at least 70 percent of the tires and the top of the flaps must be parallel with the trailer's frame (Rothe, 1991a). Because mud flaps experience wear and tear from routine driving, a police officer who searched for "due cause" was generally assured entry through a mud flap violation.

Police officers were always on the lookout for the dividing line between legal and illegal behavior. One such case is the presence of yellow reflector lights on trailers. Typically, a truck's lighting system includes red reflectorization for taillights and backup lights. Yellow lights are used for turning and/or braking (Rothe, 1991a). To show their nonconformity some truckers install a unique, yet illegal rear light scheme. They replace two red reflectors with yellow ones. This subtle act of individuality is sufficient cause for state troopers to move on truckers. According to one trooper, yellow lights and broken reflectors allow him a "foot in the door to do a trucker's log audit."

A "must" for truck investigation officers was to keep an invigilant eye on improperly placarded trucks. The law states that vehicles must have placards displayed so that they are easily seen from the direction they face, their letters or numbers are level and easy to read from left to right and each placard is at least three inches from commercial trailer markings (Washington, The State of, 1989).

Because a hazardous load may pose environmental disaster, police officers were less flexible in their use of discretion. One American trooper had come to expect that "one out of every ten hazardous materials loads is improperly packed."

Cosmetic trucks and "beaters" also catch the officers' attention. The former are usually owner operator vehicles customized to perfection, worth in excess of $120,000. They represent "everything truckers own." According to members of truck investigation squads, to keep ahead of payments, the drivers of such vehicles must "drive long and hard." This made them favorite suspects for exceeding the legally allowed ten hour consecutive driving time. It was not uncommon for troopers to search for obvious violations so they could investigate the truckers' log books. Witness a California highway patrol member's corroborating account:

See how shiny their trucks are and everything? They clean up the trucks and all that. The shinier the chrome, the longer the nose and the more lights are on it, the more the guy owes. The big shiny trucks, long nosed Peterbilts, lots of chrome, lots of lights, $100,000 tractors, and all they've got to do is keep them on the road. That's their home, everything is in the truck. So they keep them shiny, drive them long and hard, and keep them looking pretty. They forget about the law, about the need to rest once in a while.

"Beater trucks" were also tip-offs. Officers characterized them as being old and dirty, running on bald tires, using misaligned brakes, and having broken headlamps and cracked windshields. The rule of thumb for the police was that the truck is an extension of the driver. If the truck is in rough shape, chances are that the driver is also in poor condition. According to the police, the beater suggests a reasonable possibility that the driver is using illicit drugs. As another officer remarked,

I'll stop a carney truck today. The carnival's moving through town, the worst trucks in the world. The lesser-class truck driver drives a carnival truck. Most of them are loonies. Stopped three of them the other day, two of them had warrants out on them for drugs.

Not only did the police exercise discretion on who to select for a roadside encounter, they also employed it to decide which truckers to avoid. For example, one state trooper hated to stop and inspect livestock haulers:

Don't ever stop a bull hauler. I won't stop them. They stink too bad. I stopped one already and had a cow take a whiz. It whizzed and it shot out of the truck. You don't crawl under to check their brakes—that's the last thing you do.

A more obvious reason for stopping truckers was speeding. At first glance the violation is obvious, direct, and self-explanatory. Yet truck investigation members did not consider speeding to be problem free. Their responses reflected measured discretions:

You have to add in everything like it's the only car on the road, its only doing 10 over the limit. If that's it I give a warning.

Every truck investigation and traffic enforcement officer interviewed, stressed the power of discretion truck investigation officers had. Before laying charges they assessed the integrity of the driver and reviewed contextual factors such as the conditions of the roadway, traffic volume, time of day, and image of the rig. Equally important was the finding that many truck investigation officers were retired truckers. In a few cases officers still drove trucks in their spare time. They exercised considerable empathy by assuming the position of truckers as a prerequisite for proper understanding of driving behavior and road safety practices. As one officer said, "If I were that trucker, how would I react?"

An officer in California listened for talk over the CB to plan his opening moves. Whenever a police roadside inspection is in process, truckers use the CB to warn each other that "Smokey is on the loose." During these procedures the highway patrol officer is sometimes described in abusive language. As the Californian explained,

> Well you'll hear it when we get out there and start working the road and in a few minutes, the first thing they'll say, "DOT's out," and then drivers say, "If he stops me I'll kick his fucken ass, or whatever." So I listen. I'll try to get him. He'll drop a hint.

In response, the officer listens for hints of location, load, destination, and make of truck. Sometimes he engages truckers over the CB, posing as a trucker to retrieve incriminating information about an abusive driver. Although taking on a false identity over the CB is a violation of the American and Canadian communications laws, for the officer it usually "gets the job done." To date of the interview, he had not received any complaints about giving false call letters.

In Canada, there is no requirement for "due cause," although truck investigation teams were sensitive to the bad public relations that might result if they randomly stopped truckers for checks. Truckers were quick to call it police harassment, something the police tried to avoid for political reasons. Some Canadian police officers related the act of stopping truckers to economics. Time is money, and being stopped without legal cause costs truckers money.

The Canadian police searched for truckers who were obviously in violation of traffic laws, including missing weigh scales. They would stop truckers and initiate a line of questions, and if warranted, engage an inspection of the rig's braking systems. Truck investigation units in western Canada are rare. The few that operate are also expected to undertake traffic accident investigations. Consequently, team members had less time to search out truckers for investigation than did their American counterparts, whose major role was truck-related investigations.

Roadside stops, however, were not always police initiated. Canadian and American police officers described how at times truckers search out officers for interactions. For example, when owner-operators lease their trucks to a construction contractor or a shipper, they may be required to "run heavy," placing excess burden on their equipment. Furthermore, company drivers may be forced to operate improperly maintained rigs. So truckers may flag down a police officer and request maximum number of charges on the truck, thereby pressuring the owners and shippers to abide by the law. One Canadian truck investigation officer explained,

> You know, inadequate brakes, maybe there's no brake lights, bald tires, stuff like that. The fines add up pretty fast. Its about fifty bucks for each offense. And then he goes back to his boss and says, "Look I got all these tickets for this thing" and the boss generally, if it's a decent company, generally pays the fines. He gets the vehicle fixed if its going to cost him a lot of money. That's the bottom line. If its not going to cost him any money, he's not going to fix it.

Avoiding Roadside Encounters

It is to the truck drivers' advantage to shy away from the police officers' advances. They know that once an officer has contacted them they will, at minimum, receive a traffic citation and at maximum, have their rigs placed out of service for repairs and receive large fines. Unless it is a random roadside check, truckers take precautions to avoid invitations from the police. Although some truckers may know that they are running poorly maintained equipment, they do not repair it. Instead, they try to eliminate any "due cause" tip-offs the police might use to stop them. A trooper described the strategy:

> Oh they know they're running bad equipment, they know we don't stop them unless we find a reason. So they have chained their mudflaps down, they've done everything they can do to keep us from stopping them.

The most effective way to avoid being selected is to refrain from breaching the police officer's tolerance level on speeding. It is a common practice for truckers, especially owner operators, to speed whenever they can, to can gain time. Part of the procedural rule in trucking is that whenever truckers witness a "Smokey on the loose," they inform other truckers over the CB airwaves (Agar, 1986). As a result, a truck stopped by a police officer at the side of the road will lead to active CB airwaves; truckers informing other truckers that a police cruiser was spotted. Truckers in the vicinity will likely abide by traffic laws to reduce the chance of being marked.

On one occasion a police officer followed a driver for a period of time. Other truckers spotted the patrol car and immediately warned the driver that a "cop was tailing him." On another occasion a driver was "wasting down the road just giving her." On the way he spotted a police officer who had stopped a truck. The driver warned oncoming truckers to slow down because "there was a cop working." After a short distance another trucker hit the CB and told this driver, "No, no, the cop isn't busy now, better tell everybody to take it easy." The driver answered, "No, no, he was busy. I seen him there. He was out of his car and writing the guy up." After a little more back and forth chatter, the driver finally said, "Look, you're full of shit. He's writing the guy a ticket." The person on the other end of the CB then responded, "As a matter of fact I'm right here," whereupon the cop pulled out into the center lane and turned on all the flashers. Fortunately for the driver the officer had a sense of humor and was not preparing him for a roadside stop. He allowed the driver to proceed.

A similar strategy was evident when troopers were out doing roadside checks at weigh scales. Truckers hit the airwaves and recommended that the site be bypassed if possible. Truckers who knew they were running illegal tried to miss the check. To counter the truckers' ploy, some police detachments run "wolf packs," in which a number of officers search nearby ramps, overpasses, and roadways for renegade truckers. With the presence of officers at bipasses, truckers are cut off from escape routes. According to one trooper:

Then the truck stops fill up. Its funny, it's kind of a game I guess. We've done our job, if we go out there and we don't stop a truck they pull into the truck stops. If they pull into the truck stops we'll get the fatigued driver off the road. He says, "Hey, I got to wait them out."

A California trooper suggested that he does not appreciate logging truck drivers who avoid roadside checks. By using townspeople to spot for him, he and his colleagues know which operators purposefully missed the inspection site. Because logging truck drivers are regulars in the vicinity, rigs and drivers can easily be found and identified. Once the officer knows "who the asshole is," he purposefully checks the truck in a "lonely isolated area" and finds that, "Guess what, your brakes aren't so good. Guess you'll have to wait it out here."

A less obvious, but nevertheless observed strategy truckers used to shy away from the highway patrol advances, was intimate knowledge of the officer in a designated area. In Arizona and California some regular long haul truckers were familiar with the truck investigator's name, background, routine and schedule, pet peeve, and tolerance level. They drove according to their knowledge of the officer's personality and schedule. Sometimes they waited until the officer was off duty before they made a run that would involve deviant driving or illegal loading procedures. For example, one constable stepped out of his routine and for the first time ever patrolled the freeway on a Sunday morning. The CB came alive with warnings that the unusual was happening. Amusing stories entailed. Did the Smokey lose his watch? Was he kicked out of bed? Was he "pissed of because he didn't get any last night?" Is he "bucking for a promotion?" Is he lost? Some truckers spoke to him on first-name basis. Two of the five truckers the trooper stopped that morning showed complete surprise that he was patrolling the streets on a Sunday morning. They shook their heads in dismay at having been outwitted.

For the everyday motorist, avoidance is more problematic than it is for the trucker. Obviously, if drivers follow traffic laws to the letter, they are not likely to be selected. Although this is ideal, it is not real, for according to officers, nine out of ten drivers occasionally speed, and the tenth one breaks some other rule for which she can be held accountable.

A prevalent practice followed by motorists and truckers alike is to flick their headlight at oncoming traffic, signaling oncoming drivers that a speed trap or roadside police action is in progess. Although officers knew this happens, they expressed little concern. Their view was that speeding is so prevalent that finding quarries is easy. Chances are good that those people who reduce their speed are regulars and will be eventually caught.

Some constables interpreted flashing headlights as an effective deterrence. Although a primary goal for a speed trap is to catch violators, an important secondary purpose is for drivers to see that the police are out making stops. Just the presence of the police slows down drivers. According to members of the traffic squad, when motorists decelerate, they drive more safely, fulfilling an important purpose of situational deterrence.

A ploy used by some drivers is to take advantage of fast motorists, or as the police call them, "jackrabbits." They stay back a ways behind a speeding driver and follow. An oncoming police officer is more likely to stop the leader than to stop the follower. If the follower is too close to the jackrabbit and speeds are extreme, there is a chance that both drivers will be stopped. By the same token, neither one may get stopped because the officer may not be able to distinguish the vehicles and have trouble identifying the detected car in court. Regardless, such strategy has a good chance of avoiding a face-to-face meeting with police officers. Still, avoidance techniques available to motorists are more random than those practiced by truckers. As a subculture, truckers generally share the norm of warning each other about police actions.

Engaging Interaction

Once truck investigation officers selected truckers for investigation, they flashed their emergency lights and gave chase. Usually officers used their CB radios to inform truckers that a Smoky or a Bear was on their tail and that they pull over at the first safe site. If no CB was available, the officers followed trucks with emergency lights flashing. If no reaction was forthcoming from marked truckers, the officers would tend to drive near the center line so that the truck drivers could spot the flashing police lights in their rear view mirrors.

In the case of weigh scale checks, officers attended to truckers as they drove over the scales and presented their papers to the attendants.

Once trucks were stopped, the officers took the initiative. They walked up to the tractors, opened the doors and greeted the drivers. This initiative was more than interpersonal tactics. It was designed to frame the oncoming encounter as friendly yet businesslike. The greetings were tactful openers usually followed by the officers' explanations of why a truck was stopped. Surprise, disbelief, amazement, and anger were typical trucker responses whenever they were stopped for mud flap violations or improper placarding. It was common knowledge among truckers that the violations were baits—rights of entry, or, according to one trucker from Portland, "a way to get us."

Once introductions were made, officers began to lead. They requested all papers pertaining to freight, insurance, registration, and other legal documentation required for interstate or interprovincial commerce. If the papers were in order, the officers began a visual overview of the rig, inspecting the tires, lights, and signal lights. They then completed a survey look at the tractor and trailer brakes. The odds of troopers discovering misaligned or worn-out brakes were good. If some troopers spotted problems they retrieved a heavy blanket and tools, crawled underneath the trailer, and thoroughly inspected the tractor and trailer's brakes. For hazardous materials carriers, constables were likely to extend their investigations by checking the loads and assessing the low-air warning devices, instruments that warn truckers if their systems have air leaks.

On one of the ride-alongs a trooper stopped a truck that was transporting chlorine. His "due cause" was that the oxidizer sign on the side of the trailer was only one and a half inches from the commercial print rather than the legal three inches. The trooper discovered that the low-air warning device was out of order. After he marked the violation on the inspection form, the officer informed the trucker of the dangers involved in running such defective equipment.

Once the officer completed the truck inspection, he requested the trucker's log book and engaged in a series of uncovering moves (Lyman and Scott, 1970). He asked whether the trucker was running more than one log book; whether the trucker was hiding another book; whether the driver was hiding receipts, liquor, or drugs. The final question was a clincher: "If I was to search the cab, would I find anything hidden?" The intent behind the last question was to "shake them [truckers] up a bit."

During this phase of the inspection, the trooper "called the shots." He searched for a variety of clues and cues—some obvious, others subtle; some recognized and few missed. He structured the questions, demanded precise explanations, and enforced his status as a police officer (Rothe, 1991a). He carefully scrutinized the log book with the help of a large atlas to help him locate towns truckers use as their points of departure or destination, and to assist him in determining real highway miles between sites.

The particular trucker that the trooper stopped omitted four hours of driving time or two hundred miles in the log book. According to the officer, "there's no way in the world you can do 570 miles at an average of 60 MPH in six hours." The trooper told the driver that he cheated him out of about four hours driving time. The trucker was aware of where the discussion was going. So he made his move with an excuse formulated according to an appeal to defensibility. The trucker excused himself from the obvious error because he was overly tired while completing his log book. Rather than cheat he just forgot a few details. The officer now stepped out of his enforcer role and suggested that he was going to save the trucker a $400 fine and a citation for log book violation if he told the guest researcher, the "real reason" for the log book discrepancy. The trucker refused to change his line. Although the trooper was disappointed that the trucker failed to act nobly, he kept his promise by not charging him. The trucker did, however get red placarded for the broken low-air warning device. The officer would have accepted an excuse appealing to the trucker's basic need to cheat. He realized that truckers consider the log book as a comic book or fairy tale, a perception shared by every trucker involved in the study. However the officer did not appreciate looking like a fool. He was going to make sure that the next time the trucker was in the vicinity, he would be held accountable.

Whenever troopers found trucker's eyes in "rough shape," they tightened the inspection. If there was enough suspicion that illicit drugs were involved, troopers had the legal right to search the cab. According to one officer, a fatigued trucker taking drugs is the "scariest thing on the road. He is a loose cannon ready to kill some innocent people." For this kind of violation there is no discretion or tolerance. There was consensus among all of the officers involved in this study that such drivers must be removed from the road.

The length of the encounter depended on three factors. One was the impression the trucker made on the officer during the routine interview. The second was the shape of the truck during the initial inspection. The third factor was the reputation or lack thereof of a certain carrier regarding safety. Police officers suggested that in some cases the encounters last up to seven hours, while at other times they stop in a few minutes. It is incumbent on truckers to make the kind of moves that will most likely reduce the intensity of the police officer's investigation.

In a west coast Canadian city, the police officers found little need to negotiate the severity of a charge or the number of tickets that should be issued per trucker. As city police officers, they were not concerned about drugs, log books or fatigued drivers. Their primary interest when they engaged in truck inspections was overweight loads and bad brakes.

However, there were times when the police officer had little choice but to intervene. For example, while the officer was waiting at a red light, a loaded dump truck sped through the intersection blasting his airhorn for the driver ahead to speed up. By the time he crossed the intersection, the light had turned red. The officer flashed his lights and gave chase. For this kind of flagrant violation traffic accident investigations had to wait. As the trooper said,:

I would be amiss of duty to let it go. I mean the accident will just have to wait. Geez I hate that, that's so stupid and unsafe blasting your horn so you can run a red light.

The officer jumped on the truck's step and in a calm manner informed the trucker that he was stopped because he was speeding through the intersection and that he ran a red light. The trucker responded indignantly, claiming that he could not stop in time. The trooper retaliated by suggesting a speeding ticket instead. "No, no," replied the trucker. He now claimed that he could not stop because of the heavy clay load. The officer, becoming impatient with the interaction style, suggested to the trucker that if the driver did not stop making excuses, he would give him two tickets, one for exceeding the legal weight limit and another for running a red light. The ploy was successful. The trucker accepted the bottom-line citation for running a red light, shaking his head in disapproval. As the driver left the site, he honked his airhorn twice in defiance.

Different strategies were noted with motorists. Once a motorist was spotted and it was considered to be safe, the officer initiated a pursuit. By the time the constable turned on the flashing lights, every move the offending driver made was noted. Officers watched for sudden head movements and for signs of whether the driver was reaching for something. Many times drivers turned their shoulders, which to the officers signaled that they were putting on their seat belts. It was not uncommon to witness movements that suggested a driver was trying to hide liquor under the seat or "throw the joint out the window." However, as a rule, officers do not attend to the movements as tip-offs to other infractions unless they spell danger. Unlike truck stops where lengthy discussions pursue, with motorists the police tend to deal directly with the violations.

Traffic enforcement officers have tip offs for suspecting impaired driving. For example, a driver who takes "forever to get pulled over, slowing down . . . and. . . . slowing down," instead of stopping immediately is likely to be "popping mints" or opening the window, "trying to get some fresh air and get the smell out of the car." A more obvious sign is the way a driver pulls over. As one officer indicated, "sometimes they bounce off the curb or their motor perception is not all that good."

As was already outlined, because of the officer's adherence to personal tolerance levels, drivers selected for attention usually received tickets. But, variations were noted. If when they stopped, they noted that a headlight was burned out or a seat belt not worn, some officers laid additional charges. Others laid one charge and gave warnings for the remaining violations. Every officer did what he thought was right. As one constable joked, " There's guys who'll probably charge their grandmothers." He rationalized the actions as natural differences between officers just like there are differences between all people. For him, he was not about to clean up, "all the shit in the world." So he asked rhetorically, "Why go overboard? Whats the sense?"

A generalizable process occurred after a car was stopped. The officer, hat properly placed on head, stepped out and approached the car. The preferred strategy for officers was that drivers stay in their cars and wait for the constable's approach. They took special note if someone came out. As one constable said,

> If a person jumps out of the car and there's more than one person in the car I'll tell him to get back into the car. I want you to stay in the car. I have control over the situation.

With respect to trucking, the police considered it normal for truckers to jump out of the cab. Some officers preferred the truckers' moves because of the limited space available to stand beside the window of a cab. When a motorist jumped out of the car, officers assumed that they were likely not wearing seat belts and tried to avoid discovery by stepping out of the car before the constable arrived. Another motive the police imputed to such drivers was that they were macho. They don't like looking up to the police officer hovering over their window. So they stand up, eyeball to eyeball with officers, signaling that they are prepared to take it "like a man."

Once the interaction with drivers progressed and the constable felt in control, it made little difference whether a driver stepped outside of the car. This happened frequently on warm days when the officer returned to the police cruiser with the driver's papers in hand to write the ticket. Drivers would stand around or pace back and forth. Whereas it is accepted by the officer during the day, at night it is duly noted.

An action seldom condoned by the police is a motorist who approaches the police cruiser while the officer sits inside and writes a ticket. The driver does not have the right to disturb the officer or, unless asked, enter the police cruiser. At this time the police car becomes a private office where officers are not to be disturbed and where those receiving citations are not welcomed. The situation obviously changes at accidents, impaired driving or other major violations, and mishaps where the cruiser may become a temporary haven for a victim, interrogation quarters for a charged impaired driver, or a meeting place where information and evidence is collected from persons at an accident site.

When an officer approached the driver, the meeting was usually prefaced with two opening questions. "Do you know what the speed limit is sir/madam? Do you know how fast you were going?" After a driver delivered the answers the officer requested the driver's license, registration, and insurance papers.

The opening remarks serve several purposes. One is to introduce the reason for being stopped. Two, it signals drivers as to how long the encounter will likely last and how it will be performed. Three, it is used to establish if answers given by the driver can be used in court. A usual response that can be held against a driver is, "Maybe 60. How fast was I going?" The answer illustrates that the driver did not know his speed. It can be noted as evidence in case of a court appearance.

The questions are also designed to defuse the potential of an emotional charge and to achieve a relationship of superior (the officer has the right to question) and subordinate (the motorist is expected to answer). There was less negotiation in this matter than there was with truckers. Often motorists would ask how fast they were traveling, at which time the officers had the answer at hand. They did not invite the motorist to check the source of the speed assessment. It was taken for granted that the officer—unless otherwise proven—was correct.

After a short introductory exchange, the officers asked for relevant papers. If one or more of the papers was in a wallet or other pouch, the officers requested that the drivers remove the relevant papers and hand them over.

Whereas ongoing discourse with truckers was always likely, with motorists little talk ensued between officer and motorist. It was structured as a formal efficient encounter. Officers took the drivers' papers to their cruisers to briefly review them for dates and legitimacy. If they had a "feeling" something was amiss, a c-pick or on-board computer search was activated. One officer described it this way:

> Its the feeling you get. You deal with people long enough. You can say its the long hair, earrings, and all that shit. It really isn't. Its how you feel about the guy, how he feels toward you.

A computer check took about five minutes. The officers often wrote the tickets while waiting for the readout. The driver was not informed about the computer search. It was considered privileged information. On one occasion the officer felt that he had, "dealt with the kid before." He engaged a search, and to his surprise, the driver was clean.

Making small talk with motorists was generally not a preferred action. It may get constables into arguments, which they will likely lose. Officers felt that they had nothing to prove. If motorists did not like the tickets or treatment given by the constable, they had legal avenues. As a constable said while ticketing a motorist who was caught doing 74 km/h in a 50 km/h zone:

He knew. He was nice about it. But, there's got to be a method to your madness. Sorry—you're a nice guy and I won't give you a ticket. Either you let them all go or not.

Officers were generally determined to assign a ticket once a tolerance level was breached. They knew that the drivers would have explanations for their actions and often lie. A young driver was stopped driving 91 km/h in a 60 km/h zone. His excuse was that he was going to the pharmacy for aspirins because his mother-in-law had a headache. He conceded that he was speeding. The officer did not bite. His response was, "yes sir" and the driver received a fine for $123.75 plus four demerit points against his driving record. According to the constable, the driver thought that the reason was sufficient for getting off. But it was not! As the officer quipped, "Its expensive aspirin. He'll have the headache now."

Not only was there little room for negotiating the presentation and acceptance of a ticket, there was even less room for negotiating a lesser charge. Conversely, there was a chance for more charges being laid if the officer was insulted or if the matter became so serious that short yes and no sirs did not work. Mechanical failures or seat belt laws were then invoked. These actions, however, were invoked only in extreme situations in which the driver determinedly hassled or even threatened an officer.

The most hostile people toward the police were characterized as being "ethnic people" and "business types." The former were described as being outwardly verbal, accusing the officer of lying. The business types were considered to be more measured, showing a quiet disdain.

Some ethnic groups, which officers refused to identify, "don't believe you or they believe you but swear up and down they didn't do it." Others who are pulled over may say, "you just stopped me because I'm . . ." to which one constable responds, "No I didn't stop you because you're. . . . It is because the radar gun tells me you were speeding." To the officer it is "as simple as that."

The business types or "wheels" make the officers look like they are "trivializing their day." They demand a break threatening the officers with, "Do you know who I am?' or "I know so and so." One officer stated, "I don't care." He believed that with these motorists it is prudent to "keep you mouth shut." If he responded, he will likely end up explaining himself at a police hearing.

There is a general belief among members of the police force that they get more respect from motorists now than they did before. They suggested that it is because of tact, or the way they deal with people. "Its how you initially talk to people." Officers take pride in their careers. To have a complaint lodged against them is seen as a black mark that may ruin their credibility in the future. The rule of thumb is to treat people with respect and to say little more than the situation warrants. Politeness is a strategy that officers believe contributes to how people feel about them today. This comes on top of fairness and a professional and confident demeanor.

Negotiating a Way Out

No trucker wants the inspection to end with an "out of service" sticker, or a citation with a large fine. To help their cause, truckers came well armed with glosses or excuses to lessen the damage. For example, whenever investigating officers recognized log book falsifications, truckers responded in terms of being tired, innocently forgetting details, losing receipts, having already submitted their receipts to the dispatcher, or having forgotten to ask for them after their business dealings.   By offering practical reasons such as memory lapse, job pressure, company policy, or fatigue, truckers tried to portray their circumstances as those that happen to the average person.

For the average police officer, the ploys had a reasonable chance of succeeding. But members of specially trained truck investigation teams were not easily influenced by the trucker's conversational strategies. They were aware of why truckers "rip off" log books. It was no secret that cheating on log books was a universal practice. However officers expected truckers to be honorable, take responsibility for their actions, and not try to "bullshit" them. By trying to "hoodwink" the officers, or by trying to spoil their image as competent professionals who know the technical and street knowledge of log books, truckers made things worse for themselves. To maintain face, officers were likely to "throw the book at them."

During the American and Canadian ride-alongs, truckers routinely furnished police officers with topics of conversations such as "events they experienced on the highway," "weakness in government regulations," "members of their families that were police officers," and "their appreciation for the difficulties experienced by state troopers." On the basis of discussions with truckers, it became obvious that the drivers used sociable discourse as an attempt to influence the investigation through a a sense of "we're all together in this business." Truckers believed that by employing social poise or by conversing in a concerted, smooth, self-controlled fashion they increased their chances of not receiving serious citations.

Truckers were aware of the opportunity for using social tact or poise (Goffman, 1967). For example, one early Sunday morning an officer stopped a moving truck for traveling over 65 MPH in a 60 MPH speed zone. The trucker was in his mid-fifties, clean shaven, neatly groomed, wearing clean clothes (jeans and plaid shirt).

While the trooper explained to the trucker why he was stopped, the driver interrupted by asking, with a generous smile, why the highway patrol was active on such a nice bright Sunday morning. The trucker thought that it was unusual for the police to be working on the Lord's day. Nevertheless, he said, it was a good idea to patrol on Sunday to assure a safer highway.

The officer was caught off guard. He immediately liked the driver, and explained to him that he was caught speeding, but that he was willing to show discretion. As the trooper walked to the rear of the truck he said:

> Sunday, and here it is, he's stopped. If everything's ok, if the log book works out, I'm going to let the old fellow go, without a warning and without a ticket. Its a pleasure stopping a guy like that. He's what's left of the old school.

The officer's actions were more significant than suspected. Moving vans or as some truckers refer to them, "bed bugs" or "parking lots" share a reputation for log book infractions. To allow a driver of one to leave without serious attention is somewhat unusual in truck investigations.

Related to the interactive strategies is the physical presentation of self. Truckers suggested that a clean presentation helps to avoid visual tip-offs to the police. If they do become involved in an encounter with the police, a respectable look increased the trucker's chance of successful negotiation. A Canadian officer considered a clean trucker to be one who is least likely to cause legal problems.

Unlike truckers, motorists have less of a chance to negotiate their predicament with conversational tact or pleasing image. This does not mean that it never happens, but that it does so less frequently. Motorists are more anonymous and representative of the general public. They do not form a group that is easily distinguished by definition or description as are truckers, cabbies, and even motorcyclists. When they are stopped they are seen as little more than objects of police business.

Terminating the Encounter

Truckers hope to leave the inspection with minimal damage to their driving records or pocket books. The police officers want to be certain that drivers and their rigs are operating as safely as is reasonably possible, and that in the process of interviewing the driver they have presented an image of confidence and empathy. So the encounter ends.

The worst thing for a trucker is to be arrested for drug-related charges. Less severe, yet still major is having the truck sidelined for repair or for being overloaded. To correct a load or to have repairs done is both time-consuming and expensive.

Usually the trucker and police officer part ways after the trucker received a warning or traffic citation. In the United States police officers practice multiple citing, whereas in Canada the police assign a minimum citation believing that that gives the best chance of a guilty plea. According to one trooper, an average of thirteen citations per truck (usually equipment, load, or log book related) stopped is the rule of thumb for some members of the highway patrol. Although it happens, it was considered to be "somewhat unusual." Most troopers show more discretion than this. They were not hesitant to divulge that some action is extreme and may hurt the image of the police in the long run.

In western Canada the rule tends to be "one citation does the job." In extreme cases it may be two. For example, a Canadian officer thought that it was unfair to stack tickets. He believed that this procedure decreased a police officer's chance of receiving trucker cooperation in the future. Rather than assign tickets and fines for each mechanical violation, the officer may write one citation for general maintenance, costing the trucker about a hundred dollars. The officer's concern was that truckers not see the police as crusading against a driver or company. Yet one California Highway Patrol member has seen truckers receive as many as twenty-six tickets and as few as one. Little stacking of tickets occurs with motorists. Unless unusual circumstances arise, once motorists leave the scene, they are quickly forgotten by the officer. Ticketing is routine, a job, much like sorting letters in the post office.

If a driver threatens to take the charge to court the officer may make extra notes, "just in case." Because officers write so many citations per month, the one event, significant to the average motorist is but one of a thousand for the officer. The notes are precautions, to assure that if needed, relevant information is at hand.

Conclusion

It is apparent that police discretion involves more than the decision to take courses of action or inaction. In involves issues of morality, everyday logic, safety, political beliefs, and powers of the police agency. Using their discretion, police officers embrace personal tolerance levels on what constitutes the violation of laws.

Roadside encounters are initiated on the basis of discretionary powers and tolerance levels which differ significantly for truckers and motorists. For truckers, a pattern of negotiation is pursued that tends to be flexible, with both the police and truckers aiming for gain. With respect to motorists, the police believe that they give everyone a break through use of discretion and tolerance. Infringement of their tolerance limits invites action that invariably leads to a charge. Interaction is purposefully held to a minimum to lessen the chance of an argument or hassle.

Police discretion and tolerance are specific components of traffic life. They play a central role in the production of statistics on violations and accidents. An irony is that the police officer's subjective involvement in traffic is prized, but its broader implications in the production of statistical descriptions is almost totally ignored.

A Few Notes On Methodology

The data for this chapter were collected in western and eastern Canada and parts of the United States from 1990 to 1991, as part of a major two-year study on trucker risk behavior (Rothe, 1991). Participant observation techniques, in-depth interviews, and document analysis were used. More specifically, ride-alongs were undertaken with twenty over-the-road truckers for periods up to forty hours per trucker and ten police ride-alongs for up to three days each. In addition, thirty in-depth interviews were engaged with random law enforcement officers, weigh scale operators, dispatchers, safety supervisors, and government agents. All participant observations and separate in-depth interviews were tape recorded and transcribed. Additional field notes were entered as soon as possible after observations.

9

The Speed Ethos

[On being asked to define New Orleans jazz]
*Man when you got to ask what it is, you'll
never get to know.*

—Louis Armstrong

In today's world, speed has become a dynamic quality of social life. Over years of refinement by people, speed has come to the point where it seems to have acquired a life of its own. As a silent voice, or an ethos of modernity, speed is used to identify, arrange, and categorize objects, persons and events (Berger and Luckmann, 1967). It contributes to people's sense of "the way things are" and "the way things should be." Without overstating the case, speed has become a "symbolic universe" that makes human experiences meaningful and interpretable in an electronic age.

Berger and Berger (1975) wrote that people have the capacity to adapt their lives to a wide, continually changing range of activities and experiences. From walking, to horses, horseless carriages, steam locomotives, airplanes, jets, turbo charged sports cars, bullet trains and rocket ships, people have progressively used innovations to define their lives in terms of speed, time, and convenience; none of them necessarily exclusive. Becker (1973) summarized people's change of orientation as follows:

Man cuts for himself a manageable world: He throws himself into action uncritically, unthinkingly. He accepts the cultural pro-gramming that turns his nose where he is supposed to look; he doesn't bite the world off in one piece as a giant would, but in small manageable pieces, as a beaver does. He uses all kinds of techniques, which we call "character defenses": he learns not to expose himself, not to stand out; he learns to embed himself in other-power, both of concrete persons and of things and cultural communities. The result is that he soon comes to exist in the imagined infallibility of the world around him. (P. 23)

Increased speed has become a yardstick to judge such activities as driving cars. Qualitative expectations drivers have of the actual driving experience and purposes of trips are often redefined according to measured time. Citizens tend to envision driving as a two step mode— speed up and get there.

As drivers increasingly internalize speed and measured time they are steadily moving toward a version of Marcuse's (1968) "one dimensional man". Persons negotiate speed and time-related goals and purposes in every part of life, whether that be family, school, group affiliation, work or play. Individuals such as stockbrokers, telephone operators, fast food cooks, couriers, truckers, salespeople, and dry cleaners must decide on their actions within a consciousness of speed and time. This consciousness represents Mead's (1934) generalized other, the general standpoint of society as a whole. Persons incorporate the standards of society, or the part of society of which they are members. They form a general set of behavioral precepts.

Speed As Technologically Induced Social Speed

A brief look at history suggests that speed is relative. Excessive speed is bound to the generation that defines it. For example, in 1861 Great Britain introduced the Locomotive Act which limited the speed of all horseless vehicles to 10 MPH outside of towns and 2 MPH within them. The act was amended in 1865 to reduce maximum speed limits even further to 4 MPH outside of towns while maintaining the 2 MPH limit in town (Willett, 1964). During this era people's actions reflected a time of manual labor, some industrial machinery, proximate social circles, and the horse and carriage. The speed of transporting oneself was a direct reflection on the social speed at the time.

In the new age, technology designed for speed and efficiency has become a central form in life. It has created a milieux, an atmosphere, an environment, and a model of behavior in social relations that dominates more and more (Ellul, 1964). Etzkorn realized the danger when he wrote, "Man is always in danger of being slain by those objects of his own creation which have lost their organic coefficient" (1968: 2).

A simple example of how people's production of speed and technology in social life has come to have its own significance is the telephone. While I am enjoying a visit from a friend the telephone rings. I will likely decide in favor of the telephone, leaving a colleague sitting unattended. A friend has been subordinated for the technical promise of the telephone, a taken-for-granted device in people's lives that affects their styles of interaction, and traditional concepts of distance, time, and access to talk (Pool, 1981). It has changed geographic neighborhoods to psychological neighborhoods, connecting people who share telephone numbers. People have voluntarily governed their conduct to fit the demands of an innovation that is presently competing with faster forms of communication such as electronic mail and fax machine. The average citizen now expects to witness events as occurring rather than have them reported after-the-fact. In 1990 citizens were glued to the television to experience firsthand the invasion of Iraq by the United Nations forces under the leadership of the United States. In 1991 they were presented with minute-by-minute live action of a Senate committee hearing over the suspected improprieties of a nominated Supreme Court judge. The examples illustrate how space and time are now quasi-near (Ihde, 1983), encouraging citizens to demand rapid application, immediate solutions, and if necessary, the quickest possible counterthrust to a previous encounter. By witnessing goings-on in the world, people increasingly rely on technological innovations to find their bearings. The technology has become a trusted part of life or as James (1977) wrote, it now appears to be a "knowledge of acquaintance." If a "package just has to get there overnight," there is a courier service to satisfy the time-specific need, letters are faxed so that the communication can reach any destination in the world in minutes, and to change television stations, families have access to the convenience and quickness of remote controls.

In the workplace, time is rapidly taking on the economic meaning of a valued commodity. "Time on task," or "time theft" have been quantified and they have gained currency in organizations and businesses. Hard wired metaphorical signs such as "Rapidair,"

"Fastfrate," "Quicksilver," "Priority Mail," "Speedy Muffler," "Speed Queen," and "Minute Lube" among many others dot the social and geographical landscape. Midas Muffler has the fastest guns, IBM features the fastest computers, American Express claims that it has the fastest turnaround time for credit card acquisitions, and Japan advertises its Bullet trains as the fastest ground transportation in the world at 500 km/h. These signs are not only advertising slogans, but they provide a measure of possibilities, a cultural coherence that is immersed in the technological form (Ewen, 1976). As advertising signs, they, "help break down the barriers of individual habits" (Ewen, 1976). Their power lies in superimposing new conceptions of individual attainment and community desire (Hess, 1922).

Time, speed, rapidity, quick action, immediacy are technologically mediated concepts embedded in present culture. In addition, products such as microchips, rockets, jets, fast food, rapidly changing fads and fashions, and data transmission promote a tempo that has become internalized in people's consciousness, part of their common knowledge that permit typical ways of behaving (Cicourel, 1970). But when circumstances arise that call them into question such as a downed telephone line, broken fax machine, striking couriers, or an unexpected long line-up at a Minute Lube outlet, people recognize the unnoticed role speed plays in their lives. They become aware how speed has become instrumental in the very way in which they interpret the world and engage in action (Ihde, 1983).

Members have the capacity to resist, to say no to speed-related demands and to act on the basis of self-interest. For example, citizens can obviously step aside from speed and purposefully slow their pace, for example, by taking a leisurely drive in the country on a Sunday afternoon. The creative innovation, however, still reflects the acknowledgment of speed as a major organizing principle of daily life. They are trying to "escape the rat race" or "get away from it all" for a while (Rothe, 1990c). They want to distance themselves from the usual speed-oriented life style for a short period of time. Once the escape is completed, it's back to the "old grind."

Mass cultural events, such as the Indianapolis 500, motor cross races, stock car races, drag races, and grand prix meets bombard people with the idea that not only is speed available and positive, but that it is thrilling and rewarding. To the fastest driver goes the spoils of victory. Witness a patron parking lot after the stock car races. Squealing tires, donuts, and thrill speed pervade. Members of the audience tend to live a duality, being in and out-of-place. They duplicate the race track as an in-thing, while their actions are illegal according to traffic laws, an out- thing.

Movies illustrate the thrill of speed, synonymous with sensation, risk, and living on the edge. Who could forget the high-speed car chase in *Bullit*, a benchmark for future movies that include car pursuits. Speedboat races, and the America Cup yacht races are marvels of technology searching for faster speed. Even the Olympic Games, as illustrated in the hundred-meter dash, has become a technologically induced human speed contest. Steroids or other illegal substances are used by athletes to break previous speed barriers. Revised bicycles are used for races and swimmers now base their hopes as much on the frictionless swimsuits as they do on their skills to win. Combined, these events present an awesome display of speed consciousness dependent on technological innovation.

Restaurants like McDonald's are a modern phenomenon concerned with social speed. Pizzas are now baked in five minutes rather than the traditional time of fifteen minutes plus. Because people are busy, on the move, they often hesitate to take the time to sit down and enjoy their meal. They prefer to get in and out, or in the case of a drive- through, maneuver to a window and order without waiting. Pizza chains advertise speed. "Thirty minute delivery or your pizza is free." Walking speeds in modern cities are becoming faster. As Tsujimara, Nagayama, and Takizowa (1980) discovered in their research on walking speed, the higher the rate of fast services in an urban sector the faster the walking speed of pedestrians.

Koshi (cited in Tsujimara, Nagayama, and Takizowa, 1980) explained that as the pulse of society quickens, human beings incorporate the trend and develop desires to do as many things as possible at a high pace. This helps promote further advances in technological designs for even greater speed. The automobile serves as a fine example. Speed is an advertised feature of a car. The premise that automobiles may be driven at a high speed is a fundamental merit of a vehicle. Newspaper columnists, automobile magazine writers, and television program hosts who review automobiles, highlight features such as speed, acceleration, and power. Witness one of thousands that illustrates the common trend:

> Well, in the first place, and thanks to Subaru's full time, all-wheel-drive system, the SVX will be a 365-days-a-year rocket in the snowiest areas. And even in good weather the all-wheel-drive helps out when needed, like when the driver's exuberance surpasses his skill. Exuberance is a fine word to describe the attitude of the engine, which is a horizontally-opposed six that produces 230 horsepower at 5,400 RPM, 224 torques at 4,400 RPM and lots of all situations performance. (Law, 1991: D 1)

Cars are personalized according to their capabilities to accelerate, and their maneuverability during periods of high speed and quick acceleration. By hitting the gas pedal motorists are supposed to get a rush and save time, the latter of which Koshi considered to be indispensable to satisfy people's needs and wishes.

Blumer (1966) emphasized that actors, or more appropriate to this discussion, drivers, take account of needs, actions of others, rules (guidelines) offered by society, lived situations, and past experiences before they act. They adapt and respond to the circumstances of their milieux (Matza, 1969).   If that milieux consists of a technological mind-set that engenders speed and time benefit, it is reasonable to believe that drivers will be influenced to act in accordance with maximum efficiency; moving with the waves of a fast-flowing society. It should come as no surprise that most motorists select speeds with which they feel comfortable, meaning that they break the speed limits (Mostyn and Sheppard, 1980; Cowley, 1980; Sanderson and Corrigon, 1986). Nogushi (1990) concluded that on the basis of his research most drivers exceed the speed limit by at least 10 percent. Personal limits and desires, reflecting an internalized sense of social speed, influence the rate of travel. As Hogg (1977) claimed, this overrides the individual's emphasis on personal safety. Because drivers are not convinced of a causal relationship between speed and crash involvement, they tend to show little respect for, or rarely obey, what they consider to be unreasonable, irrelevant, or troublesome speed limits.

Driving Speed

Breaking the speeding law, according to Hutchison and Marko (1989) should be viewed as a regulatory offence. It should not be considered a crime deserving of moral condemnation. As the crown counsellor and barrister and solicitor (P. 64) explain, " As all who drive soon realize, at one point or another everyone speeds." Manraj and Haines (1985) observed:

> Some get caught and some do not and there is nothing in a speeding conviction that in any way compromises a citizen's honesty, integrity and uprightness or render him less worthy in society's eyes. (P. 198)

Speed laws are not in obvious or apparent harmony with the social speed of an advanced technological age. They proscribe behavior that is problematic within a frame of fast social, technological, and economic changes.

It is common sense that fast-driving motorists are more likely to get hurt badly in crashes than slow drivers. However, it is premature to predict or suggest that speed per se is the singular factor causing accidents. Thygerson (1977) concluded that over 50 percent of crashes occur within a twenty mile radius of the home at speeds under thirty mph. According to the British Columbia Ministry of Solicitor General official statistics (1987, 1988), of all accidents where human factors were the major contributing factor, less than 10 percent were the result of "driving at an unsafe speed." But more convincing still is the nation-wide study on speed and accidents by the United States Federal Bureau of Public Roads. The agency reported that cars traveling at 35 MPH were involved in 600 accidents per 100 miles driven, compared with those traveling at 65 MPH which sustained fewer than 100. At 65 MPH the rate began to rise, but even at 80 MPH it was still only one quarter of what it was at 35 MPH (cited in Willett, 1964: 21).

Prisk (1959) made the case that an unsafe speed is not necessarily an excessive speed. Relatively high speeds can be safe under favorable conditions. This is not unlike the turn-of-the-century debate in England over the British Motor Car Act. After a series of points and counterpoints, it was concluded that speed is often irrelevant because of the possibility of driving dangerously while within the lowest speed limit. Yet it need not be dangerous to drive fast if conditions permit. Witness the race track, where cars drive in excess of 180 MPH and the risk of an accident is moderate. Yet in a parking lot at 5 MPH two cars can collide and a driver can receive whiplash or soft tissue injuries.

Setting Speed Limits

Two questions that beg for answers are: What is a safe speed? and How does a safe speed relate to a legal speed limit? At first glance Lave and Lave (1990) may be correct in suggesting that a 5 MPH speed limit should be set for maximum safety. It would essentially prevent all highway fatalities. However, at 5 MPH the value of highway transportation would be negated and people would lose the associated mobility and convenience. But, as Lave and Lave (1990) explained, members of society have decided that the extra lives saved by traveling 5 MPH are not worth the loss of time and inconvenience this would engender. Hence, for optimal speed one must find the point where the value of lost time and convenience is balanced by the value of lives saved.

From an engineering perspective, the safety effect of speed limits is largely unknown, or in the words of Hauer (1990), such information is not on the professional engineer's bookshelf. Engineers say that a "design speed is often set as the 85th percentile observed speed" unless set otherwise by legislation (Navin, 1991).

According to Noguchi (1990), design speed is that speed at which on a day with good weather and low traffic density, when driving conditions are governed solely by the geometric conditions of the road, a driver with average driving technique is able to drive safely without losing control.

Naviin (1991) conceptualized design speed as one that consists of two separate categories. One is the highest consistent speed that can be maintained on a highway section in conventional conditions of safety and comfort. The second category includes minimum "offered" speed at tricky driving locations such as curves, under normal conditions of safety and comfort. On straightaways, speeds may be higher.

Discussions on design speed preclude the importance of traffic flow that influences driving behavior. Drivers may feel pressured to keep up with traffic, regardless of speed. Furthermore little attention is paid to how individual attitudes and abilities manifest themselves in drivers as they decide on their speed of travel.

The procedure most often used to establish speed limits is the "85th percentile" rule. It stems from Witheford (1970), who proposed that the 85th percentile is the most desirable approximated speed limit. The emphasis is on the qualifier, "approximate." According to Witheford (1970), because of the straight and steep slope of the typical speed distribution below the 85th percentile, setting speed limits a little lower will cause more drivers to be violators.

Witheford (1970) based his work on Cirillo (1968) and Solomon (1964), who suggested that accident involvement rates are lowest at the 85th percentile speed. Accident risk increases significantly at the speeds higher or lower than the 85th percentile. It should be noted that all three researchers emphasized "reasonable." That is, the 85th percentile speed seems reasonable both in terms of safety and driver desire. Based on the engineers' definition of reasonableness, the 85th percentile rule has become the benchmark for setting maximum speed limits.

To come up with the 85th percentile a team of engineers measures the speed on a particular roadway. They select a speed limit that is less than 30 MPH below the upper limit of the 85th percentile speed. Accordingly, about 15 percent of drivers will be in violation of a speed chosen and 85 percent will be in accordance with the upper limit. The emphasis is placed on violation, not on safety or possible accident causation. Fifteen percent of drivers break an artificially defined norm. But as Hauer (1990) indicated, there is no ready answer to the question of why the 85th percentile and not another number is used.

Planners cannot change the speed limit for each street according to the 85th percentile rule in urban settings. Instead they select a normative limit (usually 30 MPH or 50 km/h) and control higher speed roadways with stop signs, yield signs, and/or traffic signals. By employing this strategy they obtain a conformity in driving, which they feel increases safety.

Based on a review of speed literature, Pignataro (1973), established that there are significant differences in hourly, daily, and monthly mean speeds even though the locations are uncongested during the period of sampling. To correct for this empirical problem, engineers use a "time mean speed" under ideal conditions.

Despite claims made by some engineers and traffic safety agents, it is doubtful that an 85 percentile speed is determined on the basis of safety.   As illustrated in the "Manual For Uniform Traffic Control Devices For Streets and Highways and the Council on Uniform Traffic Control Devices for Canada," safety is a mute, undiscussed point. If it were an explicit criterion it would imply possible civil liability, which may jeopardize the engineering professional's defense of design.   Witness Hauer's remarks: "It is easier to defend your actions in the public arena when knowledge of the safety consequences of such action do not exist" (1990: 58). Because of possible legal responsibility, traffic engineers hesitate to evaluate speed limit designs against impact on safety.

Hence the national roadway grid is a landscape dotted by speed limits that do not necessarily reflect safety. They are prima facie limits, meaning that no particular rate of speed is necessarily safe or unsafe at all times.   Witness interprovincial highways, where one roadway spanning two or mor provinces has different maximum speed limits in each province. The same is true for similarly designed country roads located in different provinces.   There is little consistency.

Yet in traffic safety, speed limits are considered to be absolute. This working assumption helps standardize the roadway for legal purposes. It also contributes to an overall optimal traffic flow and it serves as the lowest common denominator for possible civil liability suits. For example, enforcement officials prefer absolute speed limits because police officers are not burdened with having to prove that the speed at which a violator traveled, was unsafe for the conditions at the time.

Related to the 85th percentile procedure is the "mean speed approach" consisting of "time mean speed" and "space mean speed." These are used to determine traffic flow and speed characteristics. A 10 MPH pace rule is commonly used to determine the value above which the maximum speed limit should be selected.   Maximum posted speed limits are usually selected on the higher limit of the pace. Speed distribution of spot speeds on a section of the roadway or space mean speed can also play a significant role in the selection of maximum speeds (Jernigan, Lynn, and Garber, 1989).

An alternative to the engineering approach for establishing speed limits is cost-benefit analysis under which speed limits are set to minimize overall transportation costs (Cowley, 1981). The classic view of optimum vehicle speed and economics was developed by Oppenlander (1962). He proposed that speed limits be established for maximally efficient highway traffic movment and minimal consumption of resources that are a function of vehicular speed. His thesis gained prominence in the 1970s when, due to a fuel crisis, speed limits in the United States were set at 55 MPH.

Speed Variance and Safety

Speed limits are normative laws. They represent desired behavior patterns based on road conditions, specifications of the car, efficient traffic flow, economic transportation, efficient judicial process, and convenient mobility. Safety tends to be more implicit than it is explicit. It might be argued, as it was with the American 55 MPH law, that safety is increased with reduced speed limits. However it would be hard to prove that city A with a speed limit of 30 MPH is less safe for driving than city B with a 35 MPH speed limit. Furthermore, there are still many questions left unanswered about studies that demonstrate that increased speed results in increased number of accidents, in light of the speed variance theory and speed context dispute.

Benchmark research often quoted in the traffic safety literature is Solomon's (1964) study later supported by Munden (1967). Both researchers concluded that there is a relationship, plotted as a U-shaped curve between crash involvement and speed. High involvement rates are found for "very low" and "very high" speed drivers. Minimum involvement rates occur at average speed. It should be duly noted that "very high speed" and not high speed was the featured descriptor. Solomon (1964) established that the accident rate is about the same whether the average speed is 55, 60, or 65 or possibly even higher as long as traffic maintains a relatively uniform pace.

Taylor's (1976) studies led to the conclusion that the accident rate is significantly higher when the speed distribution is non normal, and it is reduced when the distribution is normal. More recently, Garber and Gadiraju (1988), McCarthy (1988), Wagenaar, Straff, and Schultz (1990) and the U.S. Department of Transportation (1982) indicated that a very important consideration in the speed-safety discussion is speed variance.

Speed variance refers to the distribution of speeds on a certain road in a given area, or the number of drivers traveling faster or slower than the average speed. According to Lave (1985) and Garber and Gadiraju (1988), an increase in the number of vehicles on the road that are driving significantly slower or faster than the mean speed increases the probability of traffic crashes. Furthermore, speed variance increases as the difference between the posted speed limit and roadway design speed widens. Drivers tend to drive faster as the geometric characteristics of the roadway improve. They use common sense and experience to judge the roadway environment and proceed at speeds they consider to be reasonable for achieving their trip purposes. Posted speed limits are assigned secondary importance. The U.S. Department of Transportation handbook examined a number of studies and concluded that

> the weight of evidence would lead to the conclusion that speed variance and accident frequency are directly related. The greater the absolute deviation from traffic speed the higher the accident rate. (1982: 17)

Another perspective on speed variance concerns the characteristics of the traffic flow. Imagine a straight four-lane divided highway. If slow drivers stayed in the right-hand lane and left the passing lane for unimpaired driving by faster drivers, consistent speed for fast drivers would likely result in less risk of a crash. Because slow drivers enter the left lane, fast drivers are forced to slow down, speed up, change lanes, and so forth. The constant maneuvering increases the number of times speeds change, adding a dimension of risk for crashes. As McCarthy summarized:

Speed variation is more important to highway safety than mean speed. With respect to all roads, interstate and non-interstate, highway mean speed does not significantly affect highway safety, all else held constant, which suggests that the proportion of traffic travelling above mean speed changed little in the post law environment [change from 55 to 65 MPH speed limit in the United States]. An increase in speed variation, on the other hand, increases the incidence of fatal and injury conditions as well as the number of fatalities and injuries. (1988: 2)

Conclusion

Common sense dictates that in today's world, a situation in which there are no speed limits borders on the ridiculous. There is certainly no intent in this book to lobby for such a move. The reason for the criticisms is to introduce a measure of caution that speed or speeding is not necessarily a pathological condition on the part of drivers. Nobody is born a speeder. Drivers have learned to speed as a normal social behavior despite the threat of sanctions being held over them.

Planners may find it beneficial to establish why people speed, and how their reasons reflect the social ethos of the times. If speed is truly considered to be a major factor in accidents, it may be beneficial to address groups like car manufacturers and politicians. If a safe speed on the highways is considered to be 55 MPH, why build cars that travel 160 or even 180 MPH? They are a direct affront to speed limits in at least three different ways. One is the brute power such cars offer the driver. The second is the sensitivity of the gas pedal action required to keep a high-powered automobile at a nominal speed of 30 or 35 MPH. Third is the technology required to operate a powerful vehicle at maximum efficiency. For example, a vehicle such as Mustang 4 litre engine reads that first gear should be shifted at 60 km/h or about 35 MPH. To do otherwise may "lug the motor." Drivers are encouraged to speed to maintain the rpm's required for smooth operation of gear shifts.

On the basis of the possible conflict between technological adequacy constructed by car designers and driver decision making, there is a need to account for the sentiments, interests, roles, and set of conditions that involve auto development, marketing, and servicing. After all, cars are human creations, not absolutes. They should be evaluated accordingly.

Likewise, attention may be directed at speeding, not as an abstract, isolated piece of behavior that can be dissected from life but as something that takes place in real situations, indispersed with other acts and conduct that may well have different meanings to different people. These meanings should be negotiated with the establishment of speed limits or speed limit ranges. That is, speed limits as practical answers to complex conditions should be considered more on the basis of social conduct, as it reflects political conduct, driver meaning, auto manufacturer marketing intents, and so forth.

10

Using a Wide-Angle Lense on Impaired Driving

There must be something the matter with him
because he would not be acting as he does
unless there was.
Therefore he is acting as he is
because there is something the matter with him.

—R.D. Laing

Impaired driving may be described as the night-side of traffic safety. In recent years it has spawned a family of metaphors for roadway dread. "Killer drunks," "DWIs", "drunk drivers," and "drunks on the road" inspire fantasies of destruction that make even rational people glassy-eyed and nervous. Gusfield described the situation as

an image implying hostility, gross self-indulgence, lack of foresight, and foolhardiness. Having a high degree of hostility to others, while threatening the lives of others through indulgence in his own pleasure. (1981: 153)

Haddon and his associates produced a series of studies that first introduced the impaired driver as a significant social problem (Haddon and Brades, 1959; McCarrol and Haddon, 1961). More recently researchers like Fell (1983) fueled the moral outcry with conclusions that the consequences of alcohol-involved accidents are enormous. The numbers of fatalities, injuries, hospitalization, and workdays lost, the property damage and the overall costs to society are outrageous. Like many other traffic safety researchers, Moulden

(1985) dramatized that impaired driving has reached epidemic proportions, with a staggering annual death toll in the United States of 27,500 and over 700,800 injuries.

A growing body of research literature on impaired driving, personal accounts offered by family members who have suffered at the hands of impaired drivers, evidence of legal decisions considered by many to be soft on impaired drivers, and the prevalence of emotionally laden metaphors to describe impaired drivers, motivated citizens to become involved—to counter the threat of impaired driving. Citizen action groups arose, whose platform consisted of lobbying the government for a "war against drunk drivers" and the judicial system for stronger use of the criminal justice system against drunk drivers (Donelson, Beirness, and Mayhew, 1985). Public displays or moral outrage, such as candle burning ceremonies, were held across the continent to dramatize emotional outpourings. Grass-roots organizations such as MADD (Mothers Against Drunk Drivers), RID (Removing Intoxicated Drivers), SADD (Students Against Drunk Drivers) and Citizens for Safe Drivers have increased the pressure on the public sector and legislatures to get tough on impaired drivers. As Lightner (1986) reported, MADD favors punishment and treatment for impaired drivers; not treatment instead of punishment. The theory is that tougher legislation will provide stronger sanctions; those will change behavior.

The dramatization of impaired driving caught the attention of the media. Based on a content analysis study of the media and impaired driving, Howland (1988), established that the magazine and newspaper condemnation of impaired driving increased dramatically in the 1980s. Thousands of reports appeared. For example, the *Ladies Home Journal* (1983) included an article entitled "Teenagers and Alcohol: Holiday Hazard, Year Round Tragedy," *Consumer Reports* (1983) had an article called, "Drinking and Driving: A Serious Health Problem," and *Family Circle* (1982) published an article entitled, "Deadliest Duo: A Special Report: Teen and Cars."

While public exposure of impaired driving increased, so did the number of legislative changes. Howland's (1988) findings show that between 1981 and 1986 state jurisdictions in the United States passed 729 laws pertaining to impaired driving. This was a 300 percent increase over previous years.

The introduction of emotionally charged metaphors and mass media descriptions of mayhem and irresponsibility to describe impaired driving featured descriptions of emotion and sympathy. In the process such reports presented only one point of view. They obscured a complicated reality that features diverse patterns of involvement and outcomes of impaired driving behavior. Like speeding, impaired driving has become a public artifact based on moral condemnation, social pathology, victimization, and general irresponsibility (Donelson, Beirness, and Mayhew, 1985).

Medicalization of Drinking and Driving

Since the late 1960s a strong trend to medicalize impaired driving has arisen. Actions that were once deemed behavioral, legal, moral, or social have been brought within the orbit of medicine. Medical professionals began to postulate that the source of impaired driving is located in the physiological, organic, or psychological domains. As part of a disease configuration doctors began to mandate that intervention be practiced by medical personnel, because a disease so labeled can only be treated within the traditional medical milieu (Conrad and Schneider, 1980).

Today's expression of impaired driving as a medical problem carries a fairly clear moral overtone. Impaired driving has become defined as a public health epidemic. It is perceived to be a major health problem, not just incapacitating or dysfunctional but also bad, wrong, or deviant. Designating and treating impaired driving conditions as health risks has become a social and political act. To treat impaired driving with medical therapies is often thought to be morally neutral. However, in many cases it is clear that in the process of medicalizing impaired driving, doctors play the role of moral arbiters. They judge what is acceptable and not acceptable, what is good and what is bad, what is allowed and what should be prohibited, punished and treated.

Traffic safety agents and legal people have embraced the medical model. Some laws directly reflect medical interpretation. The example that comes to mind is "Blood Alcohol Concentration" (BAC). Impaired driving charges are laid according to an acceptable level of .08, .05, or .00. These levels were established on the basis of physiological reaction to the ingestion of alcohol.   The medical procedure of blood testing as a basis of evidence for impaired driving has become an acceptable procedure in many jurisdictions around the world.   In some Canadian and American jurisdictions the courts recommend or mandate that drivers charged with impaired driving be treated in programs developed, funded, and administered by medical personnel.

In spite of its dominance in impaired driving definition and intervention, the medical model provides only a partial explanation for how drinking and driving behaviors become defined as problems. It assumes a specific etiological pattern of cause and effect that foregoes everyday behavior. As Smith (1988) outlined, it is difficult to set standards for "normality" against which problematic or pathological behavior such as impaired driving can be assessed. The medical view of impairment and impaired driving divorces important issues from their cultural, social, economic, and political contexts by focusing on the scientific evidence of individual malfunctioning and relating it to something called socially accepted norms (Stark, Flitcraft, and Frazier, 1979). Clearly, a vaccuum of social explanation is left behind.   Perhaps Vingilis put it best: "We researchers have been afraid to explore new ground and venture into the complexities of social and psychological theories" (1983: 405).

A Broader View of Drinking and Driving

Alcohol consumption plays an integral part of people's leisure activities, celebrations, and even wakes. It serves as a symbol of comradeship, intimacy, cultural rites, and business deals.   On an individual basis drinkers seek reduction of tension, guilt, anxiety, and frustration and enhancement of fantasy, sensuality, confidence, self-esteem and escapism (Jacobs, 1989).

Intersecting the socio-psychological reality of drinking is the context of automobile use. The car is a symbol of social status and personal life-style. It satisfies people's need to declare themselves socially and individually. As Marsh and Collett (1986) described it, the parallel between the symbiotic relationship that we once enjoyed with horses and the symbolic relationship that we now enjoy with cars is inescapable. We have reached the stage when our entire livelihood depends on cars. (P: 6)

For many people, the car fulfills deep psychological needs for power, aggression, fantasy, and control (Jacobs, 1989). Furthermore, the motor vehicle may be the only reasonable access to mobility some people have within and between cities.

Combined, the social context of alcohol consumption, and automobile use form a complex reality. Impaired driving scenarios are holistic unities composed of inseparable and mutually defining psychological processes, physical and social environments, and temporal qualities. The actions of each person are understood in relation to the actions of other people and the physical/situational and temporal circumstances in which the total event unfolds (Werner, 1987). Drinkers, social and physical contexts, and time do not "cause one another." They are unified through actions, perceptual processes, rule patterns, and sequences (Altman and Rogoff, 1987). To account for the broader context, a framework has been designed that interrelates vital components of everyday actions (see fig. 10.1).

A full understanding of drinking and subsequent impaired driving requires consideration of all components. Figure 10.1 represents the drinking situation as a unity. It illustrates how public drinking is ultimately a social cultural phenomenon interconnected with social relationships, economics, politics, legalities, mass media or communication, time, and environment.

Situational Influences

The central part of the drinking and impaired driving puzzle is the situation in which the behaviors occur. The settings include both physical and social/behavioral characteristics.

People behave in ways that are compatible with or adaptive to their immediate socio-physical environment (Wicker, 1972). In short, they invest their drinking sites with meaning. The implications for drinking and impaired driving are that people engage in patterns of meaningful behavior within the boundaries of given situations. This differs significantly from the medical or psychological perspectives that address physiological and psychological characteristics as factors or causal agents for impaired driving.

Figure 10.1
Impaired Driving Situations: A Wide-Angle Perspective

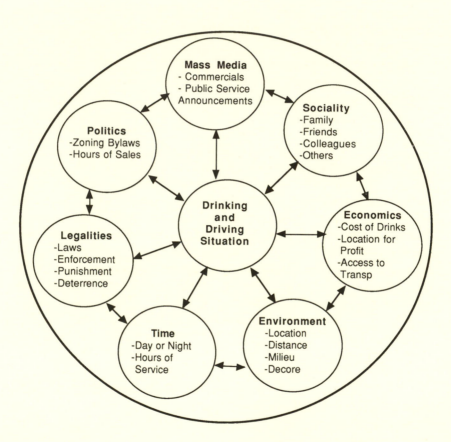

Harford (1977) wrote that the tempo of drinking, the amount consumed, and even the effects of alcohol vary among settings. Drinking in a bar is a different phenomenon than drinking at home or at a party. For example, a person feeling lonely and sad might choose to drink in a pub or the "old watering hole" to become more outgoing and cheerful.   Furthermore, differences in the location, physical characteristics, and clientele of bars influence the type of drinking and the drunken comportment. Here the risk becomes a factor that a potential drinker considers before making the decision to drink and how much.

A workshop held in Ontario addressed this perspective. A major recommendation that arose from a workshop on the use of sanctions in controlling behavior on the roads read:

> Research should be done into the "definition of the situation" by serious motoring offenders in respect to dangerous driving and drunken driving **prior** to the offence behaviour. This may assist work on motivation, another neglected aspect of knowledge in this field. (Willett, 1974: 64)

A team of American researchers analyzed a country-wide survey of adolescent drinking behavior (Rachel et al., 1982).   Their major finding was that settings in which drinking occurs appear to be related to how much alcohol is consumed and its consequences on transportation. Where teenagers do most of their drinking is related to the frequency with which they get drunk. In support, Jacobs (1989) reported that tavern drinking plays a major role in male bonding, which practically assures impaired driving in North America.

Social Influence

If the family is the home port from which individuals start out their lifelong journey through society, friends, colleagues, lovers, and acquaintances are surely ports-of-call. In their quests for independence, young people are under considerable pressure to engage in family defined appropriate behaviors. As collectors of cultural values and traits, parents pass on moral obligations to their offspring.

Ports-of-call, or relationships with other people result in the development of a new set of values, standards of behavior that may embrace or conflict with traditional family beliefs. Peer groups, economic partners or co-workers, teammates, and others produce a new zone of preferred conduct that is considered to be normal within the social circle in which persons find themselves.

In times of rapid change, or in situations in which there is a plurality of standards, social expectations may become blurred. Individuals seek relations with others in order to find meaning and support. Moral judgments about actions like drinking and impaired driving may change to avoid the potential of isolation. Social tact, politeness, social expectations, and coolness can become guides for deciding whether to partake in drinking and impaired driving.

Economic Influences

Affecting the situation of drinking and impaired driving are economic factors that shape the basic patterns of production, distribution, exchange, and consumption. Breweries and distilleries determine the taste and quality of alcohol beverages, the cost and the availability at locations for the purpose of economic gain. In some cases, major breweries directly affect situational drinking. Marketing representatives are often located on college campuses to facilitate the flow of beer. Special events vehicles visit locations and advertise their beer products. Concerts, sports tournaments, and social events are often sponsored by alcohol beverage producers.

Based on economic principles of marketing and sales, distilleries, wineries and breweries develop designer products intended to capture the interests and life-styles of different groups. For example, the cost and availability of beer helps make it the "workers drink" well illustrated by the British pubs, while expensive champagne is intended for people with more money to spend and different views on what connotes a good time. More recently wine coolers were developed with the young woman in mind (based on discussions with members of a British Columbia winery). Cheap wines often referred to as "goof" or "porch climber" are priced to satisfy low-income consumers. They are often sold in large jugs.

Prices and choices of drinks differ at neighborhood pubs, beer parlors, dining lounges, and neighborhood liquor outlets.   The selection of drinking locale and amount consumed reflects the amount of money a person has to spend on liquor.

The cost of a taxi to get home while in an inebriated state becomes a factor when motorists decide whether or not to drive home after drinking alcohol or when passengers decide on whether to take rides with impaired drivers.   Late at night when the buses stop running, a person has only one of several "basic" choices: walk, phone for a ride, take a taxi or drive while intoxicated.   Distance usually negates walking, pride often overrules phone calls for rides and taxies, are expensive.   Unless plans were made beforehand for one member of a group to stay sober to drive, the most likely decision for the inebriated person is to drive. Furthermore, the extent to which alternative transportation is available can also be defined in terms of economic viability.   In short: Is public transportation viable at certain times in the evening? and Is it cost effective to have bus routes near public drinking establishments?

Political Influences

The government influences drinking and impaired driving situations in several ways.   It controls the overall availability of alcohol by supporting the opening and closing of certain liquor outlets such as bars and neighborhood pubs through zoning bylaws.   It has the power to change the price of alcoholic beverages by manipulating the tax system, setting the hours of sale, overseeing "happy hours," regulating alcohol content in beverages, establishing minimum age for alcohol purchase, and monitoring the quantity and content of alcohol advertising.

The political will is also tested in discussions on public transportation. In short, transit systems are subsidized and controlled by local governments. According to Gusfield (1981), a government that grants licenses and a society that permits or promotes so many drinking establishments inaccessible by foot or by public transportation contributes to impaired driving.

Legal Influences

The judiciary influences drinking and impaired driving through the development, implementation, and enforcement of drinking-related laws. These may include laws on public drunkenness and disorderly conduct; impaired driving; serving liquor to minors; or consuming alcohol in public places such as beaches, parks, or public buildings. The existence of these laws leads to potential police action.

Media Influences

The media constitutes a major part of people's life curricula. Media sources do not stand apart from the social context in which they function. For example, the creative director who designs a campaign for drinking certain kinds of beer has internalized the rules and meanings of culture and social life and redraws them upon the drawing board. As Postman et al. conceptualized about commercials:

> This is not to say that commercials "merely" reflect a culture's myths and meanings. By embodying and repeating them, by projecting them over and over again in dozens of new forms, commercials also extend and perpetuate cultural assumptions, values and attitudes. (1987: 7)

The implication behind the Postman research team's announcement is that television commercials provide people with the means to enact, in their own lives, what it means to be "happy," "masculine," "feminine," "socially acceptable." They emphasize that "good times, success and friendships are the rewards of drinking." The portrayal of these life-style features serves as a generalized view of what is acceptable. It helps shape individual attitudes, beliefs and actions (Postman et al., 1987).

According to Gutenschwager (1989), the beer and wine industry alone spends over $800 million a year on advertising. No hard-headed business executive would spend that kind of money without a fairly definite idea about what kind of results to expect. With the help of psychologists working for the advertising industry, liquor advertisements have become "key socializers" in modern society.

Environmental Influence

Decorating, displaying identity, physical modeling, and geographical location of drinking sites are all ways of appropriating the environment, establishing territory, and expressing communal identity (Erikson, 1976). As Lazarus and Folkman (1984) outlined, persons subjective impressions of their immediate environment are more important than the objective environment, or to put it more strongly, there is no environment outside of persons' shared impressions of it.

The premise that persons do not exist outside of their environments cannot be avoided in discussions on drinking and subsequent impaired driving. The location of public drinking establishments, whether it be in the "downtown red light district" or "suburban west side of town" makes a difference on who accesses them, what is appropriate drinking behavior under what circumstances and how readily the sites are accessed by foot or automobile (Altman and Chemers, 1980). The decor of locales is designed to create a mood, that is intended to promote mass or moderate alcohol consumption, superficial or personal relationships.

Time Influences

The principle of time, or temporal qualities refers to measured time as, how long a public drinking establishment is open for business, how long a neighborhood party continues, and so forth. Pace refers to how rapidly events unfold, such as drinking more quickly toward the late evening as compared to early evening, or vice versa. Sequencing refers to the order of events and activities in which persons routinely engage at different drinking sites, as for example, drinking, eating, moving about, having a last one for the road, and driving. Different drinking sites promote different temporal rhythms.

Cultural Influence

Within the confines of this book, culture represents a whole way of life, embracing a wide variety or practices. It is a group of people who give similar meanings to their experiences and to ways they are symbolized. Whereas traditional culture is specific to a group of people who share norms, values, mores, celebrations, and rituals, popular culture refers to a group of people with broadly shared interests or who share a definition of reality through images of modern life. At times the two forms of culture clash, as for example, Catholic women rallying for the right to have abortions.   They question traditional beliefs, authority, and past patterns of behavior and embrace modernistic ideas, such as women's rights to their own bodies.

Impaired driving has a popular and traditional cultural dimension. A group's shared beliefs about celebration, health, responsibility, appropriate social relationships, symbolic recognition of value and custom, influence members' impaired driving behaviors. Also groups give primacy to drinking and subsequent driving behaviors according to the images they have of themselves as members.   This includes freedom, independence, life-style, change, prosperity, beliefs about the status quo, icons of achievement, excursions into modernity, and attention to mass media productions.

These factors not only influence whether persons drink and drive, and if they do, what they drink and how they drive, but also how much they drink before driving and what someone serves to others with a view to their responsible behavior concerning later driving.

How culture affects people's thoughts about drinking and impaired driving is a major part of the impaired driving puzzle. It provides the canopy of meaning for constructing the character of life events surrounding drinking and subsequent impaired driving events. It embodies a largely unconscious set of assumptions about how experience is to be understood and valued, and how drinking preferences and driving decisions are related to such other elements as status, education, conception of self, morality, success, and so forth in a web of meaning (Postman et al., 1987).

Conclusion

For those disposed to regard impaired driving as an isolated aberration, a cause-effect relationship, a personality trait, or a disease that can be cured, a review of social factors that influence alcohol consumption and follow-up impaired driving, provide sobering second thoughts. Indeed, the quest for a more broad-based approach to impaired driving has become an issue that traffic safety researchers and agents need to confront. The result is an intensification of description and an explanation of a largely neglected area of life. In terms of Erich Heller's insightful little tale, it may be the dark area upon which researchers' lights should shine:

> The late Munich comedian, Karl Vallentin —one of the greatest of the rare race of meta physical clowns—once enacted the following scene: the curtain goes up and reveals darkness; and in this darkness is a solitary circle of light thrown by a street-lamp. Vallentin, with his long-drawn and deeply worried face, walks round and round this circle of light, desperately looking for something. "What have you lost?" a policeman asks who has entered the scene. "The key to my house." Upon which the policeman joins him in his search; they find nothing; and after a while he inquires: "Are you sure you lost it here?" "No," says Vallentin, and pointing to a dark corner of the stage: "Over there." "Then why on earth are you looking for it here?" "There is no light over there," says Vallentin. (1959: 196)

By concentrating on the lit area only, researchers uncover the most rational course of action for drivers in specific contexts; and by studying the consequences of their actions, they assess the degree to which the drivers have departed from rational norms; determine what the consequences might have been had the drivers not departed from the norms; and, finally, determine whether and in what measure the behavior contributed to the outcome.

11

Drinking Sites, Impaired Driving, and Ethno-Pharmacology

In the sociology room
the children learn
that even dreams are colored
by your perspective.

I toss and turn all night.

—Theresa Burns

It is understandable that traffic safety researchers and agents seize upon the clinical gaze of the medical model to freeze impaired driving into an individual problem. It allows impaired drivers to be classified into a variety of types, such as recidivists, chronics, and first-timers, which are arranged along a graded continuum of normality. It reduces complex social activities to a simplistic pursuit of technocratic solutions. In order to escape the confines of this individualistic perspective, a salutary effort is directed at the least studied area of impaired driving: the situation in which drinking takes place and the commonsense constructions people use to make drinking a desirable activity. Such an approach invokes a closer look at the role pharmacology plays in the definition of impaired driving.

Pharmacology is defined by the *Webster's New Collegiate Dictionary* (1977) as "the science of drugs, including materia medica, toxicology, and therapeutics: their sources and properties, preparation, uses and effect." Consistent with the definitions, alcohol is billed as a drug, the use of which causes physiological and social damage. While there is ample literature that describes and accounts for the short- and long-term effects of "the drug" on driving, the bulk of it does so according to effects measured in medical and scientific ways. For example, Pikkarenen et al. (1987) researched problem drinking or alcoholism and driving, Laurell and Tornos (1986) studied hangover effect of alcohol on driver performance and Borkenstein et al. (1964), Perrine, Waller, and Harris (1971), Farris, Malone, and Lillienfors (1976) and Mayhew et al. (1987) focused on blood alcohol concentration (BAC) and risk of fatal accident involvement. The conclusion entrenched in traffic safety, is that an alcohol level exceeding .05 is associated with a significantly increased probability of being involved in a traffic accident due to decreased visual, perceptual, and judgment abilities (Shinar, 1978). Breath analysis and/or blood sampling have become the dominant pharmacological technology to assess a driver's alcohol intake.

In response to the findings of pharmacological research, a series of drinking and driving statutes were introduced in North America that reflected .0, .02, .05, .08 or 1.0 blood alcohol concentration levels. Resources for educational and behavioral modification programs were made available for first-time offenders, recidivist impaired drivers, or impaired drivers suspected of being chronic alcoholics. A highly publicized example is the Sacramento "Comprehensive Driving Under the Influence of Alcohol Offender Treatment Demonstration Project." It consists of a yearlong educational counseling program, with and without chemotherapy (disulfiram) support. It was developed for persons having two or more convictions for driving under the influence (Reiss, 1983). This program as well as others is referred to as "treatment programs" synonymous with the medical model.

The pharmacological responses to impaired driving result from rigorous and quantifiable measurements of cause and effect. Pharmacologists explain impaired driving according to the probability of therapeutic cure. Factors that influence the situations in which drinking and subsequent driving occur fall outside of their field of vision. Yet Oakely (1972), discussing the physiological effects of psychoactive drugs, claimed that ample evidence has been collected to show that user expectations derived from the setting or social mileu in which drug use occurs is a major factor in determining a drug's effects. Nigrete (1982) recognized the shortfall in the traditional pharmacological literature in the following response to Heath's account of cultural factors and drinking:

> The social scientists' view of alcoholism is one of deviant behavior, that is, a form of alcohol use which does not conform with established and socially acceptable cultural patterns. However, alcohol dependence as understood in biological terms is unlikely to be seen as noticeably different behavior in a milieu which provides so much opportunity for socially approved inebriation. Professor Heath's remark about the need to complement ethnographic observation of drinking behavior with biomedical studies is very well taken indeed (1982: 170)

Perhaps one reason among others that medical treatments have questionable long-term effects in the reduction of drinking and driving recidivism is that such interventions deny the roles played by human choice and social influence (Whitehead, Hylton, and Markosky, 1984). This omission leaves a gaping hole in impaired driving explanations. To deal with this virgin territory, an ethno-pharmacological analysis of situational drinking and subsequent driving is offered.

On Ethno-Pharmacology

Ethno-pharmacology is defined as people's commonsense knowledge or practical interest in the location of drinking, procedures of drinking, and possible impaired driving consequences. The lenses are directed at the conditions drinkers prescribe to and endorse as factual in their attempts to drink and drive "rationally," that is in ways intended to maximize the likelihood of desirable outcomes (Stoddart, 1974).

At times, people's commonsense rationalities are compared to conventional pharmacological studies and risk analyses to demonstrate how everyday defined reality in impaired driving situations relates to that defined by science. More specifically, it features risk as tied to people's commonsense beliefs about alcohol

Uncovering Ethno-Pharmacological Evidence

To formulate an ethno-pharmacological identity two forms of data gathering were used. Over one hundred face-to-face interviews with citizens chosen at random were engaged to identify typical behaviors at bars and private parties. In addition, bartenders and servers at licensed establishments were interviewed.

Exposure data on drinkers were obtained through a telephone survey. Eight hundred and fifty four subjects were interviewed. They had been drinking at least once in the seven day preceding the survey. These respondents reported a total of 1,432 drinking occasions. Of these 441 interviewees drove vehicles after alcohol consumption. For logistical and cost reasons, the survey was restricted to the Lower Mainland area of British Columbia where over half of the province's drivers live.[1]

The Ecology of Drinking

Face-to-face, open-ended interviews with 100 respondents on the West Coast elicited the perception that people drink more at private parties than at neighborhood pubs or bars. It was both a matter of economics and social taste. Some interviewees reported that when they go to bars they have preset spending limits. They enter establishments to drink "three or four beers" or "three or four glasses of wine," because they lack the financial means to buy more. Others found the bar's atmosphere to be "impersonal" and "not casual enough." They consume three to four beers within about two hours. Although the generally low consumption of alcohol is at face value a preferred outcome for traffic safety, beneath the surface it represents a troubling scenario. The short time span in which drinks were consumed neutralizes the benefits of moderate drinking. It results in sufficient impairment to produce driving difficulties. The time-consumption ratio is generally unknown to the average drinker.

There are groups who have the financial ability and social inclination to drink in bars for extended periods of time. For example, sports enthusiasts may park themselves before a bar's big-screen television and watch their sport of choice. Some enjoy the music and comraderie of drinking and socializing for the evening.

Still others visit bars to find romance. These patrons are in the minority. Because of economics, they may indulge occasionally, but as respondents suggested, usually their financial resources control their alcohol consumption.

Patrons seldom expressed concern about getting home. Interviewees felt that there was little need to preplan for transportation. The decision was usually made toward the end of the evening. The person who had "drunk the least" was most likely to be chosen as driver. This did not mean that the driver-to-be deliberately chose to abstain from consuming alcohol or was the least impaired member of the group. Rather it was the group member who "felt" the least drunk. That feeling was assessed on a personal or subjective basis: he was not "feeling high" or she felt okay. One may ask how someone who has been drinking alcohol for a period of time can accurately assess drunkenness and risk-free driving. When this issue was posed, most bar patrons did not consider it a problem. Their collective position was that they knew how they felt; they have successfully depended on their feelings for years without adverse affect.

It also became evident that a bar's business patterns influence patron decisionmaking about how much alcohol to consume. For example, a long-standing procedure is for bar patrons to buy rounds. Generally each party sitting at a table pays for a round of drinks. The member who purchased the first round is unlikely to leave before he receives just measure in return. The person who has not yet paid may feel compelled to stay and pay for the round because to do otherwise would bring social sanctions from other members. Often the drinking continues until the circle of obligations has been fulfilled, sometimes twice around. Obviously the larger the group the more likely it is that their drinking will be of long duration and that they will consume more (Skog, 1981). The bigger the groups the faster the drinking (Dight, 1976).

Also, rounds make it easier for servers to deliver drinks and to retrieve payment. Because servers make fewer trips, they can handle more tables at a reasonable work pace. The system becomes even more efficient when patrons are able to run tabs. In fact, a customary opening remark made by a server to a newly arrived group is designed to structure "round" buying. Finally, ordering and paying for rounds enhances the server's chance for a large tip. According to some servers, patrons tend to become more generous as the sum of money to be collected for payment of rounds increases, and as patrons become increasingly inebriated.

Within the extended family of bars are neighborhood pubs, upbeat locales with a theme decor that usually copies British or German customs; a "laid-back" atmosphere where patrons can play darts, stand about leisurely and visit while drinking, sit at the bar, or settle at tables. Pubs use atmosphere to sell alcohol. "Soft rock" music or folk music is preferred, whereas bars typically feature loud rock and roll or country and western bands and/or big-screen televisions tuned to the twenty four hour sport channel. Usually drinks are more expensive at pubs than they are at bars, and food offerings are more "refined" than the usual bar fare of hot dogs, hamburgers, chips, and french fries. Toward the end of the evening, servers at pubs uniformly inform patrons to reduce their drinking for the rest of the evening. They hesitate to sell "one for the road." However, at bars servers and managers agreed that it was common for groups to order a "whole pitcher" or a "last round" during last call.

Based on the social environment, neighborhood pubs appeal to an older, more mature clientele, with a liberal mix of men and women. Here managers and servers uniformly described their clientele as being persons "older than their mid-twenties." Young people, if they come in at all, usually arrive later in the evening for a quick drink. They tend to move on to other places. Sometimes they come to "chug a couple of pints" to quench their thirst after they played fastball, slow-pitch, or flag football.

At home parties, the norm may not be excessive group drinking but social drinking to have a "good time". Food is usually available, as is exercise in the form of dancing. Hence frequenters of parties are not as likely to be sedentary drinkers like bar patrons. Of late, hosts have become more interested in the possible legal and physically harmful consequences of drinking and driving. They are more likely to monitor the number of drinks and amount of alcohol consumed and have food, coffee, and nonalcoholic beverages readily available.

Because home parties go on for extended periods of time that exceed the time that patrons can remain at bars and neighborhood pubs, partygoers are more inclined to drink for longer periods of time, estimated to be on the average of five hours. The longer period of time for party attendance plus the trend for party goers to stop drinking about forty-five minutes to an hour before driving home allows for greater blood-alcohol elimination.

While many people attend private parties as couples, they are more inclined to agree that one member should stay relatively sober for the purpose of driving home. Most often the designated driver was the woman. This has become a recent phenomenon. The designated driver has the responsibility of monitoring her alcohol consumption in an environment where setting out bottles and glasses, putting up decorations, and playing music are structured for alcohol consumption (Wittman, 1983). To maintain sobriety, the designated driver must overcome the interpersonal, spatial, and situational variables conducive to drinking.

Monitoring Consequences

Unlike bar patrons, party goers tend to think about the consequences of drinking and driving. To "treat" the risks, people are likely to engage in commonsense activities that they believe negate the effect of alcohol on driving ability. The most commonly used treatment is gulping a cup of coffee before leaving a party. Respondents generally believed that caffeine has a pharmaceutical quality that keeps them sober enough to drive home. Other procedures party goers used to enhance sobriety were counting the number of drinks consumed, nursing a particular drink for an extended period of time, refusing to drink "hard stuff" such as whiskey, rum, or vodka, staying with beer or wine, and stopping drinking about one hour before leaving the event. Eating while drinking or preparing oneself for drinking by "lining the stomach" with butter, buttermilk, or greasy foods comprised another set of preemptor strategies that were learned from friends or parents. The extent to which the practices are carried through with sufficient rigor to make a difference in chemical properties in the body can only be hypothesized.

Transport Canada (1987) reported that the significant aspect of blood alcohol concentration level in the body (BAC's) depends on how fast the alcohol is absorbed in the bloodstream. It is stated in terms of milligrams of alcohol per millimeter of blood. The slower the rate of absorption the lower the BAC level. Although sipping a drink and eating do lower the BAC level, drinking coffee has no effect. The caffeine only helps drivers stay awake. However the blood alcohol concentration does vary with body weight, because blood volume is related to to body weight (Transport Canada, 1987). Shinar (1978) explained that a heavy drinker will suffer less driving impairment than a moderate drinker when both consume the same amount of alcohol per body weight. However, he noted that heavier drinkers, by definition, drink more than moderate drinkers and therefore seldom enjoy this advantage in actual driving performance. Medical experts consider the remaining monitoring strategies to be ineffective for reducing the impact drinking has on driving (Transport Canada, 1987).

Even though people may exercise some control over their use of alcohol, there is no way for them to accurately estimate or calculate their alcohol content. Few respondents in the study knew the meaning of BAC, how it was measured, and its medical/pharmacological influences on the body and the mind. Beirness and Donelson (1983) suggested that this state of affairs is analogous to enforcing speed limits when drivers have no speedometers in their vehicles. The notion that "people should know better" leaves a long shadow of doubt.

Conclusion

The problem of drinking alcohol and impaired driving as under-stood by drinkers is made up of a variety of personal and environ-mental factors. Drinking situations and their unique atmospheres or organizational settings influence the amount of liquor consumed away from home. Drinkers do consider the consequences of impaired driving by engaging in certain preemptive or monitoring strategies to limit what they believe is their likelihood of getting drunk or going out of control. However the success of their strategies is limited when alcohol concentration is measured by pharmacological or epi-demeological means. Still, most people draw on successful drinking and driving histories to suggest that their strategies have merit.

Note

1. The study from which the descriptions are based was co-authored with P.J Cooper. It was presented at the Thirty Fifth International Congress on Alcoholism and Drug Dependence, Oslo, Norway, 31 July to 6th of August 1988. The sponsoring agency for the study was the Insurance Corporation of British Columbia.

12

Claim Making and the Drive for
Greater Control

*What is truth on one side of the Pyrenees
is error on the other*

—Pascal

To further chart the social evolution of traffic safety and its
relation to society raises the thorny problems: Who defines traffic
safety? How do the definitions affect driving activities? This chapter
addresses these questions. It describes how groups transform the
traffic scene through control of interpretation. The following pages
illustrate how certain definitions of morality are intricately linked to
government safety policies, and community involvement for the
increased control of the roadways. Laws, intervention strategies, re-
education opportunities, public awareness programs, and technological innovations have been introduced on the basis of thepower
some groups have to define traffic morality.

Over the last ten years, special-interest groups from the community, industry, government, business, and research sectors have
mobilized for the common goal of reducing the number and severity
of traffic accidents. Although they range widely in influence, power,
and expertise, they share the same podium, basing their deliveries on
the same master code: Get tough on deviant drivers. Despite the
evidence produced in the previous chapters that shows that driving
decisions entail a series of social characteristics, they believe that
driving standards are nonnegotiable sanctioned norms—immutable
facts of life. Road users who deviate from these norms, they argue,

are negligent, amoral, deviant risk-takers who willfully bring financial, emotional, and social hardship on others and threaten the unity of
a smooth functioning roadway system (Macmillan, 1975).

Traffic safety interest groups broadcast a victim blaming ideology,
attuned to the belief that roadusers are entirely to blame for accidents.
Witness Dollinger, the 1984 German Minister of Transportation:

> Every road user—be he driver, cyclist or pedestrian—must become aware of the
> fact that he himself determines road safety to a large extent. It is his own
> behavior which endangers the safety of himself or others. (1984: 1)

The uncritical assignment of responsibility to the human factor is
shared by a broad spectrum of traffic researchers such as Carsten,
Tight, and Southwell (1989), Barjonet (1988), White (1988), Jessor
(1987), Slovic (1985) and Waller (1985), who among others suggest
that driver error, or human negligence, is the main contributory factor
in accidents.

Insurance companies, government agencies, traffic safety lobby
groups, traffic safety research organizations, and auto manufacturers
embrace the research stance; an approach that in a sense erases road
users as individuals and redraws them as human factors. Road users
are redefined as products of safety codes or causal agents of
accidents. Generally speaking, drivers are regarded as "maladjusted"
if, for example, they fail to comply with traffic signs or overdrive the
traffic environment by traveling faster than the traffic flow (Guastello
and Guastello, 1987; McKelvie, 1986; Shinar, 1978).

Although claim makers play significant roles in traffic and safety
standards, policy, law enforcement, accident analysis, and research,
they reject the possibility of blaming themselves (Ryan, 1976). For
example, a government's fiscal policy may reduce the amount of road
sanding or snow clearance in the winter. This may result in increased
hazardous driving during the very early hours of the morning. By
blaming motorists for not driving according to conditions, the
government effectively immunizes itself from blame and removes the
possibility that radical social change may be invoked that may
threaten its own role as a safety overseer.

The emphasis on the driver, or "human factor" became an
accepted stance ever since Myers (1935) argued that 80 to 90 percent

of road accidents are attributable to human causes. Since then, the National Highway Traffic Safety Administration in the United States (NHTSA), provincial solicitor general departments in Canada, and various national government bodies around the world have monopolized the explanatory framework for public policy. Witness the following quote by the Ontario Minister of Transportation:

> Vehicle and highways had been improved to the point where there is little left that can be substantially improved. . . . as a result of the 1,200 deaths and the reported 122,000 injuries in the report. . . . bad drivers [must] be retrained [and punished]. . . road infractions [must] be stiffened. . . and the demerit point system be modified to better identify high risk drivers. (1987: 4)

By emphasizing standard and routine versions of human factors, claimmakers deny the validity of such alternative possibilities for road accidents as:

- the construction of highways with unsatisfactory engineering safety standards (Hauer, 1990);

- social pressures on the driver that induces or influences behavior, marketing strategies that feature speed, sensation, and lifestyle (Leiss, 1990);

- lobbying efforts by large auto manufacturers to limit innovations that increase safety (Nader, 1966);

- economic advantages of auto accidents (Lave and Lave, 1990);

- maintenance crews that have not properly maintained a stretch of highway because of government funding policies (Rothe, 1991b); and

- data on age of vehicle, make and model, weight, automobile maintenance and other factors of vehicle design (Stacey, 1985).

Automakers applaud the human factor rationale. Such an interpretation encourages people to view automakers as responsible corporate citizens who support police enforcement to stem the frequency and intensity of accidents. From a practical point of view the interpretation steers citizens away from images that cars may be defective or unsafe (Schneider, 1972). From 1966 to 1985 over 100 million American-made vehicles have been recalled to correct safety defects. The number of vehicles recalled for safety-related defects was 7.2 million in 1984 and 5.6 million in 1985 (Blomquist, 1988). Of course the numbers would rise if European and Japanses vehicles were included in the count. Yet General Motors vice president Barr commented in the *New York Times*, "We feel that our cars are quite reliable. If drivers do everything they should, there wouldn't be any accidents would there?" (Gikas, 1983: 332).

Highway builders are relieved of the responsibility of constructing safer roadways. Government departments need not worry about increased costs of highway construction or facing the wrath of automakers if they oppose vehicle designs that are profitable but unsafe. Police departments can continue their investigative techniques according to their customary ways, and insurance companies can repeat their call for tighter legislation that may improve their economic positions through a reduction in claims.

When traffic safety officials invoke human factor claims they often assume that road users are human resources whose value is determined by medical, social, and emotional costs. Safety is a resource, calculated according to the worth of a human life, body part, or indexes of a person's utility to society. Life becomes reified. Injury becomes a market failure (Linder, 1987). Weighell wrote,

> How does one put a price on the loss of hearing, facial disfigurement, loss of life? Insurance societies and the courts frequently do this even though the concept requires an equation between man and money which is dependent more on a judgment of equity than on any universal validation of human suffering. (1974: 117)

As a resource, life can be refined, managed, and controlled. Witness Bonnie's much publicized resurrection of John Stuart Mill's thesis that

> coercive interventions may be justifiable if the social benefits (measured by reduction in social burden derived from reduction in the unsafe or unhealthy behavior) demonstrably outweigh[s] the costs of the intervention. (1985: 133)

Rhetoric is often used to gather political support for increased management of the resource. A group of allied claim-making groups and experts help set policy by popularizing research methods and findings that fit their worldviews. Witness Haight's account:

Sponsors of accident research often demand that, before being funded, the research worker first demonstrate how any knowledge which might be forthcoming can be transformed into a "life-saving" intervention during the current budget year. . . . Most research proposals require a good deal of ingenuity and often some downright prevarication to satisfy sponsors of immediate payoff. (1988: 11)

By stressing particular problem definitions and research designs that assure findings consistent with the thinking of agents and researchers, a loose consensus between the two groups is formed. A typical outcome is a call for rational intervention such as minimum driving or drinking ages and disincentives such as license suspension or revocation and fines.

Constructing Numbers through Police Reports

Of all driver violations, speeding has of late, received much attention from claim makers such as insurance companies, government traffic safety officers, and researchers. Their case against speeders is typically based on accident rates correlated with high rates of speed. Researchers consider casualty rates based on deaths and injuries resulting from involvement in certain driving behavior and roadway exposure to be objective facts sui generis, error free, collected through organized police investigations. They are presented as quantitative features, assigned epistemological and ontological privileges, to be accepted on faith (see annual traffic accident statistics reports supplied by NHTSA, state administrations and provincial solicitor general departments).

Yet a number of researchers have shown that official accident statistics are little more than numerical artifacts based on police accident assessments. They are inexact, decontextualized indexes with limited definitive substance. For example, Shinar (1978) noted that police accident reports are highly variable, depending on the type of accident, the time of occurrence, the jurisdictions, and the locations. Baracik and Fife (1985) compared the number of traffic-related injuries reported in police accident reports to that reported by hospitals (emergency admissions). The authors established that police report statistics consistently omitted information such as demographic, social, and crash factors and the severity of the injuries incurred.

Official causes of accidents are typically determined as human factors based on the character of accident reporting. A principal rule followed by the police is to articulate driver fault (Rothe, 1992). If this expectation is not met, insurance adjusters fill the void, often leading to split fault on a 50 - 50 or 75 25 percent basis. Possible factors such as roadway design, signs or vehicle manufacture receive scant attention. They reflect Garfinkel's (1967) thesis, that roadway and vehicle factors are not rendered observable and understandable according to traditional methods of investigation and interpretation. They are extraneous variables to the police, removed from officers' interest in human factors such as drivers and other road users.

Human factors do not encompass many human actions. They only represent recognized and accepted empirical categories of behavior. For example, speeding is an official category included in the official accident report form upon which information is collected and fault is attributed. Momentary inattention or pauses of natural driving action created by smoking, eating, daydreaming, music, or interaction with passengers are a few factors relevant to accidents that are not designated categories on accident report forms (Rothe, 1991c). They do not form part of the "of-course" assumptions or properties that support the empirical definition of "human factor."

Also omitted in police records are possible contributing factors such as emotional instability, irritability, impulsiveness, moodiness, confidence and driver perceptual capabilities (Chan, 1987). The evidence is too difficult to locate or the characteristics are too far removed from the officers' fact-finding routines. Yet, with respect to perceptual difficulties, Hughes and Cole (1986), Milosevic and Gajic (1986), and Shinar and Drory (1983) established that up to 50 percent of drivers' visual attention is not focused on the driving act. It is directed toward nondriving-related objects. Drivers see signs but may not necessarily read them. To further underscore the perceptual problems of driving, Hughes and Cole (1986) described the "spare capacity" phenomenon; that is, only 15 to 20 percent of a driver's visual attention is directed toward traffic procedures. Thirty to 50 percent of their visual attention is directed toward nondriving-related objects (e.g. commercial advertising on side of the road). By discounting "other" accident-relevant human qualities, the police consistently produce similar primary causes for accidents, or as Gusfield (1981) wrote, law officers maintain certainty in a field of ambiguity.

In studies on young drivers (Rothe, 1991c), elderly drivers (Rothe, 1990a) and truckers (1991a) the author relied on official police data. Conservatively speaking, at least 15 percent of the recorded information contained errors on location of accident, extent of injury (e.g. soft-tissue injury), traffic flow, gender of driver, and time of day. Lyles, Stamatiadis, and Lightizer (1991) pointed out that there is always a potential for bias when police officers assign responsibility to crash-involved drivers. A Michigan study using 1982-1984 data found that 16 per cent of the responsibility designations were incorrectly coded (Lyles, Stamatiadis, and Lightizer 1991: 278).

City police officers in large metropolitan areas such as Vancouver, Los Angeles, Toronto, or Chicago are so busy investigating accidents—among other police duties—that they are compelled to streamline the accident investigation procedures in order to master the work flow. For example, in Vancouver, accidents are prioritized and stacked on police on-board computers, requiring quick, efficient responses by the officers. The emphasis on time and efficiency increases the probability for error or omission of certain information by constables and reduces the possibility that officers will move outside of their normal accident investigation routine (Rothe, 1992).

Statistical descriptions based on police interviews may also be messy. Police interviews are usually pointed and direct. "What happened?" "Were you wearing seat belts?" Answers to these questions are processed for the courts, after which they become grist for the statistical mill. Yet, according to Shinar (1978), the accuracy of a driver's recall of accident circumstances in light of the tendency to justify preaccident behavior, is questionable. Furthermore, according to Shinar (1978), the accuracy of witness accounts is suspect. The knowledge that an accident has occurred can influence a witness' recall of selected details preceding the accident and lead to the perceived need for a culprit. The apparently objective process of analyzing and reconstructing the precipitating factors of an accident is, thus, influenced by numerous interpretive factors.

To illustrate the questionable nature of police post- accident interviews it is necessary to introduce a short footnote. Non-seat belt wearing is illegal in all Canadian provinces. If caught unbelted the occupant can receive a fine of up to seventy-eight dollars. It is, therefore, difficult to imagine drivers or passengers volunteering to answer that they were not wearing seat belts when asked by the officer. Yet provincial solicitor general departments report seat belt-wearing counts of accident victims on the basis of such interviews. They become the province's official statistics.

Statistical Bias of Speed and Accidents

A case study often used to infer a causal relationship between speed and accidents is that of the United States 55 MPH law that was passed in 1974 and was revised to 65 MPH on selected roadways in 1987. Researchers have lined up to demonstrate how the increased speed limit led to increases in fatal accidents and deaths. Witness the consensus drawn by Wagenaar, Straff, and Schultz (1990: 578): "We believe these results reflect increased morbidity, mortality and property damage causally attributable to the policy of raising the speed limit. . . ." Two reasons were provided. One was that the increases in damage began immediately after the signs of the higher speed limit were posted and the second was that increases were found only on those specific road segments where the posted speed limits were changed. Studies by the American Association of State Highway and Transportation Officials (1977), Michaels and Schneider (1976), Cerrelli (1983), Transportation Research Board (1984), National Highway Traffic Safety Administration (1988, 1989) and Baum, Lund, and Wells (1989), among others, concluded that due to the 55 MPH speed limit in the United States there was a reduction of 20 to 70 percent in fatalities; that is 3,200 to 5,900 lives were saved, a figure that engenders little confidence.

The researchers recognized that there are a large number of contributing factors that lead to accidents besides speed. Their analysis assumes that if everything else is held constant (eg., roadway maintenance, characteristics of the driving public, economic growth, etc.) and if the speed limit is reduced and the number of accidents decrease, then it is likely that speed is the precipitating causal variable. The difficulty with this line of reasoning is that "everything else does not stay constant," clouding the conclusions drawn. For example, more compact and subcompact cars began to populate the roadway. In 1974, 30 precent of the vehicle fleet was made up of small cars; by 1984, this figure had risen to 45 percent (Jernigan, Lynn, and Harber, 1986). The proportion of small Japanese and American cars increased even more in 1991 (Womack, Jones, and Roos, 1991) If smaller cars are less able to withstand the kinetic energy created by another car, the struck vehicle increases the chance of being involved in a more serious crash. Also, by reviewing statistics provided by the U.S. Department of Commerce (1987) and those illustrated by Desmond (1989), a conclusion can be drawn that greater numbers of larger and heavier commercial vehicles were pressed into service and that the American freeway infrastructure was physically deteriorating to the point that it created greater opportunities for high-speed crashes.

Economists like Lave and Lave (1990) and Mela (1977) found that traffic fatalities increase during good economic times and decrease during bad. According to Mela, the factors that correlate most closely with fatalities are industrial production and retail sales. In 1973-74, North America was in a recession, a very different economic scenario from the 1980s.

Furthermore, technology has created a generally faster pace of life (Noguchi, 1990). Since the 1970s and 1980s auto manufacturers again built faster, sportier and more powerful vehicles. Automobile fads and fashions have changed. Small high-powered sports cars like the Toyota Supra, Mazda RX-7, Ford Mustang and Datsun Z-28 among others once again became popular as convertible models. They were re-introduced without roll bars or extra safety protection. These vehicle designs are more likely to produce fatalities in crashes.

Localizing Claims

Claim making against road users also centers on locally organized events. For example, periodically the police, with the assistance of

local media and community safety organizations and with government sponsorship engage in traffic enforcement blitzes with the
ostensible purpose of apprehending the maximum number of traffic
violators in compressed periods of time.   Although the manifest
intent of enforcement is to deter traffic violation, public relations is a
latent benefit that is not lost on the police.

Police enforcement blitzes are based on the assumption that
decreased traffic violations are a function of increased police
visibility.   Statistics play a significant role in the affirmation of this
hypothesis.   Accidents and predefined violations before and after a
well publicized police enforcement blitz are counted and correlated.
Unfortunately, problems with the design are seldom publicized. First,
the true number of traffic violations committed in a defined sector are
at best approximataed, because only some fraction of them are ever
observed or reported.   More importantly, to engage in pre- and
postenforcement studies and to generalize from them a measure of
effectiveness is to gloss.   There are numerous uncontrolled factors
involved during the time of measurement that produce questionable
external and internal validity (Haight, 1972, Campbell and Stanley,
1966).   Other variables interact with the dependent factor to threaten
general conclusions of success. For example, how can driving in a
rainstorm during the pre- or postmeasurement time be correlated with
driving on a clear sunny day, when it is widely known that weather
influences both the volume of traffic and the risk of an accident
(Haight, 1972)? On certain days there are special events like football
games or holiday celebrations that increase traffic flow which may be
entirely different on other days.   In the summer, the traffic mix
includes a greater number of out-of-town tourists and this challenges
the research numbers in terms of attentiveness to the safety message
and motivation to comply with local police-community efforts.

Still, claim makers proclaim time and time again that after
counting preintervention accidents and/or observed violations and
comparing them to postintervention behavior, police intervention
allied with media publicity was a success. For support they point to
the numbers. The rhetoric of proof often becomes another opportunity
for certain groups to call for increased police involvement in the
streets.

Claim Making as Staging

The quantitative approach has been used to gain prestige and to give the appearance of scientific rigor. It has, by and large, been molded into a presentation format that reflects Nisbet's introduction to a sociological text:

> A social problem cannot be said to exist until it is defined as one. The way of behavior involved may be fixed and may be found among many people. But unless the behavior is defined as a violation of some norm, unless it is regarded by large numbers of people as being repugnant to moral consciousness, it cannot be termed a social problem. (1971: 2)

The purpose behind much of the traffic safety research is to construct a driving problem based on the driver as a human factor, announce it, sensationalize it, and use it to appeal for change. Continuous reinforcement of the problem definition is vital for the claim makers because without it people may not embrace the public definition as private knowledge. For example, speeding trend statistics provided by Noguchi (1990), Jernigan, Lynn, and Garber (1988) and others illustrate that the majority of drivers do not believe or behave as if speeding is an everyday concern. They are not predisposed to define speeding as a personal problem. To counter this scenario, some interest groups design communication techniques to channel free-floating driving-related anxiety to the public through empiricist vocabulary that represents the invariant features of speeding. The most common is the announcement that "speed kills," followed by statistics. The presentation is usually followed by specific punitive prevention strategies such as the use of electronic surveillance or increased visible policing. To reach the public, claim makers increase the salience of both speeding and speed prevention.

One way of accomplishing this is to spread the salience of traffic violation across communities. For example, youth conferences in British Columbia, New Brunswick, California, and Minnesota, among other jurisdictions, are organized to convince high school students that collectively, traffic safety violators comprise an unimpeachable moral problem that demands serious attention. The conferences take on a theatrical frame, treating traffic as a drama or fiction rather than real life. The problem is defined, statistics are reviewed, rational authority figures such as police officers or attorneys are invited to speak, and accident victims discuss their horrible experiences. These dramatic episodes are designed to suspend student disbelief. A high level of traffic-related anxiety is created, which some attending teachers at one conference explained was akin to a "revival meeting." Students are chastised for being passive and are then encouraged to involve themselves in the struggle to convince drivers to become virtuous. As one guest speaker at an Ontario conference screamed to the audience, "We're not gonna take it anymore. Give us back the roads." Such emotional outpourings help claim makers to sustain a sense of moral panic and thereby enlist and organize a new generation of claim makers.

However routine and ordinary speeding may be, claim makers cast it in a certain light to activate a certain response. An example is the introduction of the photo radar camera in British Columbia (Rothe, 1991d). In the spring of 1990, seven medical doctors working from the Lions Gate and Squamish Hospitals united to hold a news conference and present a formal brief to the government. As classic moral entrepreneurs (Gusfield, 1981), they developed and sensationalized the problem of the carnage on Highway 99 caused by speeding and reckless driving. After they cited statistics, portrayed by them as unscientific but relevant, they demanded immediate action.

In response, British Columbia's provincial insurance company, a provincial crown corporation, the local print media, and the police department's public relations officers teamed up to alert citizens that speeding is the leading cause of traffic accidents. At news conferences held in May 1990, and in news bulletins and research reports government agents characterized an identifiable group of drivers as speeders and portrayed them as people who take unwarranted risks, seek thrills, disobey traffic laws, and selfishly place innocent people's lives in peril. Speeders were represented as nonconformists, guilty of failing to observe the sanctioned moral order of the roadway.

Once the public was shaken into a view that there is a conflict between "us," the good average drivers and "them," the reckless drivers, the government, with the support of the police and the insurance company, introduced the need for a radical solution. To punish and deter, the government introduced the photo radar camera on Highway 99.

Claim Making as an Industry:
The Insurance Company Case

Traffic safety claim making has become an industry. The National Highway Traffic Safety Administration (NHTSA) in the United States regularly presents statistics to the media and government officials, leaving the impression that there is a problem and that they have defined it.   Inquiries are commissioned, policy papers are presented to legislatures, and seminars are organized with helping professions such as medical doctors (AAAM) and other public health officials. As a group they consume information, and share data. In this way organizations such as NHTSA highlight their view that traffic violations are a threat to public safety, that the government is attentive to the welfare of road users, and that there are a large number of deviant drivers.

Recent players supporting organizations such as NHTSA are insurance companies. However, the attention they assign to traffic safety intervention may be questioned on the grounds of altruism. Naturally an expanded explanation is warranted.

Insurance is more than simply a commodity bought and sold in the marketplace. It is a social arrangement organized around a set of procedures for allocating risk across a community of risk takers (Reichman, 1986: 151).   The Insurance Corporation of British Columbia, Canadian Insurance Bureau, the American Insurance Institute for Highway Safety, the Comite' Europe'en des Assurances in Paris, and HUK Verband in Germany focus on traffic violations as a contingency for which the technology of insurance provides an effective management ethos. Part of their strategy is to minimize or neutralize hazards such as improperly maintained roadways that complicate the accident risk calculus. A Blue Cross and Blue Shield advertisement, illustrates the theme:

> If we take better care of ourselves, we're going to need less health care. And this will slow down the rise in health care costs. . . . We're not asking you to become a Puritan, to stop enjoying life. Just to take better care of yourself. Please don't

overeat, don't oversmoke, don't overwork. And, if you are going to drink to someone's health, don't overdo it. (Cited in Bonnie, 1985: 132)

To further their aim, insurance organizations contract research companies and university faculties to focus their attention entirely on human factor issues such as young drivers, drinking drivers, motorcyclists, and lately, speeders. Because they are in the actuarial business, risk taking, or the probability that losses will occur, regardless of the form or social context, is considered to be negative, and risk-takers, so defined, are viewed within the medical model as social health culprits.

Insurance firms benefit from pressure on risk taking because they believe it helps reduce the number and severity of claims. They not only support, but perpetuate, claims making by subsidizing intervention strategies such as community monitoring (eg., providing radar to neighborhoods so that people can detect speeders, or advising people to call the police if they witness a severe traffic violations such as impaired driving or erratic driving), increased police enforcement, punitive punishments, and revised licensing strategies. Such strategies are constructed on the belief that there is a need for "instrumental discipline" or control on the opportunities that permit violations to occur (Shearing and Stenning, 1981). As part of the behavioral management approach, they have many seeming advantages. They are direct. The target is clearly discernible as some specific behavior to be changed. They are immediate. Results can be immediately observed and assessed. Finally, techniques can frequently be applied with or without the recipient's request. The following recommendation for a graduated licensing program in Canada, made by the Insurance Bureau of Canada and the Traffic Injury Foundation illustrates the theme poignantly:

Risk is minimized by managing the conditions and circumstances arising from age-related factors, such as thrill-seeking or from inexperience. This is accomplished by restricting new drivers in terms of when, where, or with whom they can drive. . . . It is now time to implement and evaluate its effectiveness in Canada. (1991: 35)

To assist their cause, insurance companies present themselves to the public as concerned altruistic problem solving organizations.

Because of their strong lobbying power, insurance companies, allied with public health officials, policymakers, and law enforcement agencies are successfully getting their claims established and registered with influential agencies. They attempt to blend private and public authorities and the creation of large public-private enterprises (Reichman, 1983). Their strength of presentation lies in emphasizing human factors as a simple problem about the severity of which there is ample data. This form of presentation makes solutions possible, perceptible, nameable and actionable (Spector and Kitsuse, 1977). Through statistical probabilities, exclusionary decisions are reached. Through selective attention, insurance firms define the needs they wish to serve.

In some jurisdictions, such as California the courts have invoked the "deep pocket" theory of liability. In short, those organizations that can best afford to pay for damage, should do so. Organizations such as insurance companies have been ordered to pay millions of dollars to the victims of crashes. As a result, the medical costs of major injuries have increased substantially. In response to this trend, insurance companies are now more inclined to focus on prevention in order to control funds than they are on harnessing premiums. According to Nader (cited in Reichman, 1986), insurance companies previously had little interest in diminishing losses in auto crashes because, among other considerations, as long as they could raise premiums, increased losses were balanced by increased premiums and reinvestments. With increasing public hostility against insurance company premium increases witnessed in Ontario and California, among other jurisdictions, insurance companies hesitate to continue yearly increases in premiums. Hence insurers shifted their attention to prevention, one of the few opportunities left to control costs while winning public acceptance.

Conclusion

Traffic safety as a public concern is not above criticism. It is difficult not to see controversial issues such as total faith in measurement procedures, unsubstantiated myths, self-interest, ideologies, designed economic values, distribution of social justice and specific versions of morality. Claim makers insist that they are the sovereign center, the ultimate source of truth, of empirical evidence, and of meaning, in whose terms traffic safety should be defined.

Traffic safety is a creature of modern business, government, and community lobby groups. As such it is the vehicle for providing authoritative concepts capable of rendering traffic situations meaningful. These meanings are manufactured so that people can easily grasp their significance. Traffic safety claims makers arouse emotion, rhetorically celebrating the individual while in reality moving toward greater control of the person's life. The individual driver has been rendered obsolete as an "I" and has been redefined as a human factor, a general concept of maladjustment, responsibility, and blame. Through emphasis on the human factor and victim blaming, interest groups such as insurance companies and government safety agencies have cleared the way for paternalistic interventions that increase the use of power and control. Paraphrasing Horowitz ((1989), they work toward the constant expansion of state power and the increase in administrative domination and disposition of people.

13

Surveillance on the Roadway

Every breath you take
Every move you make
Every bond you break
Every step you take
I'll be watching you.

—Sting

The notion that traffic safety problems ought to and can be solved or minimized is closely related to acknowledgment that problems exist. Indeed, the relationship between the recognition of traffic safety problems and the desire to solve them represents a faith in technology. Planned technological interventions are rapidly becoming a part of the traffic safety landscape. So they become part of the data and ideas upon which understanding of traffic behavior is based.

To define and solve the impaired driving problem, legal officials use an array of examinations and intrusive technological screening and intervention devices. Field sobriety tests, breathalyzers and Alcosensors are used to provide blood alcohol concentration readings, HGN procedures are used to test drivers' eyes for involuntary jerking motion (Jacobs, 1989); biochemical measurements of such bodily fluids as serum, urine, and blood are used to test problem drinkers (Harper and Martin, 1983), psychometric screening is employed to characterize drinking and predict recidivism (Hagart et al., 1983); and walking a straight line, balancing on one foot, and touching the nose with the index finger are used to screen for co-ordination.

A long-term trend allegedly designed to promote safe driving behavior is the growth of electronic surveillance and the consequent appearance of a new set of values and norms. In earlier times, police officers engaged in speedometer pacing, they followed drivers and ascertained speedometer readings. There was no guarantee that drivers who were stopped would be charged. They were as likely to be lectured on the morals of the roadway or safety risks involved in speeding and breaking traffic laws. There was a reasonable chance that drivers would be let off with warnings because the emphasis was more on traffic safety than it was on punishment (Franklin, 1990).

The introduction of traffic radar in the 1960s altered the contours of police work. Emphasis on safety was superseded by individual deterrence. Police action no longer had its roots in the promotion of safety through roadside interactions comprised of warnings, discussions or on-site education. Instead, law officers shifted their attention to apprehension and punishment with minimal concern about individual driver well-being, safety and caution. A transition from rational guidance to behavioral modification based on negative reinforcement occurred (Uglow, 1988).

The technological readout of speeds removed the "subjective factor" of determining speed by pacing, vision, and assessment. In a way, radio-frequency energy and transmission replaced human brain waves. Straight documentation of technological readouts replaced the police officers' interpretations of roadway behavior. On a series of police ride-alongs it became obvious that police officers subscribed to the total accuracy of the speed readout produced by the radar unit (Rothe, 1992). In their daily work routines, law officers were more concerned about the number displayed on the screen than they were about the unit's potential for distortion or the radar's effect on police-driver interaction. They had an unshakable faith that radar could and should be used properly to solve speeding problems and to enhance the quality of driver behavior.

As technology increasingly became the organizing framework for policing, some drivers oriented themselves to the particular qualities of apprehension. They tailored their actions to the new demands of traffic surveillance by purchasing radar detectors or "fuzz busters." Their function was simple: to make radar patrols electronically "visible" to motorists (Smith and Tomerlin, 1990).

To reciprocate, some American states such as New York and Connecticut and Canadian provinces such as like Ontario and Alberta passed laws to constrain the use of radar detection devices. The measures were based more on the belief that the law cannot be broken through technological innovation than it was on empirical proof that users were more unsafe, or that they were proportionately overrepresented in accidents than were motorists without radar detectors. This does not mean that such findings were not sought. For example, a team of British Columbia researchers attempted to correlate presence of radar detectors with violations and accidents. The search proved to be fruitless because of everyday factors that ruined the data. For example, radar detectors that were installed were not always spotted by the police; some radar detectors that were found had not been used, while others that were had been used.

Although no evidence to date has shown that drivers who own radar detectors are more likely to be violators, risk-takers or accident promoters, regulations against the ownership of these detectors, a legal consumer product, were passed. The argument for stopping the use of radar detectors appears to rest on teleology. It goes something like this. Radar detector owners possess the characteristics of speeders. The purpose for them having radar detectors is to speed without the risk of apprehension. On the basis of this commonsense logic, radar detector owners are consequently considered to be blameworthy. The sense-making scheme, invoked by traffic safety professionals, is that people who purchase such devices are motivated to break the law without experiencing risk of apprehension.

If the police use traffic radar entirely to promote safety, rather than to mete out punishment, radar detectors may prove to be valuable assets. For example, some police officers believe that roadside radars help slow down drivers through visible police action (Rothe, 1992). Assuming for a moment that some motorists with radar detectors are speeding, then they would surely be motivated to decelerate once the detector was activated. A form of deterrence has been achieved. However, the dominant assumption still is that the apprehension of speeders supersedes slower speed for safety, or that apprehension is more likely to deter speeding.

In rhythm with the cycle of technological one-upmanship, the police began deploying advanced technological devices that detect radar detectors. In the early 1990s devices such as laser guns, sensors embedded in the road and video speed recorders were being tested and will soon be used. They will render the conventional radar detectors obsolete (Gooderham, 1993; Lagac, 1992)). VASCAR (Visual Average Speed Computer and Recorder) is used from low-flying aircraft, and new radar instruments are designed to delay radar transmissions until target vehicles are well within range, making it impossible for long-distance warning.

In the midst of the cat-and-mouse game of detecting the detector, new technological systems called photo radar have been developed. It states in the *Royal Canadian Mounted Police User Manual* (undated) that the technology is designed to escape conventional radar detector detection because its beams operate at an accelerated rate. Whereas traditional traffic radars operate within the X-band at frequencies of about 10.525 billion waves per second (or 10.525 gigahertz), and K-band radars operate on frequencies of 24.15 gigahertz, the photo radar unit's rate of frequency is 34.3 gigahertz. Antiradar devices are incapable of locating the 34 gigahertz emissions—for now.

The Photo Radar Camera

Unlike traditional traffic radar, photo radar cameras consist of Doppler radars linked to cameras. The radar "acquires" an oncoming car and determines its speed. A preprogrammed microprocessor triggers the camera on a vehicle exceeding the programmed speed, taking a photograph of the oncoming car and driver (Lesce, 1988).

Once a driver has been spotted by the camera a negative is produced that includes a photo of the marked car, along with the date, time, and speed recorded. A postcard-sized print is developed and mailed to the vehicle's registered owner with an official letter. Roadside interactions between the police and drivers are eliminated. The police now assume that the driver is guilty as accused by the photograph. However, it should be noted that the owner of the car is in violation and not the driver, a case of "vicarious liability." There is the legal assumption that registered owners are responsible for any violations committed in their cars, whether they were driving or not (Smith and Tomerlin, 1990).

The photographic evidence on license plate numbers is collected by an agency that is appointed or sub-contracted by the Department of the Attorney General in Canada or District Attorney in the United States. It obtains a list of vehicle owners, then matches them to the license plate numbers in photographs. Traffic citations are then mailed to the vehicles' registered owners, who can either pay their fines by mail or appear in court if they wish to contest the notice (Lesce, 1988).

Freedman, Williams, and Lund (1989) outlined five advantages photo radar has over conventional speed enforcement techniques. One, it can positively identify speeding vehicles in a non-discriminatory fashion, producing evidence that shows speed, time, date, location, and other relevant information. Two, it detects and records nearly all speeders, photographing successive vehicles as close as a half a second apart, while providing safeguards that ensure that the speed measurements will be associated with the correct vehicle. Three, it emits a low-powered microwave signal that is effective against radar detectors. Four, it reduces hazardous exposure of police officers, speeders, other vehicles, and pedestrians because law enforcement officers do not pursue and stop offenders. Five, it is an efficient means of operation that requires minimum officer time on the site, freeing other members of the police force to engage in more valuable work. These advantages are believed to outweigh individual police officers' discretion, interpretation, and accuracy.

Photo Radar and Profit

During an interview with French scholars, Foucoult (1980) stated that delinquents are necessary for economic reasons. Without crime there would be less need for legal personnel, criminologists, emergency response professionals judiciaries, prison guards, and so on. Producers and directors would be deprived of story lines for popular movies and pulp writers would have fewer plots for detective serials. According to Hagan (1985), if there were no crime society would have to invent it because of its significance in the economic sector. It is little wonder that Stgt. Howie of the Calgary City Police Services proudly stated that he "issued $1.7 million in tickets last year with a little help from photo radar technology (Gooderham, 1993: A1). To emphasize Hagan's theme, a case study on the use of photo radar in

Paradise Valley, Arizona, is featured. It demonstrates the many social implications that underlay the implementation of the technology.

The Paradise Valley Case

Foucoult's position on deviance has direct relevance to the photo radar debate. For example, in Paradise Valley, Arizona, one of two American locations where the photo radar camera has been used, critics accused the town of using a technology that "grinds on people" or that fills the town coffers at the expense of motorists.   The accusation resulted from the town manager's confession that photo radar grossed $400,000 a year (1988), of which Paradise Valley received about 30 percent as net income (Lesce, 1988).

When photo radar was first introduced in Paradise Valley, it was used for nineteen hours per week. During an average week 1,025 photographs were taken, and 301 citations issued. According to the district attorney's office, the percentage of citations will increase once officers gain experience. By assuming that the average fine is about $75, the net profit can be determined.

Lamm and Kloeckner (1989) provided substantiation for the claim. In Germany, photo radar cameras have been used on a seven kilometer stretch of the Autobahn called Elzer Mountain. Between the years 1974 and 1983, at $20 per ticket, the government grossed 15 million dollars (Lamm and Kloeckner, 1989). Furthermore, judicial expenses were reduced. Several times a year the police were set up at the side of roads demanding that identified drivers pay fines on the spot or have their cars impounded. It has since become a standard practice in Germany (Traffic Watch, 1974).

Lamm and Kloeckner editorialized that the process is worthwhile, because it controls the number of speeders, who would otherwise go to court and fight the charges on the basis that they were not the drivers in the vehicles photographed. The pay-on-the-spot strategy has been deemed an economic success because of numbers caught, imposition of immediate payment, and limited judicial involvement. Because of the high net intake of funds, a suggestion has appeared in German newspapers that Elzer Mountain is no more than a successful taxation exercise (Felke, 1983). Enough money was collected in the first two years of operation to pay for all installations, labor, and accompanying electronic equipment. Since the technological devices have been amortized, an average of $1.5 million was collected per year on the basis of two hundred cars receiving fines per day.

The numbers are modest because the police can increase usage and lower tolerance levels to produce a greater volume of drivers. If "zero tolerance" ever becomes realized, significant increases in profit are assured.

During a photo radar pilot study in British Columbia, the attorney general recommended that the police use a tolerance level of 20 km/h. The standard was not enforced. Because it was a guideline, and not a policy the final decisions on tolerance were deferred to individual police detachments. Consequently some officers reduced the tolerance level to 15 km/h (discussions with ICBC photo radar personnel, 1990). As Marx (1989) discussed, failure by legislators to regulate potentially problematic tactics in surveillance represents legislative acquiescence.

An original goal for introducing the technology in British Columbia was to control high risk-roadway environments where physical policing was difficult and dangerous due to roadway geometry and exceedingly heavy traffic. However, during the pilot study the police deviated significantly from the original design. Members used the photo radar camera at sites where traditional policing could be continued. Observed locations were on straightaway sections of the highway where visibility was good, and at the foot of mountain grades where it was correctly expected that drivers would speed as they travel down steep inclines.

It appears that despite all good safety intentions, the photo radar camera can be, and is, used in harmony with a jurisdiction's economic interests. It has the potential to increase gross and net incomes and make apprehension, prosecution, and collection of fines more efficient. As Judge Alfred North of the Dade County Circuit Court warned, it could become an arm of the revenue collecting office (Smith and Tomerlin, 1990). Numerous editorials have appeared in daily newspapers across Canada about revenue production. For example, one of many letters that appeared in the *Toronto Star* stated that the sole purpose of speed limits is to raise revenue; it [the government] depended on mass contempt for speed limits to yield $72 million dollars in the last fiscal year, which will grow at least $100 million in the current one resulting from increased police patrols, massive increases in penalties, and the so called "zero-tolerance" approach to enforcement. (Saturday, 18 August, 1990)

Government agents are assured of maximum apprehensions in minimum time. The greater the number of tickets issued, the larger the amount of money collected in fines! If the payment of fines goes into general revenue, then as some motorists, such as the members of POSTL (Proponents of Sensible Traffic Legislation) point out, the money may not even be used for traffic safety interests, but is simply a hidden tax.

Privatization trend. The Paradise Valley photo radar equipment is owned and promoted by a company called TMT (Traffic Monitoring Technologies). Its service includes vehicles, radars, cameras, film processing, forms control, and data handling. As a private business, economic viability and profit are obvious concerns.   Profits are dependant on the number of drivers photographed and cited. Consequently, aggressive use of the technological system is economically advantageous. If the emphasis becomes quantity, speeding becomes a commodity, a defined profit margin irrespective of safety, and inattentive to contextual or psychological factors that influence driving.

Due to market pressures, TMT has undoubtedly rationalized its services along   business lines.   Factors are the cost of leasing or purchasing surveillance equipment, labor, transportation, and data processing.   Elementary arithmetic suggests that if insufficient numbers of speeders are caught or tolerance levels are too high, the company's involvement becomes uneconomical. Also at a 30 percent net profit per violation, the government stands to gain with any increase in the number of charges laid. In a way the legal system has taken on an auxiliary to the economic system, one in which private enterprise is in a position to collaborate with judges, lawmakers and law enforcement officers. Still, safety-related discourse is offered to the public. Witness the following quote offered by the Paradise Valley police chief: " We didn't introduce it [photo radar] to raise revenue, but to promote traffic safety. If we accomplish this, we'll be happy even if we were to issue no citations at all" (Lesce, 1988: 38).

The police chief's rationalization borders on the edge of absurdity, considering that police officers assume that nine out of ten drivers speed (Rothe, 1992). As has been outlined in chapters 7 and 8, speeding is such a built-in feature of people's driving lives that a "no speeding scenario" is unimaginable (Ross, 1960).

A second privatization issue arose in Paradise Valley. The state of Arizona supports retraining by providing apprehended speeders the option of taking an "American Consortium for Traffic Safety" driving course in lieu of paying a fine and receiving points in their driving record. A relevant supposition is that speeding, "a popular" driving violation, is believed to require re-education. Followed to its logical yet absurd conclusion, this would mean that nearly every motorist in North America may need to be re-educated. Although they may not have been caught, they would have the characteristics agents in Paradise Valley believe to be inherent in speeders.

The town has three "hearing officers" whose role it is to identify vehicle owners' faces with photo radar pictures, read standardized statements to the defendants describing the options of fines or re-education, and document defendants' choices. On this basis Stephen Clark, plaintiff accused Paradise Valley of conflict of interest. The claim he presented in 1989 rested on the fact that one of the town's three hearing officers owns Arizona Consortium for Traffic Safety (Manson, 1989).

The superior court commissioner determined there was no real conflict of interest because there was no financial advantage to the driver who took the school option. The fine for speeding is the same as the cost of attending classes.

Although the decision addressed legal factors, it did not focus on social considerations. For example, the costs of taking the course and paying the fines may be similar, but drivers' decisions to opt for "re-education" may reflect their concerns about receiving demerit points on their driving records. Because drivers who choose re-education are spared points in their driving records, they avoid possible increased insurance premiums. The merits of the training course may be less of an influence than the potential for higher insurance premiums (Lesce, 1988). Also it is possible that the officer, to whom drivers submit their options, could influence the drivers' decision to select the driving course that the company manages.

Changing the Laws to Suit Technology

Ellul (1964) wrote that technique integrates technology into society. It constructs the kind of world the technology needs. It clarifies, arranges, and rationalizes. More importantly, Ellul explained, "modern men are so enthusiastic about technique, so assured of its superiority, so immersed in the technical milieu, that without exception they are oriented toward technical progress" (1964: 85).

In traffic law, charges are laid on drivers. They are considered to be responsible for observed violations. With the introduction of the photo radar camera "direct liability" changed to "vicarious liability." The violation is now against the car owner, proven by the registration number of the vehicle. In Galveston, Texas, a local judge took exception to the change in law. Because the registered owner of a vehicle was not necessarily the driver at the moment the photo radar took the picture, under the law, the owner's registration was not adequate probable cause for issuing a citation.

To gather proof, an officer would have to visit the registered owner's home and verify the identity of the driver. The problem of time and effort needed to serve the law proved to be sufficiently great for Galveston officials to decide against continued use of the technology.

Paradise Valley's strategy was to change the law to suite the photo radar camera.   Policymakers made the vehicle owners responsible for the way their vehicles were operated. City ordinance 297 paved the way for the unrestricted operation of photo radar in Paradise Valley. It states:

A.   If any vehicle unoccupied by a licensed driver is found upon a street or roadway in violation of any provision of this Article Title 28, Chapter 6, Article 14 of the Arizona Revised Statutes, or if any vehicle has been driven in violation of the speed restrictions of this Article or Title 28, Chapter 6, Article 6 of the Arizona Revised Statutes or A.R.S. 28-797, then proof of the identity of the person in whose name such vehicle is registered pursuant to Title 28, Chapter 3 of the Arizona Revised Statutes may be sufficient evidence that such person was responsible for such violation, in the absence of probative contrary evidence and if the magistrate is so persuaded. (Paradise Valley Town Attorney, 1988)

At a Supreme Court hearing, *Cortright vs Paradise Valley*, 1989, Cortright argued that the photo radar ordinance used by the police to enforce speed laws should be struck down because it assumed that the registered owner was the driver of any vehicle photographed speeding. Manson (1989) commented on the case:

"This system should be struck down based on how they [Paradise Valley officials] operate it," said Joseph Mott, an attorney arguing against the photo radar system for Cartright and the Arizona Civil Liberties Union. Mott said that having a police officer stationed at the machine "creates a sham" by giving the impression that the officer is actually identifying the person who was speeding. In fact, the registered owner always is the person cited, whether the owner was driving or not. (P. B4)

The state attorney conceded that law officers who sign tickets do not examine photos to determine whether drivers who are pictured are the registered owners. However, he continued, the notice sent to owners informed them that photographs could be examined at City Hall. If the picture was not of the owner, the ticket could be dismissed. The emphasis was on the assumed guilty party to prove innocence. The individual had to verify that the evidence submitted by the state was insufficient.

The Paradise Valley district attorney retorted that registered owners who had not committed the cited offenses had their charges dropped. This occurs at the pre-trial hearing when the owners' faces are matched with photo radar pictures. However, under a city ordinance, officials can require owner to disclose who was driving. The ordinance empowers law officials to enforce "squealing" (Lesce, 1988). It would be interesting to see how the attorney would handle a transvestite who owned the car as a male but drove as a female. The two pictures would not match, and forced squealing would lend itself to self-incrimination.

Cortright's lawyer pointed out, that with the exception of the grand jury, the law does not permit officials to force an accused person to assist in an investigation until that person is in court. A city ordinance was passed to overcome this basic legal right.

It appears that if the weakest link of the technological process of law enforcement is threatened, policymakers bolster it with a revised ordinance. The intent is to keep the traffic violation structure from collapsing under the weight of constitutional and civil rights for drivers accused of speeding.

The emphasis is less on helping individuals maintain their rights under the traditional legal code, and more on efficiently employing technology that is capable of detaching the power of proof and process from the traditional legal pattern.

With the introduction of the photo radar camera, police officers no longer need to provide evidence to establish speed violation (Royal Canadian Mounted Police, undated). They no longer have to adhere to the elements of valid identification of target vehicles or, in police jargon, presenting the "tracking history," whose elements are:

1.   Visual estimate of target speed.   Testimony must substantiate that the vehicle in question was observed to be speeding.   An officer's ability to estimate speeds is established separately from the RADAR evidence.

2.   Audio tracking. The audio feature common on many police traffic RADARS allows the operator to hear the incoming Doppler signal. A stable target signal will result in a single pure, clear audio tone. The higher the pitch of the signal, the faster the speed of the target producing the signal.   With experience, an officer can correlate this pitch with actual speeds.

3.   Target speed displays. The target speed displayed by the RADAR must correspond reasonably with the visual and audio estimations. Each of the three must reinforce each other. If any of them is incompatible, the reading must be disregarded. (Royal Canadian Mounted Police, undated: 16)

The police training manual states that officers should never lay charges based entirely on radar measurements.   They must watch speed measurement and listen to the audio output for a least a few seconds to make sure that the signal received is from an identifiable vehicle.

With the introduction of the photo radar camera, many of the double checks are eliminated or they are subsumed in electronics. Tracking history is programmed into the machine by a Doppler signal that originates from the radar unit, reflects off the target vehicle and is received by a central control unit. The legitimacy of the task is now assumed and not questioned as a safeguard for radar use.

Due Process of the Law and Photo Radar

Due process is another issue worthy of discussion. Photo radar pictures and charges are mailed to the registered owner ten to fourteen days after the event. The claim made by some lawyers is that a citation mailed ten days after-the-fact prohibits the vehicle owners from gathering facts for their offenses. Knowing the details of the citations' circumstances is an integral part of the defendants' presentations. It is difficult to imagine a driver remembering every speed limit sign and location she passed fourteen days earlier.

The Arizona district attorney responded to the due process debate by arguing that if a driver had good reason to speed, it would be memorable ten to fourteen days later. If the incident cannot be remembered, the drivers would be admitting that they," speed on a regular basis." In light of the assumption that the majority of drivers speed, that the average distances traveled per week is about four hundred miles per week, and that there are important social factors that influence speeding behavior, it is nearly impossible to remember precise conditions at precise times. In fact, because of strict liability, intent is not considered a legitimate defense (Hutchison and Marko, 1989). On the basis of implausibility, the defense lawyer for Cortright stated cryptically, "I'm not even going to make a statement. I hope the reader can see the problem with that logic" (Samson, 1989: B2).

Recall can be prompted by some current happening. It is always a task of reconstruction, and because this is so, avenues for imaginative interpretations are opened. Because people engage in hundreds, if not thousands, of microsituations during any lengthy trip, many of which are routine commutes, to serialize one experience into one episode is a fallible process (Jamieson, 1985).

When motorists are physically stopped by a police officer they anticipate the likelihood of re-using needed information collected at the time of the event. Because the scenario has special legal significance, accused violators are more likely to remember information on location, situational factors, and time. They may even make notes on the situation to sharpen their attention and retention, to recall, recognize, and link pieces of information for defense. In fact, the police advise victims of violence to write an account of events in case they are called upon to attend court or are needed for future reference.

If or when drivers take the initiative to counter the photo radar technology by, for example, removing the front license plate, placing mud on the numbers, or using a reflecting substance that may block the radar beam, the police are quick to respond. In Vancouver, the police used the local media to warn drivers that law officials would pay special attention to cars whose license plates have been deliberately altered. The warning resulted from a photographed speeder whose plate numbers could not be read. Vancouver's traffic unit was on the alert for the car.

By assigning special attention to eluders of technology, a situation is created where apprehension becomes the focus of a secondary intent of technology. Drivers manipulating their plates are no longer spotted by chance. They are sought because they attempted to elude the power and influence of surveillance technology. From a safety perspective, altering one's registration plates is not a risk factor. Law officers now emphasize the premise that drivers cannot beat the law and those who try to upstage the photo radar camera will be pursued.

The police in Paradise Valley utilized additional technology to catch the drivers who attempted to counter the photo radar camera. A manually operated auxiliary camera is mounted to photograph the rear of receding vehicles. A Canon camera with "Databack" records the date and time on the film with small LED's. The net result is that motorists who are caught, receive two citations, one for excessive speed and one for lacking the required front plate.

The Power of the Photo Radar Photograph

Photographs do not represent reality. They are merely reproductions of reality comprised of social codes that influence viewers to see the picture as intended. As Picasso and Muggeridge suggested, photographs are a form of plausible lies.

From a lay person's perspective, pictorial images appear to be natural, objective, and uncoded. But behind pictures are interventionist devices that are not always apparent at the viewing level. Concealed treatment effects such as lighting, camera angles, focusing, editing, or montage help form the pictorial message, to influence interpretation in a direction desired by the presenter (Jamieson, 1985).

A snapshot is an index of values, a collection of meaning that shows a certain setting within a context of meaning (Berger, 1980; Desnoes, 1985). In the case of the photo radar photograph, the meaning context is officialism, inferring evidence, legality—trouble with the law.

The photo radar picture may be considered a text that presupposes a code. Although the image bears a relationship or resemblance to its referent, the thing photographed, it does so according to a preconceived form of reality that has been amputated from its context. The photo is structured on a formula of symbols to influence observers' interpretations of it. The front or back of the vehicle signifies driving. The license plate illustrates that the automobile is registered, and it defines the registration number. The viewer combines the two signs to engender an understanding of "my car." The image of the driver creates the final clue for personal identity of the viewer as driver.

The overall design of the picture as a small postcard and the dimensions and ingredients of the picture add to the conventional system of legality. The picture is standardized, removing the possibility of anyone placing aesthetic meanings and emotions on the basis of color, composition, or angle. The accompanying data registered in the corner of the picture as text is a printout of time, speed, and date. It anchors or guides the viewer toward the desired interpretation of formality, technological sophistication, and legal evidence. The data items are simple signs, to persuade the viewer that the image is value-free. The card induces a feeling of authority, power of technology, and verification of event to promote a concession of guilt. McLuhan (1964) would consider the photograph an example of hot media that incurs low participation in original thinking.

There is little opportunity for the receiver of the photograph to misconstrue the intent of the picture. But there is another side to the coin. The expression on the face or the enthusiasm of the driver is muted. Motorists are stripped of individuality, organizational rank, social status, and self-image. They become simple objects of the law. The photograph results from a camera setting that records particular drivers from defined perspectives, packaged in signs to induce the impression that "seeing is believing." The visual field is restricted to represent an image of truth, objectivity, and evidence. The picture leaves little room for ambiguity. It utilizes legal codes to induce people to come to the same conclusion when given identical imagery and textual information (Barthes, 1968).

Not only does the photo radar photograph reflect the legal interpretation of reality, it also affects reality. It intimates guilt. Drivers become guilty parties through the identification of selves in the picture, recognition of the car and license plate, and the numerical text supporting the visual text. The legal institution is presented through the photograph.

A footnote is now necessary. No sign may also be a sign. Absent signs reveal meaning. For example, the photo radar photograph does not include detail of the driving context. It omits variation in roadway designs such as lane merges that may force drivers to temporarily increase their speeds, traffic flow, and actions of other drivers that influence one's driving.

By omitting the traffic context, the photo radar camera distorts the roadway reality at the time of the happening. If it was included, the propriety of the guilty verdict might be questioned by the receiver of the ticket, leading to court cases. Such action contradicts the efficiency of the technology. The intent is to keep the evidence simple and direct; to reduce the possibility of alternative interpretations.

Conclusion

In summary, searching for the traffic offender under the rhetorical claim of traffic safety has become a technological boom. As part of today's technical matrix, the new electronic surveillance devices are reshaping the legal landscape. Instead of traffic safety, they have become means of exercising instrumental or disciplinary control over drivers. They manifest as much affinity with the economic marketplace, profit, and efficiency than they do with weeding out "bad drivers."

14

Electronic Traffic Surveillance and the Character of Experience

No more privacy than a goldfish

—Irvin S. Cobb

So far traffic safety has been described as a social process that relates a complex social world to situational interests. Forms and realities that constitute traffic laws, driving behavior, risk, impaired driving, speeding, lobbying, and surveillance have been expressed. Conceptual, factual, theoretical, and projective information was presented to portray actualities and possibilities. However, there has not yet been a description of the structure of perception as a driver experiences the photo radar camera.

This chapter departs from the traditional and attends to some perceptual possibilities that are activated in experience. Attention is drawn to the problematic and situated nature of meaningful experience that is far richer and more complex and subtle than one ordinarily takes it to be (Douglas and Johnson, 1977; Ihde, 1983). A case is offered that portrays individual freedom and societal constraints as they come together at a particular moment. More specifically, it reflects the feelings and emotions of a driver experiencing the photo radar camera. The description is based on Kotarba's proposition that

This chapter was originally presented as a paper entitled "Electronic Highway Surveillance and the Glance" written for the Canadian Learned Societies Conference, Canadian Association of Sociology and Anthropology, held in Kingston, Ontario, 26 May-9 June 1991.

underlying all the work, . . . is an emphasis on and a deep commitment to understanding how feelings form the foundations of our lives, as well as the intricate social realities we construct. (1979: 350)

The study of how distinct human feelings are particular features of experience contributes to a better understanding of a driver's self-presence before the photo radar camera. According to Smith (1987, 1990), the standpoint of actual individuals located in the everyday world is the point of d'appui.

The following description is written in the first person to better describe personal experience in a photo radar camera pilot program. As a "being-in-context" my experiences are located in the generalized and generalizing relations of an institutional process. As a researcher I was engaged in planning a study on the effectiveness of implementing photo radar cameras. At the same time, the highway on which I commuted was one of the locations where photo radar cameras were installed. Hence I experienced them as a driver.

I reflect on the character of human experience to impress on the reader the perceptions, needs, and emotions that affect the moment of experience. These are difficult to isolate, and they are generally taken for granted when universal validations are invoked in social science. Because psychological and sociological statements, however precise, never express fully the living process of experience, I shall reveal my awareness of the extensive field of driving under the watchful eye of electronic surveillance.

Introducing Electronic Surveillance

At the outset, I am a driver who occasionally violates speed laws. Although I drive beyond the speed limit for reasons I consider to be legitimate, like other drivers I do not consider myself to be a "real speeder." For example, I do not believe that I am unique when I speed to make a meeting on time, or to pass a driver because he was driving "too slow." My working assumption is that there is a stereotype of "real speeder," who is defined by traffic safety agents as a "devil-may-care risk-taker" living the thrill of breaking the law—a conception I believe does not invoke my behavior. With the introduction of the photo radar camera, legal representatives negate my personal view of self as speeder and relocate me within a generalized category of speeding, a driving behavior that necessitates legal sanction.

Before I continue, a brief description of the events that led up to my experience is provided. Recently the British Columbia Solicitor General's Department publicized that it had the fiduciary responsibility to solve the safety problem on the highway. The two options that received attention from the government were education or public awareness and technological intervention! Education through social awareness strategies was dismissed by the solicitor general because it was considered to be a formidable task. Officials reasoned that it was impossible to persuade speeders to forego immediate personal gain in favor of a long-term social safety gain. Overwhelming drivers with a barrage of moral and educational programs intended to change people's motives to speed was considered to be time-consuming and expensive. The conclusion reached was that the implementation of a relatively cheap, simple, and expedient technological device was preferred.

An important component of implementing photo radar cameras on the roadways was the erection of road signs that advised drivers that the highway was patrolled by the photo radar camera. The government erected four such signs on the Squamish Highway, a sixty-mile stretch of weaving, coast-hugging roadway between Vancouver and Whistler. They warned drivers that there was a possibility, in fact a probability, that the speed traps would be in operation, paralleling Bentham's view that liberty is constantly sacrificed for the sake of security (Long, 1977). As I will now discuss, these signs transformed my perception of driving as everyday experience.

Driving in Privacy

Like other drivers I place great value and meaning on my car, the countryside, and other road users. My vehicle has symbolic value for me that extends beyond utility and movement. Although the automobile typically symbolizes movement and transportation, to me it represents "a living room on wheels," "an extension of myself." My car is a symbolic boundary, a private territory. Through the vehicle I carve out a space on public roadways that I control (Lyman and Scott, 1970). It "provides us with a shield and a feeling of invulnerability, a shelter for all manners of activity" (Marsh and Collett, 1986: 11).

In a way the car is part of my home turf, immediately realized by the design of seating arrangements, walls and opportunity for entertainment. It has distinctive features with which I feel totally comfortable. Its outside (style, color, model degree of cleanliness, etc.) and the inside (organization of the interior, the smell, the personal adornments) serve as personal "identity pegs" (Schutz and Luckmann, 1973). Through continuous and usually unreflective action I steer, accelerate, shift gears, brake, signal, and observe events with little thought. These behaviors comprise "a set of integrated gestures and movements which sustains a particular task or aim," or as Seamon (1979: 64) described, a body ballet of driving.

While driving I attend to others without really noticing them. I scan the horizon, yet I escape the public presence, bypassing much of the remaining world, like a parent who gets lost in thought watching a television show, not fully listening to a child's chatter, shutting out the demands of life (Fisher, 1975; Chin, 1975). I am situated inside my car, "my space," a zone established by imaginary one-way windows. I look out and notice things without establishing heightened contact with the things I notice. I become the focal point around which other road users are engaged. Because of the symbolic membrane surrounding my automobile, much like tinted windows, I assume that others do not pay unwarranted attention to me. I control and protect my individuality, autonomy, and solitude (Fisher, 1975). I may pick my nose, comb my hair or steal a kiss from my wife, assuming that other people are not attentive to my actions. As Simmel (1957) wrote, "Alone, the visual feeling of the window goes almost exclusively from inward to outward: it is there for looking out, not for seeing in" (P. 5).

When a motoring crisis arises, my stream of consciousness is shattered and my body ballet is broken. I now look outward. The event becomes a significant occasion that obliges me to re-orient myself to the other person (Goffman, 1963). I step out of my privacy and interact, focusing my attention to the affairs at hand.

The Gaze

During normal driving times I withdraw myself not only into the bubble of my car but into myself. Unless I have passengers, I enter the world of solitude in which I isolate myself (Berdeyav, 1947). I create a world for myself—a psychic zone in which there is no trace of strangeness, or threat of unwarranted intrusion. I feel like a free person moving about as I wish. I am conscious of other road users in the sense that I have apprehended myself as a person who is peaceful and coherent without being unresponsive and exclusive. I do not wish to be disturbed, so that I may fulfill my driving project.

Whenever another person looks at me judgmentally, my view of self changes. For the moment I may feel alienated. In the words of Sartre (1956) I change from a "being-for-itself" to a "being-in-itself," from a free person to an apprized object. With this shift comes a sense of "there is something wrong with me," a feeling that I have a deficiency upon which another person is focusing, much like Aristotle's reminder that shame dwells in the eyes of others (Morano, 1973). Through a critical look, another person makes me feel that I am under direct scrutiny.

Similarly, the signs on the roadway inform me that I may be under the watchful eye of the photo radar camera. I become conscious of myself, feeling a need to protect my integrity.

The photo radar camera's image of me is unlike a picture a neighbor or family member takes with my approval. I acknowledge that any picture is but a caricature that presents a frozen image. Whenever I consent to a person taking my picture, I voluntarily pose for the camera's welcoming look. The lense's gaze is part of my intentionality, to have a picture taken for some specific purpose. I trust that the audience for the picture is known to me, unlike the hidden photographer or the photo radar camera where the camera's gaze is outside of my immediate plans and the picture is intended for an unknown or invisible audience (Mead, 1964).

Also, the photo radar camera's gaze is different from other driver's generalized look. While driving, the eyes of road users pass over my eyes, but no "recognition" typically takes place. It represents Spiegelberg's (1989) concept of "plain looking" in which I glance casually at others, paying only indiscriminate attention. I have nothing to fear by being seen and being seen, seeing (Goffman, 1963a). In outstanding or unusual situations, in which I look and expect to be looked at, the true dialectic of seeing and being seen socially cancels itself out, in the sense that while others objectify me through their looks, I in return objectify them, gaining some form of equilibrium.

This reciprocity is not true of the photo radar camera. Roadway signs warn me that an anonymous onlooker may be peering. The possibility of being seen and noticed without myself seeing and noticing changes me to a robotlike creature without control of my territory, privacy, perceptual field, or body. The technological gaze, according to van den Berg (1962) is like the malicious look of an unknown person, the look that causes one to shiver from neck to ankle. I become keenly aware of any awkward behaviors that I may produce lest they be interpreted by anonymous others as unbecoming.

The roadway warning signs shatter my sense of lived privacy. I no longer experience a feeling of security, driving naturally without having to explain my actions to myself or to anyone, without having to be on guard. I suspend trust in my everyday reality and feel as if I am being thrust into the reality of electronic surveillance, spying, and police action. My stock of knowledge, or pre- organized scheme for sensemaking is insufficient to normalize the event. A feeling of impotence overcomes me. I have moved from a mild awareness of things around me to a heightened state of intrusion on my sanctuary.

The shift of awareness, oncoming anxiety, and uncertainty occurs in four stages, originally described by Chin (1975). Step one, I begin my driving experience by entering the car and closing the doors behind me. Step two, I concentrate on driving, forgetting about the walls or doors. They move into the background. I am privacy personified. Step three, I read the photo radar camera warning signs on the highway. A disruption occurs. I look at my speedometer. I become vigilant and glance at the physiognomy of the landscape for visual proof of a possible intrusion. My coveted psychic space becomes threatened and begins to lose some of its value. I realize that my privacy can be invaded at will. Step four, I become anxious, realizing that the automobile's physical structure cannot keep out a camera's glance. The speedometer becomes ominous and relentless in its portrayal of my foot action on the gas pedal and brakes. This gives way to an overwhelming proximity of being violated, crowding me out of my own space.

My trust in the normal pattern of driving turns to doubt, suspicion, fear, and later to thoughts about freedom, and civil rights. As I enter the world of electronic monitoring, my typical means and solutions for typical problems under typical situations do not apply any more. Information has been created and disseminated about me, to which I have little access and which I cannot verify. I lack the concept of certainty of outcomes or standardized results. As Schutz wrote:

> The subjective meaning-context has been abandoned as a tool of interpretation. It has been replaced by a series of highly complex and systematically interrelated objective meaning-contexts. The result is that the contemporary is anonymized. (1972:184)

The distinctions between electronic or technological and legal schemes of interpretation and my schemes of interpretation become obscured. Rather than being seen as a person driving a vehicle, acting within my realm of possibilities, I am made to feel like Laing's (1971) schizophrenic, at whom someone looks for signs of schizophrenia. Before the "stare" of the photo radar camera there is no guiltless way to be (van den Berg, 1962). Like the modest maiden who feels ashamed walking before a group of leering men with looks that unclothe her, I feel the camera's gaze scrutinizing my anonymity. The photo radar camera leaves me unmasked and unprotected (Hora, 1962), looking to find me guilty.

I reflect upon myself through the viewpoint or perspective of the lense. I become what the lense sees: guilty. Once I interchange the "him" and "he" in Laing's (1970) *Knots* with a "me" and "I," the dialectics of self definition become more obvious:

> There must be something the matter with [me] because [I] would not be acting as [I] do unless there was. Therefore [I] am acting as [I] am because there is something the matter with [me]. (1970: 5)

Because trust turns to doubt, presumed innocence turns to assumed guilt, and concerns of safety turns to interests of the law, I may become psychically disoriented (Franklin, 1990). With heightened awareness, I look about, searching for the camera, thinking I can evade its gaze, but as a researcher, knowing that I cannot.   Through analysis of the literature and government information I know that once a driver spots the camera, it is too late. The picture has already been taken.

I am confronted by an object that I do not see because it may be hidden in the trees, beside a parked car, in front of an oncoming vehicle or atop a telephone pole. I have little in-depth understanding of its operational principles. Because I know where the information goes, and how it is processed, I try to exercise appropriate critical restraint in my normal appearance before others.

Whereas at the beginning of the journey my car represents a symbolic yet real gesture of privacy, when I read the signs about surveillance, I become a public entity. My perception of the police and the government changes. Meanings of the police change from law enforcers to personal threats. They become peeping toms, lacking in the moral fiber that would be necessary to confront me in person. Secrecy and suspicion become features of driving that I must now thematize into experiences. As a result, trust, privacy, psychological coherence of lived personal space degenerate into guardedness, suspicion, cut-off dialogue, and a questioned sense of identity and even shame.

When a police officer stops me for a driving infraction, I do not expect deception in face-to-face interaction, nor do I experience an illusory sense of guilt. I have my say as does the officer to establish or reinforce guilt or innocence. With the photo radar camera there is an immediate uncompromising sense of guilt. I become what the technology has identified me as being.

The Call to Sacrifice

Altman wrote that a person's ability to regulate contact with others contributes to a sense of self-worth.

> Privacy mechanisms define the limits and boundaries of the self. When the permeability of these boundaries is under the control of a person, a sense of individuality develops. But it is not the inclusion or exclusion of others that is vital to self-definition; it is the ability to regulate contact when desired. If I can control what is me and what is not me, if I can define what is me and not me, and if I can observe the limits and scope of my control, then I have taken major steps

toward understanding and defining what I am. Thus, privacy mechanisms serve to help me define me. (1975: 50)

As a driver I exalt in my privacy distilled into solitude (where I am free from surveillance) and anonymity (where my behavior is not expected to be identified with me personally). Naturally, by driving in public I am conspicuous, however it is a selective conspicuousness that hinges on brief nonattentive visual exposure by others. Whenever I disclose more of myself I may become vulnerable to influence and possible exploitation and hence lose my independence (Derlago and Charikin, 1977).

The impact of shattered trust or intrusions into personal feelings of faith, confidence, reliance and security (Shapiro, 1987) can be presented by Garfinkel's (1967) social experiments in which he demonstrated how basic trust in the moral social order can be destroyed by changing familiar roles, expectations, and contexts. When the familiar was made problematic people demonstrated feelings of consternation, confusion, anxiety, shame, guilt, and indignation. Such reactions parallel my feelings when new age surveillance techniques challenge my trust in the assumed moral order of the roadway and society's normative policing practices.

In its rhetoric, designed to establish a boundary between those who are morally right and those who are wrong, the British Columbia government requested citizens to concede their determination of privacy and self-disclosure for the sake of public morality and safety. To preserve the law and to curtail harm, every driver was asked to sacrifice a degree of liberty, privacy, and anonymity and to support the surveillance scheme. The rationalization offered by government agents and police officers was that drivers who uphold the law suffer little by having a hidden camera directed at them.

As a driver I was asked to accept encroachment of privacy and place my faith in "neutral" security technology for greater roadway safety. Because I do not have the opportunity to interact directly with my accuser, if photographed I am considered to be deficient without anyone establishing whether I affirm my deficiency or whether I am cognizant of it. Instead, the government expects me to live with shame, or as Morano (1973) labeled it, ontological guilt before another person. I am asked to curtail the exclusiveness of my access to, or disposal of, my self (van den Haag, 1971: 151). For

> the right to privacy entitles me to withhold the contribution of my private realm to the contents of someone else's mind—to his image of me—even if no further use of it is contemplated. (van den Haag, 1971: 151)

Before the camera's gaze, I am forced to modify my private behavior or to control the image being formed by the police to avoid a bad image or label. I have become out of role (Goffman, 1963b) and I have been forced into contact with anonymous others. Rather than the police producing a legitimate reason for engagement, now there is an encroachment on my being, merely because I am driving through a particular point at a particular time. I am pursued by quiet feet all around me. There is no frontal attack or confrontation by an overpowering foe, but instead a subtle siege, an unrelenting surveillance of me—a surveillance that I can never escape as I scan the environment from the corner of my eyes. The government demands that I sacrifice my solitude and anonymity for a constant dull gnawing enervating dyspepsia.

Government officials have placed a societal scheme of reference upon me to legitimize their intrusion on my privacy. Due to the reported urgency of the increasing vandalization of the roads as portrayed by accident statistics, I am expected to understand the request and offer my commitment to the Napoleonic view that I am guilty and must prove my innocence (Marx, 1989). This parallels Mead's (1964) attitude of the generalized other, in which the generalized other is the attitude of the whole community as expressed by members of the government. Because the government has implied that I am a law-abiding person, the sacrifice is not seen by officials as a major issue for the individual driver.

Conclusion

I have repeatedly heard that the only reason for keeping something from others is that the secret keeper is ashamed of it. In the example described, public agents were content to disregard my interests in privacy and solitude. They played on the notion that if I am decent and innocent, I have no cause for shame and no need to worry about an invasion of privacy.

But as I have already described, my claim to privacy is more than a matter of shame (Gross, 1971). It is a wholesome regard for the self, an expression of respect, a right of self-definition. When the photo radar camera is used, I lose control over myself: there is curtailment of my natural attitude and impingement on my stream of consciousness. The streets no longer disclose themselves comfortably through my movement.

To experience an encroachment on my existence, to be usurped of my natural attitude about the social world of driving and privacy, and to expect that I integrate estrangement in the world of driving for the sake of social harmony is a highly problematic sacrifice that requires further empirical clarification.

15

The Emergence of Traffic Sociology

Life can only be understood backwards,
but it must be lived forward

—Kierkegaard

In the broadest and most fundemental terms, traffic is a socially created and maintained reality. Individual drivers operate in multiple ways—with respect to themselves, other people, immediate circumstances, as well as past experiences. However, law officers, government agents, traffic safety professionals, engineers, roadway maintenance crews, and others also play major roles in the construction of roadway traffic. Consequently, researchers and agents must contend with the observation that things often seem otherwise to different members involved in traffic-related matters. They are not as likely to agree that certain features are givens, sets of objects naturally exist, and things are the way they are and must be.

New drivers enter traffic as a more or less intact, already-labeled reality. Laws appear firm, even if they are often broken, roadways are defined; the driver's license is a tangible and constituent part of driving; family life, friends and peers, legal organizations, traffic safety agencies, and the like seem natural and inevitable. Yet motorists are not circumscribed by these features. They deal with unexpected circumstances, not as automotons, but as problem solvers who regularly violate laws, regulations, and safety policies for reasons they consider legitimate. The image is one of contrast, if not contradiction of opposing tendencies in traffic safety. On the one hand, drivers cope with traffic on the roadways in a normal unproblematic way and in so doing create a sense of order, trust and responsibility. On the other hand, they seem disposed to overstep the responsibility for their driving behavior, to ignore the dependence of social order on their diving acts. What makes traffic safety a fascinating topic, among other reasons, is that it dramatizes this contrast between general conceptions of normality, safety, control and health and the everyday perspective that suggests that reality is constructed according to motorists' beliefs, projects, and interests. These are vital for the study of traffic safety. As Thomas (1928: 56) wrote, "things perceived as real, are real in their consequences." Traffic safety in general is a striking example of the contrast between the social creation of reality and the disposition to view it as real and objective.

Controlling Diversity

As a constructed reality, traffic has a natural diversity of meaning. This is a publicly prized value in a democratic society. However, one cannot escape realism. Absolute deviance-blind tolerance in traffic behavior is as unachieveable as is international harmony. It is not clear that a totally forgiving traffic safety community would be a desirable one.

Examples in traffic safety point to the potential complexity between driving behavior and the number of intervention strategies to control that behavior. The rapid growth of the number of drivers, the presence of political processes, established empirical findings, and relevant economic circumstances generated considerable negative feelings toward certain groups such as the young and senior drivers. The critical portrayals are usually directed toward adaptation and matters of origin. With respect to adaptation, the focus is on how individual behavior can be modified to cope with traffic circumstances and how a safer driver can be developed through use of deterrence, punishment, and cure. The emphasis on the origin of the prototype driver is usually related to a normative definition of "the safe driver." For example, impaired driving is spoken of in the same way as a disease or medical condition, a fault not found in "normal drivers."

The examples mentioned share currency in traffic safety as benchmark definitions to control diverse behavior. Traffic safety agents come to grips with individual drivers by designating them predefined objects of attention. They are created by researchers and agents in relation to assumed standards of normal conduct.

The range of situations and circumstances in traffic that persons experience suggests that different kinds of lenses whould be applied to account for traffic safety.   There is a need to understand the drivers' subjective state of mind, and the intersubjective relations between drivers and other relevant persons or organizations. Such an approach, referred to by Bogdan and Taylor (1990) as "optimistic research" advances the efforts of change. It shifts the attention from documenting the dark side to looking at the bright side, to identifying positive examples of driving with a view toward creating change.

Furthermore, by attending to the driver as a social being, researchers and traffic safety agents are in a better position to detail the life of accidents, violations, and safe driving. Perhaps it is time to take a page out of the Federal Bureau of Investigation's handbook on criminal investigations.   Agents develop criminal profiles through regular informal interviews with criminals about their experiences, knowledge, relationships, intents and meanings of events.   Using these experiential revelations that other methods fail to provide, agents can make assessments or profile certain types of criminals. (Canadian Press, 1992)

Given the relative merits of a social analysis of drivers, the process becomes a vehicle for understanding why drivers take the risks that they do. The prospect exists that such research will help provide not only a stronger theory of risk in traffic, but also an enhanced understanding of the experience of risk and driving as perceived by drivers. In this way the dark shadow between research, policy, and practice has a better chance of being removed.

If traffic sociology as defined in this book is to be of any benefit, it requires work, the active engagement of thought and reflection. As was already described, such an engagement requires a grasp of principles that can affect social policy.

Social Policy

The practical application of traffic sociology is to sensitize policy planners to the fact that the mere existence of traditional research and conceptions of what should be is not enough. For example, to know the causes of traffic accidents is no assurance that people will agree on how they are to be reduced, that the reduction is worth the cost of doing so, or that those in control will use their knowledge to design effective policies. There may be wide agreement that traffic safety ought to be a valued goal, and research may discover that greater control of drivers will help to reach this goal. But, as experience in other social problem domains has demonstrated, it is not scientific knowledge or rigorous empirical evidence, but human attitudes, beliefs, interpretations, and conduct that determine whether drivers will accept control measures at all, or any given techniques such as photo radar cameras. This premise is important in terms of whether drivers feel obliged or committed to follow controls on their behaviors.

As was previously discussed, social policy designers, legislators, bureaucrats, and heads of traffic safety agencies, to name a few influential groups, generally develop and apply social policy in the manner they think best for a mobile society. If they do so on the basis of self-interest, institutional mandates, positivistic research, and psychological or medical theory, then the average citizen continues to be left out of decision making. Even though influential people develop and implement interventions for what they believe will enhance safety, they must take time to debate the extent to which laws, regulations, and policies affect average drivers as competent members of society. Imposing control by the fiat of those holding the power to make decisions leaves an open door for driver discontent. As Mills (1959: 15) so aptly wrote, there is a need for "an understanding of the intimate realities of ourselves in connection with larger social realities."

Traffic sociology is a special way of applying the sociological imagination. Its focus is on the common elements in traffic behavior that find expression in different groups and organizations but nevertheless retain an underlying emphasis on trust and assumed roadway morality. Traffic sociology concepts described in the book do not form a storehouse of facts and formulas to be applied mechanically to traffic safety problems. Instead they represent a way of looking at the reality of traffic conditions not as a set of tools only for those in control but also for those over whom control is exercised.

Attending to individuals' self-conceptions affords no guarantee to greater safety. There is little certainty that a heightened awareness of drivers' interpretations and meanings will promote adjustments. Nor, indeed are sociological conceptions particularly easy to apply to traffic safety with any accuracy. However, by considering things road users do on the basis of insights, meanings, reasons, and interpretations provides for a greater magnitude of the safety task and serves as a democratic ideal. To recognize people struggling with traffic is a goal worth pursuing in and of itself.

The Future of Traffic Sociology

Serious students of traffic safety sometimes ask what future lies ahead for this challenging field of study. It seems appropriate to offer some reflections on this topic. First, by invoking a wide-angle lense to capture social factors, traffic safety will continue to develop and change both as a disciplinary subspeciality within the academic arena and as a field of potentially important contributions in the social policy field. Moreover, the boundaries of the field will become looser as the social sciences begin to examine the human dimensions of traffic safety-related structures and processes. Urban planning and public administration are also among some of the newer practicing professions whose focus includes traffic concerns.

More importantly, traffic safety professionals must break loose of their normal field of operation. Without serious investment of research and theory, alternative perspectives offered by subfields such as traffic sociology cannot grow as progressively as desired. Traffic sociology offers a venue for researchers and agents to find new modes of adapting traffic safety-related issues to political realities and contributing to the design of traffic safety policies.

The relationship between policy and research must be better defined. It must be better understood that policy research includes intelligible and convincing data that can be translated for various audiences and be effective for making decisions that motorists can accept. Too often traffic safety discussions are short-sighted, overly dramatic or sensational, simplistic in clarifying complex factors, and devoid of social perspectives. Data become removed from people's everyday actions and understandings. Hence drivers cannot appreciate the consequences of the choices they make on the streets. It is essential that well-written, interesting, relevant, and clearly presented syntheses of traffic behavior be available for many more people than professional practitioners.

Ethical concerns will become critical considerations in undertaking traffic safety studies. This does not necessarily mean continuing to "do good" in the way that has sparked past traffic safety movements with both beneficial and detrimental results. It means that a greater commitment be given to examine traffic safety conditions with an overall concern for enhancing a quality of safe driving.

Although social scientists have a common commitment to work as objectively as possible, the essence of human involvement guarantees that one can never be totally objective or value free. No researchers or traffic safety professionals can escape making ethical choices. Those who professionally continue the examination or control of traffic safety in the years ahead may well find that this task is most overwhelming of all. Attention to the use of technology and social control must be clearly thought out in terms of commitment to a humanized world that includes meaning and sociability.

Final Reflections

The argument so far has touched on traffic safety as a sophisticated form of victim-blaming; and on driving choices as constrained and conditioned by specific social, moral, and legal context. It is well worth noting that the various research studies, policy and problem definitions, and risk categories of traffic safety contain the tacit, pervasive assumption that accidents are wholly individual pheno-mena.

An alternative perspective is offered in this book. Accidents should be understood as complex social phenomena that demand social change through collective forms of action. This includes provisions for group activities such as mutual support, self-help, "relevant" education, and dialogue for critical analysis. Furthermore, institutions such as the judiciary, insurance lobbies, governments, auto manufacturers, civil engineers, medicine, and traffic safety researchers should be analyzed to establish if and how they are interwoven in the production of structural pathogenesis. Such a process would entail reflecting upon problems of traffic, looking behind these immediate problems to their root causes, examining the implications and consequences of these issues, and, finally, developing a plan of action to deal with the problems as collectively identified and defined (Minkler and Cox, 1980).

It is important for the reader to remember that any attempt to broaden the base of an already well established paradigm of problem development and problem solving is risky. As Kuhn (1970) wrote about normal science,

> Normal science is predicated on the assumption that the scientific community knows what the world is like. Much of the success of the enterprise derives from the community's willingness to define the assumption if necessary at considerable cost. *Normal science, for example, often suppresses fundamental novelties because they are necessarily subversive of its basic commitments* (P. 5, emphasis added)

So it is with traffic safety. By introducing a critical perspective to the enterprise, old beliefs are shaken. It debunks the long-standing premise that when in vehicles, drivers demonstrate unsocial, irresponsible, and even antisocial traits (Canty, 1956). Upon calm review and reflection, traffic safety agents and researchers may recognize that a broader point of view is to the benefit of all. To this end, traffic sociology becomes a valued pillar in the study of traffic safety.

References

Adams, D.L. (1971). Correlates of satisfaction among the elderly. *The Gerontologist* 11: 64-68.

Adams, J. (1985). *Risk and Freedom*. Cardiff: Transport Publishing Projects.

Agar, M.H. (1986). *Independents Declared*. Washington, DC: Smithsonian Institute Press.

Altman, I. (1975). *The Environment and Social Behavior: Privacy, Personal Space, Territory and Crowding*. Monterey, CA: Brookes.

Altman, I., & Chemers, M. (1980). *Culture and Environment*. Monterey, CA: Brooks-Cole.

Altman, I., & Rogoff, B. (1987). World views in psychology: Trait, interactionist, organismic and transactionalist approaches In D. Stokolos & I. Altman (Eds.), *Handbook of Environmental Psychology: Vol. 1*. New York: John Wiley.

American Association of State Highway and Transportation Officials. (1977). *Safety Impact of the 55 mph Speed Limit*. Washington, DC: American Association of State Highway and Transportation Officials.

Andenaes, J. (1984). "Drinking and driving laws in Scandinavia." *Journal of Scandinavian Studies in Law*, 4, 13-23.

Atkins, A. (1984). *The Relation of Written Examination Performance to Safe Driving: A Literature Review With Recommended Methods For Developing Exams. Report No. VHTRC 84-R41*. Charlottesville, VA: Virginia Highway and Transportation Research Council.

Avis, N. E., Smith, K. W., & MacKinley, J. B. (1989). Accuracy of perceptions of heart attack risk: What influences perceptions and can they be changed? *American Journal of Public Health*, 70(12), 1608-1612.

Baker Publishing Company. (1988). U.S. love of automobile revives with new power. *Michigan Roads and Construction*, 85(41).

Baracik, J.I., & Fife, D. (1985). Discrepancy in vehicular crash injury reporting: Northwestern Ohio Trauma Study IV. *Accident Analysis and Prevention*, 17(2), 147-54.

Barber, B. (1983). *The Logic and Limits of Trust*. New Brunswick, NJ: Rutgers University Press.

Barjonet, P.E. (1988). Understanding driver behaviour: Sociological theories and surveys. In SWOV (Ed.), *Traffic Safety Theory and Research Methods*. Amsterdam: SWOV.

Barry, P.Z. (1975). Individual versus collective responsibility for safety: On unexamined policy issue. In *Proceedings, Fourth International Congress on Automotive Safety*, Washington, DC: USGPO.

Barthes, R. (1977). *Image, Music, Text*. London: Fontana.

_____.(1968). *Elements of Semiology*. New York: Hill & Wang.

Bates, A.P (1964). Privacy—a useful concept? *Social Forces*, 42, 429-34.

Baum, H.M., Lund, A.K., & Wells, J.K. (1989). The mortality consequences of raising the speed limit to 65 mph on rural interstates. *American Journal of Public Health*, 79, 1329-95.

Baumrind, D. (1987). A developmental perspective on adolescent risk taking in contemporary America. In C.E. Irwin Jr. (Ed.), *Adolescent Behavior and Health.* San Francisco: Jossey-Bass.

———. (1978). Reciprocal rights and responsibilities in parent-child relations. *Journal of Social Issues* 34 (2), 176-79.

Becker, E. (1973). *The Denial of Death.* New York: Free Press.

Becker, H.S. (1963). *Outsiders: Studies in the Sociology of Deviance.* New York: Free Press.

Bedard, P. (1983, July). The 55 mph speed limit. *Car and Driver.*

Beirness, D.J., & Donelson, A.C. (1983, November 13-18). Noncompliance with per se laws: Ignorance or inability? Paper presented at the 9th International Conference on Alcohol and Drugs and Traffic Safety, San Juan, Puerto Rico.

Bellah, R.N., Madsen, R., Sullivan, W.M., Swidler, A. & Tipton, S.M. (1985). *Habits of the Heart: Individualism and Commitment in American Life.* Berkeley: University of California Press.

Bentham, J. (1970). *Principles of Legislation, 1/An Introduction to the Principles of Morals and Legislation.* London: Athlone Press.

Berdeyaev, N. (1947). *Solitude and Society.* London: Geoffrey Bless.

Berger, A.A. (1980). *Signs in Contemporary Culture.* New York: Longman.

Berger, P., & Berger, B. (1975). *Sociology: A Biographical Approach.* New York: Basic Books.

Berger, P., & Kellner, H. (1964). Marriage and the construction of reality. *Diogenes,* 46, 1-24.

Berger, P., & Luckmann, T. (1967). *The Social Construction of Reality.* New York: Anchor Books.

Bierenbaum, A., & Sagarin, E. (1973). Introduction: Understanding the familiar. In A. Bierenbaum & E. Sagarin (Eds.), *People in Places: The Sociology of the Familiar.* New York: Praeger Publishers.

Bittner, E., & Platt, E.M. (1966). The meaning of punishment. *Issues in Criminology,* 79.

Black, D.(1976). *The Behavior of Law.* New York: Academic Press.

Blau, P. (1964). *Exchange and Power in Social Life.* New York: John Wiley and Sons.

Blau, Z.S. (1973). *Old Age in a Changing Society.* NY: New Viewpoints.

Blomquist, G. (1988), *The Regulation of Motor Vehicle and Traffic Safety.* Stockholm: Kluwer Publishers

Blumer, H. (1971). Social problems as collective behaviour. *Social Problems,* 18(3), 298-306.

———. (1969). *Symbolic Interactionism, Perspective and Method.* Englewood Cliffs, NJ: Prentice Hall.

———. (1966). Sociological implications of the thoughts of G.H. Mead. *American Journal of Sociology,* 71(5), 535-44.

——— Bogdan, P., & Taylor, S.J. (1990). Looking at the bright side: A positive approach to qualitative policy and evaluation research. *Qualitative Sociology,* 13 (2), 183-92.

Bok, S. (1978). *Lying: Moral Choice in Public and Private Life.* New York: Pantheon Books.

Bonnie, R.J. (1985). The efficacy of law as a paternalistic instrument. *Nebraska Symposium on Motivation.* Omaha: University of Nebraska Press.

Borkenstein, R., Crawther, R., Shumate, R., Ziel, W. & Zylman, R. (1964). *The Role of the Drinking Driver in Traffic Accidents*. Indiana: Indiana University.

Boughton, C., Carrick, C., & Noonan, G. (1987). Development of graduated licensing in Autralia. In T. Benjamin (Ed.), *Young Drivers Impaired by Alcohol and Other Drugs*. London, UK: Royal Society of Medicine Services.

Braddock, Dunn and McDonald, Inc. (1974, September). *Impact Considerations of the National 55 mph Speed Limit (Interim Report)*.

Brehmer, B. (1987). The psychology of risk. In W.T. Singleton & J. Hovden (Eds.), *Risks and Decisions*. New York: John Wiley and Sons.

British Columbia Ministry of Solicitor Genral (1990). *1989 Traffic Accident Statistics*. Victoria BC: Motor Vehicle Branch.

_____. (1989). *1988 Traffic Accident Statistics*. Victoria BC: Motor Vehicle Branch.

Bronfenbrenner, U. (1979). *The Ecology of Human Development: Experiments by Nature and Design*. Cambridge MA: Harvard University Press.

Brown, L.R., Flavin, C., & Norman, C. (1979). *Running On Empty*. New York: W.W. Norton and Co.

BSSR. (1985). *Techno Cop, New Police Technologies*. London: Free Association Books.

Burnham, D. (1961, December). The gasoline tax and the automobile revolution. *Mississippi Historical Review* 48, 435-59.

Burt, R. (1982). *Toward a Structural Theory of Action: Network Models of Social Structure, Perception and Action*. New York: Academic Press.

Butler, R. and Lewis, M. (1977). *Aging and Mental Health*. St. Louis, MO: Mosby.

Campbell, D., & Ross, L. (1968). The Connecticut crackdown on speeding. *Law and Society Review*, 3, 63-77.

Campbell, D.C., & Stanley, J. (1966). *Experimental and Quasi-Experimental Designs for Research*. Chicago: Rand McNally and Company.

Canadian Public Health Association. (1974). Health promotion. *Canadian Journal of Public Health*, 65 (2), 140.

Canadian Press. (1993, February, 13). Sped to sick baby, MD must pay fine. *Kitchener-Waterloo Record*. A8.

Canadian Press. (1992, July 25). Doomed killers often help FBI concoct profiles. *Kitchener-Waterloo Record*, A3.

Canty, A. (1956). Problem drivers and criminal offenders. *Canadian Services Medical Journal*, 7, 136-43.

Carr, A.F., & Schnelle, J.F. (1986). Police crackdowns and slowdowns: A naturalistic evaluation of changes in police traffic. *Behavioral Assessment*, 33.

Carsten. O.M.J., Tight, M.R. and Southwell, T. (1986). Urban accidents: Why do they happen? Leeds, UK: Institute for Transport Studies, University of Leeds, AA Foundation for Road Research.

Cavan, S. (1963). Interaction in home territories. *Journal of Sociology*, 8.

Centre of Criminology, University of Toronto (1972). *Workshop on the Use of Sanctions in Controlling Behavior on the Roads*. Toronto: University of Toronto.

Cerrelli, E. (1983, January). *Alcohol in fatal accidents-National estimates—USA*. (National Highway Traffic Safety Administration Technical Report DOT-HS-806-371. Washington DC.) January.

Chambliss, W., & Seidman, R. (1971). *Law, Order and Power*. Reading MA: Addison-Wesley.

Chan, A. (1987). Factors affecting the drinking driver. *Drug and Alcohol Dependence*, 19, 99-119.

Chin, M. (1975). Lived privacy and personal space. *Humanitas*, 11 (1), 45-55.

Cicourel, A. (1970). The acquisition of social structure. In J. Douglas (Ed.), *Understanding Everyday Life*. Chicago: Aldine Pub. Co.

_____. (1964). *Method and Measurement in Sociology*. New York: Free Press.

Cirillo, J.A. (1968). Interstate system accident research study II, Interim Report II. *Public Roads*, 35 (3). Washington, DC: Federal Highway Administration.

Clark, J.P. (1965, September). Isolation of the police: A comparison of the British and American situations. *Journal of Criminal Law*, 56, 307-19.

Cohen, A. K. (1956). The study of social disorganization and deviant behavior. In R. Merton (Ed.), *Sociology Today*. New York: Basic Books, Inc.

Cohen, A.P. (1985). *The Symbolic Construction of Community*. London: Tavistock Publications.

Cohen, J. (1960). *Chance, Skill, Luck*. Hammandsworth, UK: Penguin Books.

Cohen, S. (1985), *Visions of Social Control: Crime, Punishment and Classification*. Cambridge, England: Polity Press.

_____. (1983). Social control talk: Telling stories about correctional change. In D. Garland & P Yung (Eds.), *The Power to Punish*. London: Heineman.

Coleman, J. (1957, January). The effect of speed limit signs. *Traffic Engineering*.

Coleman, J.S. (1975). Current contradictions in adolescent theory. *Journal of Youth and Adolescence*, 1-11.

Collins, R. (1989, February), Sociology: Proscience or antiscience? *American Sociological Review*, 54, 124-39.

Combs, A. (1979). *Myths in Education*. Boston: Allyn and Bacon Inc.

Conley, B.C. (1976). The value of human life in the demand for safety. *American Economic Review*, 61 (1), 45-55.

Cooley, C.H. (1966). *Social Processes*. Ill: Southern Illinois University Press.

Conrad, P., & Schneider, J.W. (1980). *Deviance and Medicalization: From Badness to Sickness*. St. Louis, MO: C. Mosby.

Coppin, R.S. (1977). *Driver Licence and Driver Improvement Program: A National Review*. Canberra, Australia: Department of Transport.

Cowley, J.E. (1981). *A Review of Rural Speed Limits in Australia*. (Report CR20, Federal Office of Road Safety). Canberra, Australia: Commonwealth Department of Transport.

_____. (1980). A review of rural speed limits in Australia. Canberra, Australia: Federal Office of Road Safety, Commonwealth Department of Transport. Davis, K.C. (1975). *Police Discretion*. St. Paul MI: West Publishing.

Dawe. A. (1970). Two sociologies. *British Journal of Sociology*, 21, 207-18.

Deen, L. (1959, April). Effectiveness of speed limit signs. *Traffic Engineering*.

Derlago, V.J., & Charikin, A.L. (1977). Privacy and self-disclosures in social relationships. *Journal of Social Issues*, 33 (3), 102-16.

Desmond, P. (1989, July). 1988: Bigger, better but no boomer. *Commercial Carrier Journal*, 70-84

Desnoes, E. (1985). Cuba made me so. In M. Blasky (Ed.), *On Signs*. Baltimore: John Hopkins University Press.

Dight, S. (1976). *Scottish Drinking Habits: A Survey of Scottish Drinking Habits and Attitudes Towards Alcohol Carried Out in 1972 for the Scottish Home and Health Department*. London: Her Majesty's Stationary Office.

Dollinger, W. 1984). Forward. In German Federal Ministry of Transport, Traffic Division (Ed), *Road Safety Through Education and Training*. Bonn, Germany: Federal Ministry of transportation.

Donelson, A.C., Beirness, D.J., & Mayhew, D.R. (1985). *Characteristics of Drinking Drivers*. Ottawa: Department of Justice Canada.

Dorf, R.C. (1974). *Technology and Society*. San Francisco: Boyd and Fraser Publishing Co.

Douglas, J. (1976). *Investigative Social Research*. Beverly Hills, CA: Sage.

Douglas, J. (Ed.). (1970a). *Deviance and Respectability*. New York: Basic Books.

_____. (1970b). *Understanding Everyday Life*. Chicago: Aldine.

Douglas, J., & Johnson, J. (1977). Introduction. In J. Douglas & J. Johnson (Eds.), *Existential Sociology*. Cambridge: Cambridge University Press.

Douglas, M., & Wildavsky, A. (1982). *Risk and Culture*. Berkeley: University of California Press.

Drew, E. B. (1966, October). The politics of auto safety. *Atlantic*, 218, pp. 95-102.

Drummond, A. & Torpey, L. (1985). *Driver Improvement Program Evaluation Report No. 11/85*. Hawthorne, Victoria: Road Traffic Authority.

Durkheim, E. (1966). *The Rules of Sociological Method*. New York: Free Press.

_____. (1953). *Sociology and Philosophy*. London: Cohen and West, Ltd.

Eagan, J.M. (1990). *A Speeder's Guide to Avoiding Tickets*. New York: Caretaker Publishing.

Eco, U. (1976). *A Theory of Semiotics*. Bloomington: University of Indiana Press.

Economos, J.P. (1967). The legal environment and traffic safety. In The National Academy of Engineering (Ed.), *Traffic Safety: A National Problem*. Saugatuck, CN: The ENO Foundation for Highway Traffic Control.

Eisenhandler, S. A. (1990). The asphlt identikit: Old age and the driver's license. *International Journal of Aging and Human Development*, 30 (1), 1-14.

Elliot, B.J. (1981). *Attitudes to exceeding the speed limits*. (Report to Road Traffic Authority of Victoria, Australia).

Ellul, J. (1964). *The Technological Society*. New York: Vintage Books.

Elmberg, H., & Michael, D. (1961). Effect of speed limit signs on speeds on suburban arterial streets. *HRBB, 303*.

Erickson, K.T. (1976). *Everything in Its Path*. New York: Simon and Schuster.

Etzkorn, P. K. (Ed.). (1968). *Georg Simmel: The Conflict in Modern Culture and Other Essays*. New York: Teacher's College, Columbia University.

Ewen, S. (1976). *Captains of Consciousness, Advertising and the Social Roots of the Consumer Culture*. New York: McGraw-Hill Book Company.

Ewing, A.C. (1962). *Ethics*. New York: Collier Books.

Faberman, H., & Goode, E. (1973). Introduction. In H. Faberman & E. Goode (Eds.), *Social Reality*. Englewood Cliffs, NJ: Prentice Hall.

Fagothey, A. (1976). *Right and Reason, Ethics in Theory and Practice*. Saint Louis, MO: C.V. Mosby Company.

Farris, R., Malone, T. & Lillienfors, H. (1976). *A comparison of alcohol involvement in exposed and injured drivers, phase I and II*. (Report No. DOT-HS-4-00954). Alexandria, VT: National Highway Traffic Safety Administration.

Federal Highway Administration. (1976). *Interstate System Accident Research Study*. Washington DC: FHA.

Federal Minister of Transport, Germany. (1984). *German Bundestag*. (Publication No. 10/1479), Bonn.

Feest, J. (1968). Compliance with legal regulations: Observation of stop sign behavior, *Law and Sociological Review*. 2 (3), 447-71.

Felke, D. (1988). 15 Jahre Verkehrsuberwachung am Elzer Berg. *Hessiche Polizei Rundschau*, 11, 19-22.

———. (1983). Polizeiliche Massnahmen in Strassenverkehr al Beitrag zur Verkehrssicherheit *Zeitschrift Fur Verkehrsicherheit*, 29, 63-66.

———. (1980). The effectiveness of speed limits by police surveillance. *Police Information of the State of Hessen*. 2, 10-15.

Fell, J.C. (1983). Tracking the alcohol problem in U.S. highway crashes. *Annual Proceedings*. Arlington, VI: American Association for Automotive Medicine.

Fisher, C. (1975). Privacy as a profile of authentic consciousness. *Humanitas*, 11 (1): 27-45.

Flaherty, M.G. (1987). Multiple realities and the experience of duration. *The Sociological Quarterly*, 28 (3), 313-26.

Flink, J. J. (1975). *The Car Culture*. Cambridge, MA: MIT Press.

Forsyth, E.(1991). The relationship between methods used in learning to drive and performance in the driving test? In A.S. Hakkert & A. Katz, (Eds.), *Proceedings: New Ways for Improved Safety and Quality of Life*. Tel Aviv: Transportation Research Institute.

Foucoult, M. (1980). *Power/Knowledge: Selected Interviews and Other Writings 1972-1977*. (Colin Gordon, Ed.). New York: Pantheon Books.

Fowler, R. (1985). Power. In *Handbook of Discourse Analysis Vol. 4.*, Norwood, NJ.

Frankena, W. K. (1963). *Ethics*. Englewood Cliffs, NJ: Prentice-Hall.

Franklin, U. (1990). *The Real World of Technology*. Toronto: CBC Enterprise.

Freedman, M., Williams, A.F., & Lund, A.K. (1989). *Public opinion regarding photo radar*. (A report by the Insurance Institute for Highway Safety).

Friedland, M., Trebilock, M., & Roach, K. (1988). *Regulating Traffic Safety: A Survey of the Effectiveness of COntrol Strategies*. Toronto: Canadian Institute for Advanced Research.

Frier, B., Steel, J., Matthews, D., & Duncan, L. (1980, June 7). Driving and insulin-dependent diabetes. *Lancet*, pp. 1232-34.

Fuller, R. (1984). A conceptualization of driving behavior as threat avoidance. *Ergonomics*, 27(11), 1139-55.

Garber, N.J., & Gadiraju, R. (1988). Factors affecting speed variance and its influence on accidents. *Transportation Research Record*, 1213, 64-71.

Gardiner, J.A. (1964). *Traffic and the Police: Variations in Law Enforcement Policy*. Cambridge, MA: Harvard University Press.

Garfinkel, H. (1967). *Studies in Ethnomethodology*. Englewood Cliffs, NJ: Prentice-Hall.

Gehlen, A. (1980). *Man in the Age of Technology*. New York: Columbia University Press.

Gentry, M., & Shulman, A. (1988). Remarriage as a coping response for widowhood. *Psychology and Aging*, 3 (2), 191-96.

Giddens, A. (1984). *The Constitution of Society*. Berkeley, CA: University of California Press.

Gikas, P.W. (1983). Crash worthiness as a cultural ideal. In D.L. Lewis & L. Goldstein (Eds.), *The Automobile and American Culture*. Ann Arbor: University of Michigan Press.

Giorgi, A. (1990). The phenomenological (experiential) approach to traffic problems."In P. Rothe (Ed.), *Challenging the Old Order: Towards New Directions in Traffic Safety Theory.* New Brunswick, NJ: Transaction.

Goffman, I. (1967). *Interaction Ritual: Essays on Face-to-Face Behavior.* Garden City, NY: Anchor Books.

_____. 1963a). *Behavior in Public Places.* New York: The Free Press.

_____. (1963b). *Stigma: Notes on the Management of Spoiled Identity.* Englewood Cliffs, NJ: Prentice-Hall.

_____. (1961). *Encounters.* New York: Bobbs-Merrill Co.

_____. (1956). *Presentation of Self in Everyday Society.* New York: Vintage Press.

Gold, H. (1982). *The Sociology of Urban Life.* Englewood Cliffs, NJ: Prentice-Hall.

Gooderham, M. (1993, February 27). Catching speeders in stop-action photos. *The Globe and Mail,* A1.

Graham, J. & Shakow, D. (1981). Risks and rewards: Hazard pay for workers. *Environment,* 23 (8), 13-16.

Gross, H. (1971). Privacy and autonomy. In R. Pennock & J.W. Chapman (Eds.), *Privacy.* New York: Atherton Press.

Gurin, P., & Brim, O.G. Jr. (1984). Change in self in adulthood: The example of sense of control. In P.B. Bates & O.G. Brim (Eds.), *Life Span Development* and *Behavior,* Vol. 6: New York: Academic Press.

Gusfield, J.R. (1981). *The Culture of Public Problems: Drinking and Driving and the Symbolic Order.* Chicago: University of Chicago Press.

Guastello, S.J., & Guastello, D.D. (1987). The relation between the locus of control construct and involvement in traffic accidents. *The Journal of Psychology,* 120 (3), 293-97.

Gutenschwager, G. (1989). *The Political Economy of Health in Modern Greece.* Athens, Greece: National Center of Social Research.

Haddon, W., Jr. (1973). Energy damage and the ten countermeasure strategies. *Journal of Trauma,* 13, 321-31.

Haddon, W., & Bradess, V.A. (1959). Alcohol and the single fatal accident experience in Westchester County. *Journal of the American Medical Association,* 169, 1587-93.

Haddon, W., Suchman, E.A., & Klein, D. (1964). *Accident Research: Methods and Approaches.* New York: Harper and Row.

Hagan, J. (1985). *Crime, Criminal Behavior, and its Control.* NY: McGraw-Hill Book Company.

Hagart, J., Dunbar, J.A., Ritchie, A., Devgun, M.S., Ogston, S.A., & Martin, B.T. (1983). Detection of problem drinkers using perception of risk test: A preliminary statement. Paper presented at the 9th International Conference on Alcohol, Drugs and Traffic Safety, held in San Juan, Puerto Rico.

Haight, F.A. (1988). Research and theory in traffic safety. In Institute for Road Research (Ed.), *Traffic Safety Theory and Research Methods.* Amsterdam: Institute for Road Research.

_____. (1980). "What causes accidents—A semantic analysis." In Society of Automotive Engineers (Ed.), *Accident Causation.* Warrendale, PA: Society of Automotive Engineers.

_____ (1972). Do speed limits reduce traffic accidents? In J. Tanur, F. Mosteller, W. Kruskal, R. Link, R. Pieters, & G. Rising (Eds), *Statistics: A Guide to the Unknown.* San Francisco CA: Holden-Gay, Inc.

Hammer, U. (1991). Children and traffic. In A.S. Hakkert & A. Katz (Eds.), *Proceedings: New Ways for Improved Safety and Quality of Life.* Tel Aviv: Transportation Research Institute. Harford, T.C. (1977). Ecological factors in drinking. In H.T. Blane & M.E. Chavez (Eds.), *Youth Alcohol and Social Policy.* New York: Plenum Press.

Harford, T.C., & Gaines, L.S. (Eds). (1979). *Social Drinking Contexts.* (Research Monograph No. 7.) Rockville MD: National Institute for American Automobile Accidents.

Harper, D.R., & Martin, P.D. (1983). Isotachophoretic detection of microbial metabolites with ethanol production in urine. Paper presented at the 9th International Conference on Alcohol, Drugs and Traffic Safety, held in San Juan, Puerto Rico.

Harrington, D. (1973). The young driver follow-up study: An evaluation of the role of human factors in the first four years of driving. *Accident Analysis and Prevention* 4, 191-240.

Harvey, P., & Hopkins, A. (1983, February 19), Views of British neurologists on epilepsy, driving and the law. *Lancet,* 401-04.

Hauer, E. (1990). The engineering of safety and the safety of engineering. In J.P. Rothe (Ed.), *Challenging the Old Order: Towards New Directions in Traffic Safety Theory.* New Brunswick, NJ: Transaction Publisher.

Heath, D.B. (1982). Historical and cultural factors affecting alcohol availability and consumption in Latin America. In A. Kaplan (Ed.), *Legislative Approaches to Prevention of Alcohol-Related Problems: An Inter-American Workshop.* Washington DC: Institute of Medicine, National Academy Press.

Heidegger, M. (1977). *The Question Concerning Technology and Other Essays.* New York: Harper Colophon Books.

———. (1967). *Being and Time.* New York: Harper and Row.

Heimer, C. (1988). Social structure, psychology and the estimation of risk. *Annual Review of Sociolgy* 14, 495-519.

Heller, E. (1959). *The Disinherited Mind.* New York: Meridian Books.

Hess, H.W. (1922, May). History and present status of the 'truth-in-advertising' movement as carried on by the vigilance committee of the Associated Advertising Clubs of the World. *Annals of the American Academy of Political and Social Science.*

Hewitt, J.P. (1988). *Self and Society: A Symbolic Interactionist Social Psychology (4th ed.).* Toronto: Allyn and Bacon, Inc.

Hogg, R. (1977). *A study of male motorists' attitudes to speed restrictions and their enforcement.* (Transport and Road Research Laboratory Supplementary Report 276). Crowthorne, Berkshire: Transport and Road Research Laboratory.

Holzner, B. (1968). *Reality Construction in Society.* Cambridge, MA: Schenkman Publishig Co.

Homans, G. C. (1961). *Social Behavior.* New York: Harcourt, Brace and World.

Hood, R. (1972), *Sentencing the Motoring Offender.* London, UK: Heinemann.

Hora, T. (1962). Existential Psychiatry and Group Psychiatry. In H. Ruitenbeek (Ed.), *Psychoanalysis and Existential Philosophy.* New York: E.P. Dutton.

Horowitz, I.L. (1989). *Taking Lives: Genocide and State Power.* New Brunswick NJ: Transaction Publishers

Horowitz, I.L., & Liebowitz, T. (1968, winter). Social deviance and political marginality. *Social Problems,* pp. 280-96.

Howland, J. (1988). Social norms and drunk driving countermeasures. In J. Graham (Ed.), *Preventing Automobile Injury*. Chicago: Auburn House.

Hughes, P.K., & Cole, B.L. (1986). What attracts attention when driving? *Ergonomics*, 29 (3), 377-91.

Hunt, A. (1976). Perspectives in the sociology of law." In P. Carlen (Ed.), *The Sociology of Law*. Staffordshire, UK: University of Keele Press.

Hutchison, S.C., & Marko, J.G. (1989). *The Law of Traffic Offences*. Toronto: Carswell.

Ihde, D. (1983). *Existential Technics*. Albany: State University of New York Press.

Ilchman, W.F., & Uphoff, N.I. (1969). *The Political Economy of Change*. Berkely, CQ: University of California Press.

Insurance Bureau of Canada. (1991, February 17-20)). *New to the road: Prevention measures for young or novice drivers*. A Report of the Findings of a Symposium Held in Halifax, Nova Scotia.

Irwine, A. (1985). *Risk and the Control of Technology*. Manchester: University of Manchester Press.

Jacobs, J. B. (1989). *Drunk Driving: An American Dilemma*. Chicago: University of Chicago Press.

Jacobs, J. & Dopkeen, L. (1990). Risking the qualitative study of risk. *Qualitative Sociology*, 13 (12), 169-81.

James, M., & Eagon, M. (1990). *The Speeder's Guide to Avoiding Tickets*. New York: Butterworth.

James, W. *The Writings of William James*, (J. McDermott, Ed.). (1977). Chicago: University of Chicago Press.

Jamieson, G.H. (1985). *Communication and Persuasion*. London: Croom Helm.

Jehenson, R. (1973). A phenomenological approach to the study of formal organizations." In G. Psathas (Ed.), *Phenomenological Sociology*. Toronto: John Wiley and Sons.

Jennett, B. (1983). Anticonvulsant drugs and advice about driving after head injury and intracranial surgery. *British Medical Journal*, 286, 627-28.

Jernigan, J.D., Lynn, C., & Garber, N.J. (1989). An investigation of issues related to raising the rural interstate speed limit in Virginia. Arlington, VA: Transportation Research Council.

Jessor, R. (1987). Risky driving and adolescent problem behavior. *Alcohol, Drugs and Driving* 3 (3-4). 1-12.

Jones, M. J. (1980). *Organizational Aspects of Police Behaviour*. Westmead, Farnborough, Hants, UK: Grower Publishing Co.

Jones, R. & Joscelyn, K. (1978). *Alcohol and highway safety: A review of the state of knowledge*. (Technical Report DOT HS 803 714). Washington, DC: National Highway Traffic Safety Administration.

Kalish, R., & Knudston, F.W. (1976). Attachment vs disengagement: A life-span conceptualization. *Human Development*, 19, 171-81.

Kaplan, A. (1964). *The Conduct of Inquiry*. Scranton, PA: Chandler Publishing Co.

Karpf, R. S., & Williams, A. F. (1983). Teenage drivers and motor vehicle deaths. *Accident Analysis and Prevention*, 15 (1), 55-63.

Kastner, N.S. (1987). Mistake of law and the defence of officially induced error. *Criminal Law Quarterly*, 28.

Kenlie, J. (1990, April 8). Fanatical use of speed traps is futile and wastes money, [Editorial] *Toronto Star*. Kearl, M.C. (1986). Knowing how to quit: On the finitudes of everyday life. *Sociological Inquiry*, 56 (3), 283-303.

Keyserlingk, E. W. (1990). Government paternalism in traffic safety: A new-old perspective. In J. P. Rothe (Ed.), *Challenging the Old Order: Towards New Directions in Traffic Safety Theory*. New Brunswick, NJ: Transaction Publishers.

Kirkham, G. (1963). On the etiology of police aggression in black communities. In J. Kinton (Ed.), *Police Roles in the Seventies*. Aurora: Social Science and Sociological Resources.

Klockars, C. B. (Ed.). (1983). *Thinking about the Police: Contemporary Readings*. New York: McGraw-Hill.

Kotarba, J.A. (1979) "Existential sociology." In S. Mcnall (Ed.), *Theoretical Perspectives in Sociology*. New York: St. Martin's Press.

Kuhn, T. S. (1970). *The Structure of Scientific Revolutions* (2d ed.). Chicago: University of Chicago Press.

Lagac, B. (1992, May 6)). Laser to nab aggressive speeders.*Toronto Star*.

Laing, R.D. (1971). *Self and Others*. Hammondsworth, Middlesex: Penguin Books.

_____. (1970). *Knots*. Hammondsworth, Middlesex: Penguin Books.

Lamm, R., & Kloeckner, J.H. (1989). Increase of traffic safety by surveillance of speed limits with automatic radar devices on a dangerous section of a German autobahn: A long term investigation. *Transportation Research Record*, 974, 8-14.

Laufer, R., & Wolfe, M. (1977). Privacy as a concept and a social issue: A multidimensional development theory. *Journal of Social Issues*, 33 (3), 22-42.

Laurel, H., & Tornos, J. (1986, November 13-18). Hangover effects on driver performance. Paper presented at the 9th International Conference on Alcohol and Drugs and Traffic Safety, San Juan, Puerto Rico.

Laurence, M. (1988). The legal context in the United States. In M. Laurence, J. Snortum, & F. Zimmering (Eds.), *Social Control of the Drinking Driver*. Chicago: University of Chicago Press.

Lave, C., & Lave, L. (1990). Barriers to increasing highway safety. In J. P. Rothe (Ed.), *Challenging the Old Order: Towards New Directions in Traffic Safety Theory*. New Brunswick, NJ: Transaction Publishers.

Lave, C.A. (1985). Speeding, coordination, and the 55 mph limit. *American Economic Review*, 75 (5), 1159-64.

Law, A. (1991, September 20). Subaru SVX incredible at any price. *Kitchener-Waterloo Record*.

Law Reform of Canada. (1975). *Limits of Criminal Law*. Ottawa: Information Canada.

Lawson, J.J., Arora, H.R., & Jonah, B.A. (1982). 1981 night time surveys of driver's alcohol use. *Proceedings of the 26th Annual Conference of the American Association for Automotive Medicine*. Arlington Heights, VA: American Association for Automotive Medicine.

Lazarus, R.S., & Folkman, S. (1984). *Stress, Appraisal and Coping*. New York: Springer.

LeMaire, P.H. (1982). *Personal Decisions*. Washington, DC: University Press of America.

Lesce, T. (1988, July). Photo radar controls speed. *Law and Order*, pp. 34-38.

Leiss, W. (1990). Traffic safety and the media environment: The role of communication in public policy issues. In J.P. Rothe (Ed), *Challenging the Old Order: Towards New Directions in Traffic Safety Theory*. New Brunswick, NJ: Transaction Publishers.

Lightner, C. (1986). Citizen action to reduce alcohol-crash losses: Mothers against drunk drivers (MADD). In *Proceedings of the Ninth International Conference on Alcohol, Drugs and Traffic Safety*, Washington DC: National Highway Traffic Safety Administration.

Lilienfeld, A.M., & Lilienfeld, D.E. (1980). *Foundations of Epidemeology*. New York: Oxford University Press.

Linder, S.H. (1987). Injury as metaphor: Towards an integration of perspectives. *Accident Analysis and Prevention*, 19 (1), 3-12.

Liner, S. A. (1979). *State Laws on Probationary Licensing and Licensing of Minors*. Washington, DC.: National Committee on Uniform Traffic Laws and Ordinances.

Long, D. (1977). *Bentham on Liberty*. Toronto: University of Toronto Press.

Luhmann, N. (1980). *Trust and Power*. NY: Wiley.

Lundman, R. (1979, August). Organizational norms and police discretion: An observational study of police work with traffic law violators. *Criminology*, 17 (2), 159-71.

_____. (1974). Routine police arrest practises: A commonweal perspective. *Social Problems*, 22, 127-41.

Lyles, R., Stamatiadis, P. & Lightizer, D. (1991). Quasi-induced exposure revisited. *Accident Analysis and Prevention*, 23 (4), 275-85.

Lyman, S.M. & Scott, M. (1970). *A Sociology of the Absurd*. New York: Appleton-Century-Crofts.

_____. (1968). Coolness in everyday life. In M. Truzzi (Ed.), *Sociology and Everyday Life*. Englewood CLiffs, NJ: Prentice-Hall.

Lynd, R., & Lynd, H.M. (1929). *Middletown: A Study in Modern American Culture*. New York: Harcourt, Brace.

Macmillan, J.(1975). *Deviant Drivers*. Westmead, Farnborough, Hants, UK: Sacon House.

Manraj, C., & Haines, J. (1985). *The Law on Speeding and Radar*. Toronto: Butterworth and Co.

Manson, P. (1980). Supreme court declines review of town's photo-radar system. *The Arizona Republic*. Wednesday, April 26th: B4

Marcuse, H. (1968). *One Dimensional Man*. London: Sphere Books.

Marsh, P., & Collett, P. (1986). *Driving Passion: The Psychology of the Car*. London: Johnathan Cape.

Marske, C.E. (Ed.). (1991). *Communities of Fate: Readings in the Social Organization of Risk*. Lannham, ILL: University Press of America.

Marx, G.J. (1989). *Undercover. Politics of Surveillance in America*. Berkeley: University of California Press.

Marx, G.J., & Reichman, N. (1984). Routinizing the discovery of secrets: Computers as informants. *American Behavioral Scientist*, 27 (4), 423-52.

Matza, D. (1969). *Becoming Deviant*. Englewood Cliffs, NJ: Prentice-Hall.

Mayhew, D.R., Beirness, D.J., Conelson, A.C., & Simpson, H.M. (1987). Why are young drivers at greater risk of collision? In T. Benjamin (Ed.), *Young Drivers Imparied by Alcohol and Other Drugs*. London: Royal Society of Medicine Services.

Mayhew, D. R., & Simpson, H. M. (1991). *New To The Road: Young Drivers and Novice Drivers, Similar Problems and Solutions.* Ottawa: The Traffic Injury Foundation.

McCarrol, J.R & Haddon, W. (1961). A controlled study of fatal accidents in New York city. *Journal of Chronic Diseases*, 15, 811-26

McCarthy, P.S. (1988). *Highway Safety and the 65 MPH Maximum Speed Limit: An Empirical Study.* Washington DC: AAA Foundation For Traffic Safety.

McEwen, J., & and McGuire, J. (1981). *Traffic law sanctions.* (Technical Report DOT HS 805 876). Washington, DC: National Highway Traffic Safety Administration.

McKelvie, S.J. (1986). An opinion survey and longitudinal study of driver behaviour at stop signs. *Canadian Journal of Behavioral Science*, 18 (1), 75-85.

McKenna, F.P. (1984). Measures of field dependence: Cognitive style or cognitive ability. *Journal of Personality and Social Psychology*, 47 (3), 593-603.

McKnight, A. J. (1985). *An Analysis of the Effectiveness of Written Driver License Examinations in Evaluating Applicant Driving Abilities. Taske 1: Revision of Test and Manual.* (Report no. FHWA/AZ-85/225-1). Phoenix Arizona: Arizona Department of Transportation.

McKnight, A. J., Hyle, P., & Albrecht, L. (1983). *Youth Demonstration Project.* (National Highway Traffic Safety Administration. Report No. DOT-HS-01765). Springfield, Virginia: National Technical Information Service.

McKnight, A.,& Edwards, R. (1982). An experimental evaluation of driver license manuals and written tests. *Accident Analysis and Prevention* 14 (3), 187-92.

McLuhan, M. (1964). *Understanding Media.* London: Routledge and Kegan Paul.

McEwen, J., & McGuire, J. (1981). *Traffic law sanctions.* (Technical Report DOT HS 805 876). Washington, DC: National Highway Traffic Safety Administration.

Mead, G.H. (Anselm Strauss Ed.). (1964). *On Social Psychology.* Chicago: University of Chicago Press.

———. (1932). *Mind, Self and Society.* Chicago: University of Chicago Press. Mela, D. (1977). Review on information on the safety effects of the 55 mph speed limit in the United States. Washington, DC: National Highway Traffic Safety Administration, U.S. Department of Transportation.

Melossi, D. (1987). The law and the state as practical rhetoric of motives: The case of decarceration. In J. Lowman, R.J Menzies, & T.S. Palys (Eds.), *Trancarceration: Essays in the Sociology of Social Control.* Aldershot, UK: Grower.

Mermall, T. (1970, Spring). Spain's philosopher of hope. *Thought*, 45 (176), 104-120.

Michaels, R., & Schneider, C. (1976). The energy crisis, characteristics of traffic flows and highway safety. *Accident Analysis and Prevention*, 8, 123-30.

Mill, C.W. (1959). *The Sociological Imagination.* New York: Oxford University Press.

Milosevic, S., & Gajic, R. (1986). Presentation factors and driver characteristics affecting road-sign registration. *Ergonomics*, 29 (6), 807-15.

Minkler, M., & Cox, K. (1980). Creating critical consciousness in health. *International Journal of Health Services*, 10 (2), 311-22.

Mirowsky, J., & Ross, C.E. (1986). Social patterns of distress. *Annual Review of Sociology*, 12, 23-45.

Moore, G.E. (1966), *Principa Ethica* (2nd ed). New York: Oxford University Press.

Morano, D.V. (1973). *Existential Guilt: A Phenomenological Study*. Assen, Holland: Van Gorcum and Comp. B.V.

Morton, D., & Hutchison, S.C. (1987). *The Presumption of Innocence*. Toronto: Carswell.

Mostyn, B.J., & Sheppard, D. (1980). A national survey of drivers' attitudes and knowledge about speed limits. (Transport and Road Research Laboratory, Supplementary Report 548). Crowthorne, Berkshire: Transport and Road Research Laboratory.

Mouldon, J.V. (1985). National transportation safety board alcohol initiatives." In National Highway Traffic Safety Administration (Ed.), *Proceedings of the 7th International Conference on Alcohol, Drugs and Traffic Safety*. Washington, DC: National Highway Traffic Safety Administration.

Moynihan, D.P. (1986). *Family and Nation*. San Diego, CA: Harcourt Brace Javanovich.

Munden, J.W. (1967). *The relation between a driver's speed and his accident rate*. (Transport and Road Research Laboratory Report LR88). Crowthorne, Berkshire, UK: Transport and Road Research Laboratory.

Myers, C.S. (1935). The psychological approach to the problem of road accidents. **Nature**, (86), 740-42.

Naatanen, R. & Summala, H. (1976). *Road User Behavior and Traffic Accidents*. Amsterdam: North-Holland and Elsevier.

Nader, R. (1966). *Unsafe at any Speed*. New York: Pocket Books.

Nash, J., & Spradley, J. (1976). *Sociology: A Descriptive Approach*. Chicago: Rand McNalley College Publishing Company.

National Acadamy of Science. (1984). *55: A Decade of Experience*. (Report of the Transportation Committee, NAS).

National Highway Traffic Safety Administration. (1989). *Report to Congress on the Effect of the 65 MPH Speed Limit during 1988*. Washington, DC: U.S. Department of Transportation.

_____. (1988). *Report to Congress on the Effect of the 65 MPH Speed Limit during 1987*. Washington, DC: U.S. Department of Transportation.

Navin, F. (1991, June). Speed: Some definitions and observations. Paper presented at the Canadian Multidisciplinary Road Safety Conference VII, Vancouver.

Nichols, B. (1981). *Ideology and the Image*. Bloomington: Indiana University Press.

Nigrete, J. (1982). Commentary. In A. Kaplan (Ed.), *Legislative Approaches to Prevention of Alcohol-Related Problems: An Inter-American Workshop*. Washington DC: Institute of Medicine, National Academy Press.

Nisbet, R. (1971). Introduction: The study of social problems. In R. Merton and R. Nisbet (Eds.), *Contemporary Social Problems*. New York: Harcourt Brace Javanovich.

Noguchi, K. (1990, August). In search of "optimal" speed: From the user's viewpoint. *ITE*.

Noguchi, K., Koshi, M., Okabe, F., Okano, Y., & Suzuki, H. (1978). Speed and man." *IATSS Research 2*.

Norman, E. (1962). *Road traffic accidents—epidemeology, control and prevention*. (World Health Organization Public Paper No, 12).

Normandeau, A., & Leighton, A. (1990). *A Vision of the Future of Policing in Canada: Police Challenge 2000*. Ottawa: Solicitor General.

North, R.V. (1985). The relationship between the extent of visual field and driving performance: A review. *Ophthalmology, Physiology, Optometry,* 5 (2), 205-10.

Oakely, R.S. (1972). *Drugs, Society and Human Behavior.* St. Louis: C.V. Mosby.

O'Connor, P. J. (1986). *Report on Graduated Driver Licensing and Other Road Accident Countermeasures Focusing on Young Drivers.* (Report Series 6/86). Canberra: Federal Office of Road Safety.

Ontario Ministry of Transportation. (1992). *The Driver's Handbook.* Toronto: Ontario Ministry of Transportation.

_____. (1987), *Ontario Road Safety Annual Report.* Toronto: Ministry of Transportation and Communications.

_____. (1980), *Motor Vehicle Accident Facts.* Toronto: Ministry of Transportation and Communications.

Oppenlander, J.C. (1962). A theory of vehicular speed regulation. In *Highway Research Board Bulletin 341, Accident Analysis and Characteristics.* Washington, DC: National Research Council.

Paradise Valley Town Attorney. (1988). Ordinance number 297. In *Town Code.* Paradise Valley: Paradise Valley Town Attorney.

Parry, M.H. (1968). *Aggression on the Road: A Pilot Study of Behaviour in the Driving Situation.* London: Tavistock.

Parsons, J. (1937). *The Structure of Social Action.* New York: McGraw-Hill.

Peirce, C.S. (A.W. Burk, Ed.). (1958). *Collected Papers of C.S. Peirce.* Cambridge: Harvard University Press.

Peltzman, S. (1975). The effects of automobile safety regulation. *Journal of Political Economy,* 83 (4), 677-725.

Pepinsky, H. E. (1987). Justice as information sharing. In J. Lowland, R.J Menzies, & T.S. Palys (Eds.), *Transcarceration: Essays in the Sociology of Social Control.* Aldershot: Gower.

Perinbanayagam, R.S. (1975, Autumn). The significance of others in the thought of Alfred Schutz, G. H. Mead and C.H. Cooley. *The Sociological Quarterly,* 16, 500-21.

Perrine, M., Waller, J., & Harris, L.A. (1971). *Alcohol and Highway Safety: Behavioral and Medical Aspects.* Burlington, VT: University of Vermont.

Perrow, S. (1984). *Normal Accidents, Living with High Risk Technologies.* New York: Basic Books.

Pfohl, S. (1985). *Images of Deviance and Social Control: A Sociological History.* New York: McGraw-Hill Book Co.

Philips, D. (1977). Motor vehicle fatalities increase just after publicized suicide stories. *Science,* 196, 1464-65.

Pignataro, L.J. (1973). *Traffic Engineering Theory and Practice.* Englewood Cliffs, NJ: Prentice-Hall.

Pikkarainen, J., Penttila, A., Karhunen, P.J., Kauppila, R., Liesto, K., & Tiainen, E. (1987). Young drivers in Helsinki: Drinking habits. In T. Benjamin (Ed.), *Young Drivers Impaired by Alcohol and Other Drugs.* London, UK: Royal Society of Medicine Services.

Pool, Ithiel de Sola (1981). *The Social Impact of the Telephone.* Cambridge, MA: MIT Press.

Postman, N., Nystrom, C., Strate, C., & Weingartner, C. (1987). *Myths, Men and Beer.* Falls Church VA: AAA Foundation for Traffic Safety.

Preusser, D., Zador, A.F., & Blomberg, R.D. (1984). The effect of curfew laws on motor vehicle crashes. *Law and Policy Quarterly*, 6, 115-128.

Prisk, T. (1959, August). The speed factor in highway accidents. *Traffic Engineering*, pp. 16-21.

Quigley, F.L., & DeLisa, J.A. (1983). Assessing the driving potential of cerebral vascular accident patients. *American Journal of Occupational Therapy*, 37 (7), 474-78.

Quinney, R. (1970). *The Social Reality of Crime*. New York: Little Brown and Co.

Rachel. J.V., Maisto, S.A., Guess, L.L., & Hubbard, R.L. (1982). Alcohol use among youth." In *Alcohol Consumption and Related Problems*, Alcohol and Health Monograph No. 1, Rockville, MD: NIAAA.

Reese, J. H. (1971). *Power, Politics, People: A study of Driver Licensing Administration*. Washington, DC: National Research Council.

Reichman, N. (1986). Managing crime risks: Toward an insurance based model of social control. *Research in Law, Deviance and Social Control*, 8, 151-72.

_____. (1984, November 7-11)). Screeing, sorting, classifying and excluding: Social control in the welfare state. Paper presented at the American Society of Criminology, Cincinnati, Ohio.

_____. (1983). Ferreting out fraud: The manufacture and control of fraudulent insurance claims. Unpublished doctoral dissertation, MIT, Cambridge, MA.

Reis R. E., Jr. (1983). The findings of the comprehensive driving under the influence of alcohol offender treatment demonstration project. *Abstracts and Reviews in Alcohol and Driving*, 4 (1), 10-16.

Reiss, A. J. (1984). Consequences of compliance and deterrence models of law enforcement for the exercise of police discretion. *Law and Contemporary Problems*, 83, 210-225.

_____. (1971). *The Police and the Public*. New Haven: Yale University Press.

Robertson, L. S. (1981). Patterns of teenage driver involvement in fatal motor vehicle crashes: Implications for policy choice. *Journal of Health, Policy and Law*, 6 (2), 101-13.

Ross, H. (1973). Law, science and accidents: The British Road Safety Act of 1976. *Journal of Legal Studies*, 1-78.

Ross, L. (1982). *Deterring the Drinking Driver, Legal Policy and Social Control*. Lexington, MA: Lexington Books.

_____. (1973). Folk crime revisited. *Criminology*, 11, 71-85.

_____ (1960). Traffic law violation: A folk crime. *Social Problems*, 8, 231-41.

Rothe, J.P. (1993). "Cessation of driving: a significant life event. *German Journal of Traffic Safety*, 1 (1), 12-16.

_____. (1992, May). Routine roadside police behaviour: Smokies meet knights of the road and four wheelers. Paper presented at the Qualitative Research Analysis Conference, Carlton University, Ottawa Ontario.

_____. 1991a). *The Truckers' World of Risk, Safety and Mobility*. New Brunswick, NJ: Transaction Publishers.

_____. (1991b, October). Traffic sociology: Social patterns of risk. *New Ways for Improved Road Safety and Quality of Life: Proceedings*. Tel Aviv, Israel.

_____. (Ed.). (1991c). *Rethinking Young Drivers* (2d printing). New Brunswick NJ: Transaction Publishers.

_____. (1991d, June). Electronic highway surveillance and the glance. Paper presented at the Canadian Sociology & Anthropology Association Learned Societies Conference, Kingston, Ontario.

_____. (1991e, June). Truckers and institutionally demanded driving risks. Paper presented at the Canadian Sociology & Anthropology Association Learned Societies Conference, Kingston, Ontario.

_____. (1990a). *The Safety of Elderly Drivers: Yesterdays Young in Today's Traffic*. New Brunswick, NJ: Transaction Publishers.

_____. (Ed.). (1990b). *Challenging the Old Order: Towards New Directions in Traffic Safety Theory*. New Brunswick, NJ: Transaction Publishers.

_____. (1990c). Problem definition, research and educational program development. In J.P. Rothe (Ed.), *Challenging the Old Order: Towards New Directions in Traffic Safety Theory*. New Brunswick NJ: Transaction Publishers.

Rothe, J.P., & Cooper P.J. (1989). *Never Say Always: Perspectives on Seat Belt Wearing*. New Brusnwick, NJ: Transaction Publishers.

Royal Canadian Mounted Police. (undated). *Multanova—Radar 6F Basic Training Manual*. Ottawa, Ont.: RCMP.

Rubinstein, J. (1973). *City Police*. New York: Ballantine Books.

Ryan, W. (1976). *Blaming the Victim*. New York: Vintage Books.

Rykwert, J. (1978). The street: The use of its history. In S. Anderson (Ed.), *On Streets*. Cambridge, MA: MIT Press.

Sacco, V.F., & Silverman, R.A. (1982). Crime prevention through mass media: Prospects and problems. *Journal of Criminal Justice*, 10, 257-69.

Sampson, L. (1989, May 3). Developing ruling not final for photo radar. *Phoenix Gazette*, pp.B1-B2.

Sande, T. (1987). Risk in industry. In W.T. Singleton & J. Hovden (Eds.), *Risk and Decisions*. New York: John Wiley and Sons.

Sanderson, J.T., & Corrigan J. (1986). *Arterial road speed survey: Undivided roads*. (Report No. TS84/6), Royal Automobile Club of Victoria, Australia.

Sartre, J.P. (1956). *Being and Nothingness*. New York: Washington Square Books.

Schaff, A. (1975). The individual in society. In R. Blackburn (Ed.), *Ideology in Social Science*. London, UK: Fontana Books.

Scheidt, R. (1984). A taxonomy of well-being for small-town elderly: A case of rural diversity. *The Gerontologist*, 24, 84-90.

Scheler, M. (1954). *The Nature of Sympathy*. London, UK: Routledge and Kegan.

Schlenker, B., Helm, B., Tedeschi, J. (1973). The effects of personality and situational variables on behavioral trust. *Journal of Personality and Social Psychology*, 25 (3), 419-427.

Schneider, K.R. (1972). *Autokind vs Mankind*. New York: Schoken Books.

Schutz, A. (1973). *On Phenomenolgy and Social Relations*. Chicago: University of Chicago Press.

_____. (1971). *Collected Papers I. The Problem of Social Reality*. The Hague: Martinus Nijhoff.

Schutz, A., & Luckmann, T. (1973). *The Structure of the Life-World*. Evanston, ILL: Northwestern University Press.

Schwab, J.J., & Schwab, M.E. (1978), *Sociolcultural Roots of Mental Illness: An Epidemeological Survey*. New York: Plenum Press.

Seamon, D. (1979). *A Geography of the Lifeworld: Movement, Rest and Encounter*. New York: St. Martin's Press.

Sethi, S.P. (1972). *Up Against the Corporate Wall: Modern Corporations and Social Issues of the Seventies.* Englewood Cliffs, NJ: Prentice-Hall.

Shapiro, S.P. (1987). The social control of impersonal trust. *American Journal of Sociology,* 23 (3), 623-658.

Shearing, C.D., & Stenning, P.C. (1981). Private security: Its growth and implications. In M. Tonry & N. Morris (Eds.), *Crime and Justice—An Annual Review of Research Vol 3.* Chicago: University of Chicago Press.

Shils, E.B. (1966). Privacy: Its constitution and vicissitudes. *Law and Contemporary Problems,* 31, 281-306.

Shinar, D. (1978). *Psychology On The Road: The Human Factor in Traffic Safety.* New York: John Wiley and Sons.

Shinar, D. and Drory, A. (1983). Sign registration in daytime and nighttime driving. *Human Factors,* 25 (1), 117-22.

Short, J.F. (1984). The social fabric at risk: Toward the social transformation of risk analysis. *American Sociological Review,* 49, 711-725.

Shotter, J., & Gergen, K.J. (1989). Preface and introduction. In J. Shotter & K.J. Gergen (Eds.), *Texts of Identity.* Newbury Park, CA: Sage Publications.

Simmel, G. (1971). *On Individuality and Social Forms.* Chicago: University of Chicago Press.

_____. (1957). Brucke and tur. In *Brucke and Tur.* Stuttgart, Ger.: K. F. Koehler.

Singer, E., & Endreny, P. (1987). Reporting hazards: Their benefits and costs. *Journal of Communications,* 37 (3), 10-26.

Skog, O.J. (1981). Drinking behavior in samll groups: The relationship between group size and consumption level. In T.C. Harford & L.S. Gaines (Eds.), *Social Drinking Contexts.* (Research Monograph No. 7). Rockville, MD: NIAAA.

Skolnick, J. H. (1966). *Justice Without Trial: Law Enforcement in Democratic Society.* New York: John Wiley & Sons.

Slovic, P. (1985). Risk theory: Concpetual frames for understanding risk taking in young drivers. In R. Blackman, G. Brown, D. Cox, S. Sheps & R. Tonkin (Eds.), *Adolescent Risk Taking Behavior.* Vancouver, BC: Young Driver Behavior Project.

Smith, C. J. (1988). *Public Problems: The Management of Urban Distress.* New York:The Guilford Press.

Smith, D. (1990). *The Conceptual Practises of Power, A Feminist Sociology of Knowledge.* Toronto: University of Toronto Press.

_____. (1987). *The Everyday World As Problematic, A Feminist Sociology.* Toronto: University of Toronto Press.

Smith, D. & Tomerlin, J. (1990). *Beating the Radar Rap.* Chicago: Bonus Books.

Solomon, D. (1964). *Accidents on Main Rural Highways Related to Speed, Driver and Vehicle.* Washington, DC: US Government Printing Office.

Sonntag, S. (1978), *Illness as Metaphor.* New York: Farrar, Straus and Girox.

Spector, M., & Kitsuse, J.I. (1977). *Constructing Social Problems.* Menlo Park, CA: Benjamin/Cummings Publishing.

Spencer, M.E. (1981). The idea of the person as a collective representation. *Human Studies,* 4, 257-71.

Spiegelberg, H. (1989, May). Phenomenology of the look. *British Society for Phenomenology Journal,* 20 (2), 107-15.

Stacey, B.G. (1985). Drinking and driving: Alcohol association with traffic accidents. *Journal of Alcohol and Drug Education,* 30, 25-36.

Stark, E., Flitcraft, A. & Frazier, W. (1979). Medicine and patriarchial violence: The social construction of a private event. *International Journal of Health Services*, 9, 461-83.

STAYSAFE. (1988). **Driver Licensing**. Roseberry, New South Wales: Traffic Authority of New South Wales.

Stern, A. (1967). *Sartre. His Philosophy and Existential Psychoanalysis*. New York: Delta Books.

Stevenson, A. (1972). Foreward. In R.H. Blum (Ed.), *Surveillance and Espionage in a Free Society*. New York: Praeger Publishers.

Stevenson and Kellogg, Ltd. (1975, June). *A study of the economic and social impacts of lower speed limits*. Report prepared for Ontario Ministry opf Transportation and Communications.

Stoddart, K. (1990). Erfahrung of young drivers. In J.P. Rothe (Ed.), *Rethinking Young Drivers*. New Brunswick NJ: Transaction Publishers.

_____. (1988). *Analysis of Student Interviews*. (Unpublished Report Submitted to the Insurance Corporation of British Columbia, North Vancouver, BC)

_____. (1980). *Sociology of Deviance Unit I*. Richmond, BC: The Open Learning Institute.

_____. (1974). The facts of life about dope: Observations of a local pharmacology. *Urban Life and Culture*, 3 (2), 179-204.

Stuart, D. (1982). *Canadian Criminal Law*. Toronto: Carswell.

Sykes, G. M., & Matza, D. (1957, December). Techniques of neutralization: A theory of delinquency. *American Sociological Review*, 22, 664-70.

Tabachnik, N. (1973). Accident or Suicide: Destruction by Automobile. Springfield, ILL: Charles, C Thomas.

Tara, B. (1972). Curent surveillance technology. In R.H. Blum (Ed.), *Surveillance and Espionage in a Free Society*. New York: Praeger Publishers.

Taylor, D.H. (1976). Accidents, risks and models of explanation. *Human Factors*, 18 (4), 371-80.

Taylor, W. (1962, August). Speed zoning: A theory and its proof. Ohio Department of Highways, Bureau of Traffic.

Tefft, S.T. (1980). *Secrecy, A Cross-Cultural Perspective*. New York: Human Sciences Press.

Thalen, R.H. (1983). Illusions and mirages in public policy. *Public Interest*, 73, 60-74.

Thomas, W.I. (1928). *Social Organizations and Social Personality*. Chicago, ILL: University of Chicago Press.

Thomas, W.I., & Znaniecki, F. (1917). *The Polish Peasant in Europe and America*. Boston: Richard Badger.

Thygerson, A. L. (1977), *Accidents and Disasters*. Englewood Cliffs, NJ: Prentice-Hall.

_____. (1975). *Accidents and Disasters: Causes and Countermeasures*. Englewood CLiffs, NJ: Prentice-Hall.

Tillman, W.A., & Hobbs, G.E. (1949). The accident prone automobile driver. *American Journal of Psychiatry*, 106 (5), 321-33.

Titmuss, R.M. (1974). *Social Policy: An Introduction*. London: Allen and Unwin.

Tittle, C. (1980). *Sanctions and Social Deviance: The Question of Deterrence*. New York: Praeger Publishers.

Torpey, S. (1988). *An Evaluation of the Revised Driver License Written Testing System.* (Road Traffic Authority. Report No. GR/88/1). Hawthorne, Victoria, Australia: Road Traffic Athority.

Townroe, P. M. (Ed.). (1974). *Social and Political Consequences of the Motor Car.* London: David and Charles.

Traffic Institute, Northwestern University. (1981). *Background for traffic law enforcement.* Discussion paper.

Traffic Watch. (1974, July-August). Do you follow speed limits of 80 km/h. *Traffic Watch,* 4, 102-109.

Transport Canada (1987). *Smashed.* Ottawa: Ministry of Supply and Services.

Transportation Research Board. (1984). *55: A Decade of Experience.* (Report 204., Washington, DC: Transportation Research Board.

Tsujimaru, A., Nagayama, Y., & Takizawa, K., (1980). Social speed and its indexing. *IATSS Research,* 4, 8-12.

Turner, J.H. (1988). *A Theory of Social Interaction.* Stanford, CA: University of Stanford Press.

Turner, R.H. (1972). The real self: From institution to impulse. *American Journal of Sociology,* 81 (5).

Tussman, J. (1960). *Obligation and the Body Politic.* New York: Oxford University Press.

Uglow, S. (1988). *Policing Liberal Society.* London: Methuen.

U.S. Department of Commerce. (1987). *Statistical Abstracts of the United States.* Washington, DC: U.S. Government Printing Office.

U.S. Department of Transportation (1982). *Synthesis of Safety Research Related to Traffic Control and Roadway Elements, Vol. 2.* Washington, DC: U.S. Department of Transportation.

_____. (1970). *Driver Behavior and Accident Involvements: Implications for Tort Liability.* Washington DC: U.S. Department of Transportation.

van den Berg, J.H. (1962). The human body and the significance of human movement." In H. Ruitenbeek (Ed.), *Psychoanalysis and Existential Philosophy.* New York: E.P. Dutton.

van den Haag, E. (1971). On privacy. In R. Pennock & J.W. Chapman (Eds.) *Privacy.* New York: Atherton Press.

Van DeVeer, D. (1986). *Paternalistic Intervention.* Princeton NJ: Princeton University Press.

Vingilis, E. (1983). Driving drinkers and alcoholics: Are they from the same population? In R.G. Smart, F.B. Glaser, Y. Isreal, H. Kalant, R.E. Potham, & W. Schmidt (Eds), *Research Advances in Alcohol and Drug Problems.* NY: Plenum Press.

Wagenaar, A.C., Straff, F.M., & Schultz, R. (1990). Effects of the 65 mph speed limits on injury, mobility and mortality. *Accident Analysis and Prevention,* 22 (6), 571-585.

Wallace, J., & Cramar, A. (1969). *Licensing Examinations and Their Relation to Subsequent Driving Record.* Olympia, WA: Washington Department of Motor Vehicles.

Waller, J. (1985). *Injury Control: A Guide To The Causes and Prevention of Trauma.* Lexington MA: Lexington Books.

Waller, P. F. (1986). *New Drivers: How and When Should They Learn?* Chapel Hill, NC: University of North Carolina Highway Research Center.

_____. (1974). The changing task of driver licensing. In *Future Role of Driver Licensing in Highway Safety*. Washington, DC.: Transportation Research Board.

Washington, The State of. (1989). *Commercial Driver's License*. Seattle, WA: Department of Licensing.

Wasstrom, R. A. (1980). *Philosophy and Social Issues, Five Studies*. Notre Dame: University of Notre Dame.

Weber, M. (1967). *On Law in Economy and Society*. New York: Simon and Shuster.

_____. (1949). *The Methodology of the Social Sciences*. Glencoe, ILL: The Free Press.

Webster's New Collegiate Dictionary. (1977). Springfield, Mass.: G. & C. Merriam Co.

Weighell, H. J. C. (1974). Legislation and the motor car. In J. Rose (Ed.), *Wheels of Progress? Motor Transport, Pollution and the Environment*. London: Gordon and Breach Science Publishers.

Weinberg, A. (1966). Science and public affairs. *The Bulletin of the Atomic Scientists*.

Werner, C. (1987). A transactional approach to neighborhood social relationships. In S. Oskamp & S. Spacapan (Eds.), *Interpersonal Processes*. Beverly Hills, CA: Sage.

Whitehead, P.C., Hylton, J., & Markosky, R. (1984). *Alcoholics on the road: Evaluation of an impaired driver atreatment program*. (Report prepared for the Saskatchewan Alcoholism Commission).

Werner, W. and Rothe, J.P. (1984). *Doing School Ethnography: Concepts and Cases*. Edmonton, Alta.: University of Alberta, Secondary Education Publications.

Wheatley, J. (1970). *Prolegomena to Philosophy*. Belmont CA: Wadsworth Publishing Company.

Wheaton, B. (1983). Stress, personal coping resources and psychiatric symptons: An investigation of interactive models. *Journal of Health and Social Behavior*, 24, 208-09.

White, W.T. (1988, September 14-18)). *Just how unsafe are young drivers?* Road Traffic Safety Seminar, Wellington, New Zealand.

Whitehead, P.C., Hylton, J., & Markosky, R. (1984). Alcoholics on the road: Evaluation of an impaired driver treatment program. A report submitted to the Saskatchewan Alcoholism Commission, Regina, Saskatchewan.

Wicker, A.W. (1972). Process which mediate behavior - environment congruence. *Behavioral Science*, 17, 265-77.

Wieder, D.L. (1974). *Language and Social Reality: The Case of the Convict Code*. The Hague: Mouton.

Wildavsky, A. (1987). Choosing preferences by constructing institutions: A cultural theory of preference formation. *American Political Science Review*, 8 (1), 3-21.

Wilde, G. J. S. (1982). The theory of risk homeostasis: Implications for safety and health. *Risk Analysis*, 209-25.

Wilkins, L.T. (1984). *Consumerist Criminology*. London, UK: Heinemann.

_____ (1964). *Social Deviance*. London: Tavistock

Willett, T.C. (1974). *Workshop on the Use of Sanctions in Controlling Behaviour on the Roads*. Toronto: Centre of Criminology, University of Toronto.

_____. (1964). *Criminal on the Road: A Study of Serious Motoring Offences and Those Who Commit Them*. London UK: Tavistock Publications.

Williams, A. F. (1985). Nighttime driving and fatal crash involvement in teenagers. *Accident Analysis and Prevention*, 17 (1), 1-5.

_____. (1984). *Nighttime Driving and Fatal Crash Involvement of Teenagers.* Washington, DC: Insurance Institute for Highway Safety.

Williams, A.F., & Karpf, P.S. (1984). Teenaged drivers and fatal crash responsibility. *Law and Policy*, 6 (1), 101-13.

Williams, A. F., Preusser, D., & Lund, A. (1985). Teenage driver licensing in relation to state laws. *Accident Analysis and Prevention*, 17 (2), 135-45.

Williams, E.B., & Malfetti, J. L. (1970). *Driving and Connotative Meanings.* New York: Teachers College Press.

Wilson, J.Q. (1968). *Varieties of Police Behavior.* Cambridge, MA: Harvard University Press.

Wiseman, J.P. (1979). *Stations of the Lost: The Treatment of Skid Row Alcoholics.* Chicago: The University of Chicago Press.

Witheford, D.K. (1970). *Speed Enforcement Policies and Practice.* Westport, CN: Eno Foundation for Transportation.

Wittman, F.D. (1983). The environment debate. In M. Grant & B. Ritson (Eds.), *Alcohol: The Prevention Debate.* London, UK: Croom Helm.

Wolfe, K. (1959). *Georg Simmel.* Columbus: Ohio State University Press.

Womack, J., Jones, D.T., & Roos, D. (1991). *The Machine the Changed the World.* Camridge, MA: MIT Press.

Zeitlin, I. (1973). *Rethinking Sociology, A Critique of Contemporary Thought.* Englewood Cliffs, NJ: Prentice-Hall.

Zellweger Uster Ltd. (1990). *Philosophy of application and benefit of the radar speed meters.* Information materials.

Zimmerman, D.E., & Pollner, M. (1970). The everyday world as a phenomenon. In J. Douglas (Ed.), *Understanding Everyday Life: Towards the Reconstruction of Sociological Knowledge.* Chicago: Aldine.

Zimmerman, D.H. (1970). The practicalities of rule use. In J. Douglas (Ed.), *Understanding Everyday Life: Towards the Reconstruction of Sociological Knowledge.* Chicago: Aldine.

Zylman, R. (1974). A critical evaluation of the literature on alcohol involvement in highway deaths. *Accident Analysis and Prevention*, 6, 163-204.

Index

Riley